LIBERIA AND AMERICA IN RELIGIOUS POLITICS

LIBERIA AND AMERICA IN RELIGIOUS POLITICS

WHAT IS GOD SAYING TO THE NATIONS?

DR. JALLAH YELORBAH KOIYAN

XULON PRESS

Xulon Press
2301 Lucien Way #415
Maitland, FL 32751
407.339.4217
www.xulonpress.com

Paperback ISBN-13: 978-1-66286-349-3
Hard Cover ISBN-13: 978-1-66286-350-9
Ebook ISBN-13: 978-1-66286-351-6

CONTACT:

Dr. Jallah Yelorbah Koiyan
Founder/Visionary

Praise Ministries International, Inc
Charlotte, NC 28213
United States of America

704-780-3110

jallah.11@netzero.com

For online resources, please visit:
www.praiseministriesinternational.com (Ministry)
www.praiseministriesprayerbiblestudyforum.com (Resources)

TABLE OF CONTENTS

DEDICATION

My life has been characterized with tough journey; nevertheless, the named family references in this dedicatory section have been sent by God to see me through the expedition; therefore, I am pleased to dedicate this piece of works to them based on the contribution they have made to my spiritual, emotional, and physical life. Primarily, I dedicate this work to the Mothers and Father, alive and deceased including uncles, aunties, and significant others in the family who have been the antecedents to the process of my bringing up during early childhood experience. The second group includes my children who have kept my days full of association at school and at home. Finally, I dedicate this work to Praise Ministries International, Inc. and Praise Ministries Prayer Forum whose platform onsite has been used to develop this monograph.

ACKNOWLEDGMENT

The strength of any building at the base originates with the blueprint of the building. In the blueprint, the kind of materials, the quantity of materials, the dimensions of the materials, and the cost estimate of the materials including labor are characteristics of the blueprint to build the house necessary for human habitation; similarly, education with reference to academia requires similar specifications to achieve its goal. The following named persons acknowledged in this section represent the above metaphors; therefore, I am pleased to acknowledge the following architects of my education. I begin with my parents, relatives, and significant others whom God used in my bringing up period of life nurturing in academia and conclude the acknowledgment of all professors of Charlotte Christian College and Theological Seminary.

INTRODUCTION

Book Overview

This monograph addresses the influence of religion on the government in three phased dimensions; primarily, chapter one discusses the research methodologies employed with reference to the use of the Bible, the archival research systems, the Greek tools, and program onsite while chapter two adopts the exegetical methodology in order to develop the foundation of the discourse based on the scriptural thesis with reference to the historical, the grammatical and the literary contexts of the biblical passage. Categorically, chapters three, four, five, six, and seven present the ethical dimensions that resonate with ethics, the primary and secondary holisticities in conjunction with the Liberian and American political histories and body politics in the spotlights; therefore, the monograph is theoretical and applicative in the model presentation to elucidate the roles of governments and citizens in society for solidarity and mutuality. The fact that God ordains civil government to restrain evil indicates that God has universal interest in the well-being of humanity; therefore, He has sanctioned human government to work based on universal stewardship as pre-ordained according to His divine providence.

Hypothesis and Thesis Statement

The rules of laws enacted by governments of the world for the goals of orderliness, stability, tranquility, and national security for societal members are the sum total of the influence of religion has on the government.

In the contextualization with reference to this hypothesis in respective of the government, this monograph delineates the misconceptions, the propositions, and the philosophies that resonate with the influence religion has on the government with reference to the rules of laws and ethics. While the discourse tends to explore such hypothesis in order to answer the question, the author has built the context thesis of this monograph on Romans chapter thirteen verses one to seven. The exploration of this biblical passage exegetically redresses the misconceptions, the propositions, and the philosophies lying behind the revolving questions why government and citizens should co-exist in order to relate to one another as God's established institution for collaboration and solidarity for national building and peaceful co-existence.

Synopsis

Apostle Paul's address to the Christian community of Rome to submit to the governing authority is inclusive and universal; even though, the letter being addressed to the specific group of Gentiles and Jews Christians as revealed in the epistle does not root out the universality and inclusiveness of the commandment. As the context thesis of this monograph is delineated based on Romans chapter thirteen verses one to seven, the author has adopted an exegetical approach using the historical, the grammatical, and the literary context to define the roles of civil government and citizens in the society. The universal address approach of Apostle Paul as revealed in the text asking everyone to submit to the civil authority in the obscurity of what kind of governments to submit to has created controversy on the text with reference to the text interpretation and application; nevertheless, it is understood that Apostle Paul was contextual in addressing the situation at hand imminent that could have affected believers should they rebel against the civil government of Rome and anticipate unfavorable repercussion. In this monograph, Apostle Paul's statement is exegetically examined using the historical context and proof texts to define what Apostle Paul meant when he addressed the Roman Christians urging them to submit to the governing authority.

In the primary holisticity as revealed in the text, Apostle Paul defines the roles of the government and citizens with reference to national security and taxation; nevertheless, the author has adopted national development, education, health care delivery, and social services as the roles of governments as citizens play their reciprocal roles to honor authority and to pay taxes as revealed scripturally (Rom 13:1–7); additionally, the monograph delineates the biblical view of wealth, wealth redistribution, and the dichotomy between biblical view of justice to that of the social view of justice to define ethical behaviors according to societal norms. The rationale that ethics and law reflect values and guide behaviors does not signify that ethics and law are homogenous in scope based on moral goodness across universal morality as revealed in the moral law. The reason is that law can be flawed; on the other hand, ethics is absolute and consistent with universal moral goodness of society; therefore, the controversy between the biblical views of justice to that of the social view of justice is the conflict between law and ethics based on inconsistency that conflicts with the moral law (Exod 2:1–20).

In the secondary holisticity as defined in this monograph, it explains democratization as synonymous to justice and delineates the facets of social, rehabilitation, biblical, and criminal justice systems in the context of ethics and concludes with environmental justice in the context of the preservation of the earth; therefore, this positions humanity as the steward of God according to the genesis account (Gen 1:28–31). The discourse unveils jurisprudence in chapter six of the monograph and advocates that humanity responds to law morally; however, in the midst of law that does not dictate the ethics of God, civil disobedience is necessary to guide against wrong doing as defined in this monograph. The commandment to obey government does not signify to break moral laws when the civil authority has crossed the boundary that infringes on individual's conviction; therefore, civil disobedience is necessary to keep the individual's conviction in check in order to remain obeisance to God.

Liberianization is defined as the action of making a person Liberian in character or nationality; therefore, liberianization in this context highlights the Liberia's political history, the First, the Second, and the Third Republic in such context. The discourse while examining the Liberia's political history since its independence, it has highlighted that the Liberian government had existed as the aristocratic oligarchy for 133 years of rules. The reason of the exclusion of the larger Liberian society during this period to participate into the political and civic life of the country was the result of xenophobia and ethnocentrism that had influenced the body politics of the founding fathers of the Republic of Liberia. After the end of the rule of the aristocratic oligarchy in 1980 as the result of coup d'état, Liberia had experienced dictatorial regime under the leadership of the deposed Samuel Kanyon Doe for ten years followed by the sixteen years of insurrection; then, it was climaxed by the fragile peace under the leadership of the former President, Ellen Johnson-Sirleaf; then, President George MannehWeah was elected as President for the Third Republic. Understanding that Liberia is the novice to democracy, Liberia faces the dilemmas of injustices and corrupt practices. Based on these factors, the author has recommended responsive actions with reference to envisioning, patriotism, eradication of astronomical salary, and corrupt practices in the government. To help buttress the above, the author has recommended further solutions with reference to the constitutionalization and educationalization of the law; then, the denationalization of corruption through the proposed Anti-Corruption Committee and the Informed Committee establishment. It concludes with the issue of the Liberia's elephant meat that influences aspiring politicians to adopt psychological disorder in order to practice misdeeds.

Americanization is defined as the action of making a person American in character or nationality; therefore, americanization in this context defines the American political history and body politics; additionally, the author discusses the interconnectivities between Liberia and America that resonate with body politics, commence, membership to the international organizations, and bilateral representation. While the monograph highlights these commonalities, the author has adopted the American political history and ideologies, conservatism and liberalism, the roles of the White Evangelicalism in the American body politics, flaw in the American conservatism, the legislation of morality, roles conflicts, and the rationale of the historical evidence to avoid States and church amalgamation.

CHAPTER I
RESEARCH METHODOLOGIES

Chapter Overview

This chapter gives the synopsis of the research methodologies employed to produce the monograph on the doctrine of religious politics. The methodologies deployed in this book include the use of direct quotations, indirect quotations, paraphrases, the explanation of key words, comparisons, the use of the Greek tools, and the explanation of phrases in the biblical text using the Bible as the primary resource. Such Greek tools include the *NAS Exhaustive Concordance*, the *Thayer's Greek Lexicon*, and the *Strong's Concordance*. With reference to the versions, the New International Version and the New King James Version of the Bible until otherwise stated have been adopted. Meanwhile, the use of the archival system of research via the utilization of books, articles, and credible web sources has been deployed coupled with the online group version onsite via the interactive in-group deliberation that solicits questionnaires and intellectual forum relevant to biblical subjects.

Methodologies

Methodology is defined as the mechanism used to research the particular topic under review aimed at discovering the meaning and the application of the field of studies or knowledge.[1] Understanding that religious politics is not a novel topic, but a topic that has been around for centuries, the applied research project has used the Bible, the archival system of research, the Greek tools, and program in order to research the topic while maintaining academic and scholarly integrity.

The Bible

The Bible that serves as the primary resource has been adopted and used throughout the body of the discourse using paraphrases, direct and indirect quotations. The Bible is the base for this monograph; therefore, without the Bible, the paper would not have been written since the topic chosen warrants biblical or theological authentication. The Bible has been used to build and to explain cases in the hermeneutical arenas that require the interpretation of the biblical text backed by evidence using concordances, commentaries, and dictionaries.

The Archival Research Systems

The archival system of research involves the searching for and extracting information and evidence from original archives that relate to the activities and claims of individuals, entities or both.[2] It is the very common method of conducting research in the academic settings. The use of secondary resources such as books and articles are the most common sources for archival system of research. To adequately research this topic, archival research methodology has dominated among the methodologies deployed. Books and articles on specific subjects are written by different authors with the common or dissimilar views; therefore, using the common and

---

[1] Easten Law, "Complex Currents, Contemporary Perspectives, and Converging Methods: A Review of Graduate Student Research Panel at Princeton Theological Seminary's 2018 World Christianity Conference," *World Christianity* 9, no. 1(2019): 114–121.

[2] Martha Lund Smalley, "Mountain Archival Finding Aids on the Web," *ATLA Summary of Proceedings* 53, no. 1(1999): 301–307.

contrasted views on the subject helps the researcher to see through the periscopes of different lenses or ideologies to help him or her synthesize, analyze, evaluate, and draw conclusion on the contrasting ideologies in order to make the proper judgment. The use of books and articles in the archival research system is advantageous for in-depth engagement to research the topic credibly; therefore, concordances and commentaries have been adopted in this discourse to compare the commentator's view on the particular doctrines, topics, and the biblical texts being reviewed. Reading the various commentaries from different authors better helps the researcher to compare his or her interpretation on the biblical text against other interpretations to draw the conclusion regarding the meaning of the scriptural text. The use of concordances and commentaries are secondary sources that have been used in this monograph to help the researcher interpret the primary source used in the body of the monograph.

The use of Bible dictionaries has helped to define theological terminologies in both Greek and Hebrew languages. As Greek or Hebrew words have been utilized in the book, the dictionary has been used to define each Greek or Hebrew word in the body of the book. The adoption and incorporation of the above resources in the archival system of research has helped solidified the ideologies and help the book to have meaning as defined in the doctrine of religious politics.

The Greek Tools

The use of exegesis in biblical hermeneutics using the Greek tools when it comes to textual analysis of the particular passage of the Scripture is advantageous in explaining the biblical passages looking at each word in the text with the corresponding Greek word to English's equivalence.[3] Defining the English word in the Greek's equivalence helps the biblical interpreter to interpret the scriptural text in context using the Greek tools. In this book, the Greek tools have been utilized to explain the Greek's

---

[3] Ibid.

words into the English equivalence. The original Greek form of words considering the gender used, part of speech, and word roots has been adopted to define the word in the text throughout the book.

The Program

The book has an online version written in the conversational written format submitted daily by piecemeal to group members to read and to make comments in the form of questions and statements that solicit discussion onsite. The registered group members are 100 plus memberships; however, the regular participants on an average are between 30 and 36 who read the posts daily and sometimes respond. The member participants in the group will have read the book before it is completed provided they will have been consistent in reading the daily posts.[4]

---

[4] Praise Ministries Interdenominational Prayer Bible Study Forum, "Praise Ministries Prayer Forum," accessed November 13, 2021, https://praiseministriesprayerbiblestudyforum.wordpress.com/.

CHAPTER II
HERMENEUTICAL ANALYSIS
(ROMANS 13:1–7)

Chapter Overview

I n this segment of the monograph, the hermeneutical analysis defines the context thesis of this discourse in order to lay the foundation; therefore, this subdivision of the book discusses the historical context, textual analysis of key words in the biblical text, the dichotomy between exegesis and eisegesis, and proof texting in order to define the interpretation of the biblical passage in Romans chapter thirteen verses one to seven. At the conclusion, the author has developed a reflection on the chapter to redress the subject in order to pin a mental picture in the mind of the reader for personal subjective reflection.

Exegesis

Exegesis is the critical analysis of the biblical passage using context with reference to history, geography, literary, and grammar in order to interpret the biblical passage freed from error; therefore, Romans chapter thirteen verses one to seven is exegetically approached in the context of the text interpretation and application. In Apostle Paul's address to the Christians of Rome, did he address secular or spiritual authority? A scholar of the New Testament History has argued that Apostle Paul did not refer to secular authority; instead, he referred to the Judean Spiritual authority when he addressed the Roman Christians to submit to the governing authority; therefore, he exclusively concluded that the interpretation of Romans chapter thirteen verses one to seven is being taken out of context. According to the scholar, the Gentiles believers who lived in Jerusalem did not want to submit to the Judean spiritual authority; therefore, Apostle Paul wrote the Gentiles believers urging them to submit to the Judean spiritual authority. Such scholar of the New Testament History has denied that Christians were commanded to submit to worldly governments as contextualized in Romans chapter thirteen verses one to seven.[5] It should be noted that such statement serves as a proposition; therefore, it should be proven exegetically to fix the hermeneutical controversy concerning the subject based on the scholar's exclusiveness on the passage. If Apostle Paul addressed the Gentiles believers as the New Testament Historian has said asking them to submit to the spiritual Judean authority, it should be noted that Apostle Paul's statement should have been inclusive based on the universality of his approach to the text, the historical and the grammatical context, and other proved texts in the Bible that reference submission to governmental authority in the world (Matt 22:20–24; 1 Tim 2:1–5; Col 1:15–17; Rom 13:1). The New Testament Historian needed to go further before coming to conclusion; therefore, this passage should be exegetically approached to find out the authenticity of his exclusive conclusion on the passage.

Historical Context

The book of Romans was written about AD 58 after the death of Claudius in AD 54, four or five years after the edict of Emperor Claudius at which all Jews were banished from Rome as the result of their constant disturbances at the instigation of *Chrestus*. During the edit, it is believed that Christians at the time were mixed with the

---

[5] David May, "Context Is Key to Interpreting Romans 13:1–7," accessed June 18, 2022, https://goodfaithmedia.org/context-is-key-to-interpreting-romans-13-1-7-cms-19577/.

Jews in the decree; therefore, the probability that both Jews and Christians left Rome is probable. After the death of Claudius, Nero, the step Son of Claudius ascended to the throne as the last Emperor of the Claudius dynasty and reigned between AD 41 and 68. During this era, the Jews became seditious in the land. Clarke writes,

> For what reason this edict was issued does not satisfactorily appear. Suetonius tells us that it was because the Jews were making continual disturbances under their leader *Christus*. That the Jews were in general an uneasy and seditious people are clear enough from every part of their own history. They had the most rooted aversion to the heathen government; and it was a maxim with them that the world was given to the Israelites; that they should have supreme rule everywhere, and that the Gentiles should be their vassals."[6]

Understanding that the Jews misunderstood the mission of Jesus regarding his kingdom's rule, they rejected him as the Messiah of the world (John 1:1–5). His disciples at one time asked him when he was going to restore the kingdom of Israel; in response, Jesus told them that only the Father knew when the kingdom of Israel would be restored (Acts 1:1–8); similarly, the Pharisees asked him if it was necessary to pay taxes to Caesar; in response, he commanded them to pay taxes to Caesar and to give to God what belongs to God (Matt 22:21–24).

The New Testament historian writes, "When Paul tells the Gentile believers to pay taxes and revenue (v. 6), he is telling his readers to pay the two-drachma Temple tax. Even the Roman historian Tacitus mentions Gentile converts sending contributions to the Temple."[7] In ancient Rome,

---

[6] Adam Clarke, "Commentary on Romans 13:1". "The Adam Clarke Commentary," accessed August 29, https://www.studylight.org/commentaries/acc/romans-13.html. 1832.

[7] Ibid.

taxes were paid for land, trade, military, marriage, inheritance, sales, religions, poll tax, imperial tax, sale taxes, and State's land.[8] When Apostle Paul asked believers to pay tribute to the governing authorities, he referenced one of the above mentioned taxes in the category of lands, houses, and persons. The Greek word for tribute as used in Romans chapter thirteen verse six is called *phoros*. *Phoros* is the tax that refers to lands, houses, and persons. The tax mentioned in Romans chapter thirteen verse six does not refer to the temple tax known as *didrachma* as the New Testament historian has stated in the above quotation (Matt 17:24–27). Apostle Paul did not command the Roman Christians to pay temple tax; instead, he commanded them to pay taxes that referenced individuals (imperial tax), houses (property tax), or lands according to the grammatical context. The tax known as *phoros* as mentioned in the biblical text discredits his exclusive argument that Apostle Paul did not address secular authority regarding submission. Apostle Paul commanded the believers in Rome to pay the imperial tax (*phoros*) to the Roman authority instead of the temple tax (*didrachma*). Donald's note entitled, "Duties to Rulers and Others (13:1–14)," delineates to cement Apostle Paul's reaction to the Jews' seditious behavior toward authority figures in Roman. He writes,

> Since God is the source of all authority, governments exercise power by his permission. Christians should therefore obey the ruling authorities (13:1-2). If they keep the laws of the country, Christians have nothing to fear. They should have no difficulty in cooperating with the government, because the basic functions of government are the promotion of the well-being of society and the restraint of wrongdoing, and these functions are in keeping with Christian ideals (3-4). Christians should obey the law and pay their taxes, not just because they fear the penalties, but because they see these duties as further ways of

---

[8] Peter, "Tax in the Early Days of the Roman Republic," accessed June 18, 2022, https://www.unrv.com/economy/roman-taxes.php#:~:text=Tax%20in%20the%20Early.

acknowledging God's rule in the world (5-7). Christians should also have good relations with their fellow citizens, again not just because the law tells them to, but because Christian love has changed them within (8-10). With the day of final salvation drawing nearer day by day, the time available for the development of truly Christian character grows shorter and shorter. Paul therefore urges Christians to wake up before it is too late. They must not behave as non-Christians do, and must not give the sinful nature any chance to do its evil work. They must live in the victory of Christ, with behavior that reflects his character (11-14).[9]

The claim by the New Testament Historian in his article entitled "Context Is Key to Interpreting Romans 13:1–7," appears unauthentic based on his exclusive arguments that the context of Romans chapter thirteen verses one to seven is being taken out of context. He argued that Apostle Paul did not address secular government with reference to submission. Considering the era and the historical happenings at the time in Rome, he should have been inclusive in his arguments. Apostle Paul addressed both Jews and Gentiles believers regarding submission to the Roman's authority on the subjects of respect and taxation.

In his commentary on Romans chapter thirteen verse one, Author Calvin states that Apostle Paul understood the rebelliousness of his Hebrews counterparts with reference to previous history in antiquity and commanded them to submit to Magistrates across the Greco-Roman community of his days on the subjects of honor, obedience, and the paying of tributes that due the Roman's authorities.[10] Author Coffman underscores his contributions

---

[9] Donald C Fleming, "Commentary on Romans 13:1". "Brideway Bible Commentary," accessed August 29, https://www.studylight.org/commentaries/bbc/romans-13.html. 2005.

[10] John Calvin, "Commentary on Romans 13:1". "Calvin's Commentary on the Bible," accessed August 30, 2021, https://www.studylight.org/commentaries/cal/romans-13.html. 1840-57.

towards the rebellious nature of the Hebrew nations toward their oppressors in order to galvanize Author Calvin's statement, endorse Author Donald's notes in order to invalidate the New Testament Historian's statement and delineates that the Jews nation planned to insurrect led to the destruction of Jerusalem and its temples burnt to the ground in AD 70 by the Roman soldiers led by Titus during the reign of Emperor Vespasian.[11] Apostle Paul did not speak in a vacuum; instead, he was specific in his address to them that submission was required (Rom 13:6–7).

Apostle Paul had never been to Rome when he wrote the letter to the Romans; even though, he had clearly expressed his desire to travel there in the near future (Acts 19:21; Rom 1:10–12). The Apostle greeted twenty-six different people by names, personalizing a letter from a man who would have been a personal stranger to most of the recipients. No doubt they had heard of Apostle Paul and would have been honored by his letter; however, Apostle Paul always took opportunities to personally connect with his audience so that the message of the gospel might be better received. Apostle Paul wrote to the Romans from the Greek city of Corinth in about AD 58, just three years after the 16-year-old Nero had ascended to the throne. The political situation in the Roman capital had not yet deteriorated for the Roman Christians, as King Nero would not begin his persecution of them until he made them scapegoats after the great Roman fire of AD 64; therefore, Apostle Paul wrote to a church that was experiencing a time of relative peace; however, he felt that the church needed a strong dose of the basic Gospel doctrine. Writing from Corinth, Apostle Paul likely encountered a diverse array of people and practices. Such populations of categories included gruff sailors and meticulous tradesmen to wealthy idolaters and enslaved Christians. The prominent Greek city was also a hotbed of sexual immorality and idol worship; therefore, when Apostle Paul wrote to the Roman Christians about the sinfulness of humanity, he knew that of which he spoke. It was played out before his eyes every day. The letter to

---

[11] James Burton Coffman, "Commentary on Romans 13:1". "Coffman Commentaries on the Bible" (Abilene, TX: Abilene Christian University Press, 1983–1999), accessed August 30, 2021, https://www.studylight.org/commentaries/bcc/romans-13.html.

the Romans stands as the clearest and most systematic theological presentation of Christian doctrine. Apostle Paul began by discussing that which is most easily observable in the world; hence, such includes the sinfulness of humanity. All people have been condemned due to their rebellions against God; however, God in His grace has offered them justification by faith in His Son. When believers are justified by God, they receive redemption; however, Apostle Paul made it clear that the believer's pursuit of God does not stop with salvation; therefore, it continues as each of them is sanctified, made holy, as the believer persists in following Jesus. Apostle Paul's treatment of these issues offers a logical and complete presentation of how a person can be saved from the penalty and power of his or her sin. The primary theme running through Apostle Paul's letter to the Romans is the revelation of God's righteousness in His plan for salvation. Apostle Paul writes,"For I am not ashamed of the gospel, because it is the power of God that brings salvation to everyone who believes: first to the Jews, then to the Gentiles. For in the gospel the righteousness of God is revealed—a righteousness that is by faith from first to last, just as it is written: "The righteous will live by faith"(Rom 1:16–17 NIV). Apostle Paul showed how humanity lacks God's righteousness because of her sinfulness (1–3), receives God's righteousness when God justifies her by faith (4–5), demonstrates God's righteousness by being transformed (6–8), confirms her righteousness when God saves the Jews (9–11), and applies her righteousness (12–16). The structure of Romans provides a hint into the importance of the book in humanity's everyday life. While beginning with the eleven chapters of the doctrines, the book then transitions into five chapters of practical instruction.[12]

---

[12] Ibid.

Textual Analysis
(Romans 13:1–7)

Key Words, Phrases, and Comparisons

Textual Analysis is the exegetical methodology employed in hermeneutics in order to analyze the individual word in the biblical text piecemeal with the goal to get to the true meaning of the biblical text. The words in the text are defined in the Hebrew or Greek equivalence in the English language taking into consideration the part of speech, gender, and the original Hebrew or Greek word meaning. To resolve the hermeneutical controversy in Romans chapter thirteen verses one to seven, it is prescriptive to adopt this methodology; therefore, the following words as used in the text are considered for delineation: (1) authorities, (2) rulers, (3) servant, (4) public servant, and(5) tribute. Apostle Paul writes,

> Let everyone be subject to the governing authorities, for there is no authority except that which God has established. The authorities that exist have been established by God. Consequently, whoever rebels against the authority is rebelling against what God has instituted, and those who do so will bring judgment on themselves. For rulers hold no terror for those who do right, but for those who do wrong. Do you want to be free from fear of the one in authority? Then do what is right and you will be commended. For the one in authority is God's servant for your good. But if you do wrong, be afraid, for rulers do not bear the sword for no reason. They are God's servants, agents of wrath to bring punishment on the wrongdoer. Therefore, it is necessary to submit to the authorities, not only because of possible punishment but also as a matter of conscience. This is also why you pay taxes, for the authorities are God's servants, who give their full time to governing. Give to everyone

what you owe them: If you owe taxes, pay taxes; if revenue, then revenue; if respect, then respect; if honor, then honor (Rom 13:1–7 NIV).

Reading through the lines of the above passage, there are observable words used in the passage that resonate with authorities, rulers, servant, public servant, and tribute. In Apostle Paul's address, he used four authorities as plural and four authorities as singular. The reason is that one is used as collective unit; however, it contains several members in the group. This could mean two groups of authorities Apostle Paul is addressing in the passage. The one used in the plural represents individual members in the group operating independently in their individual assignment areas that references the ranking in law enforcement division of the police force, the court systems, Para-security agency, or the military in the Roman Empire's context. The repetition of words in literature indicates emphasis; therefore, Apostle Paul's message to the Roman Christians is emphatic. Authorities are law enforcement officers such as policemen and magistrates in this context who enforce daily laws of the country for stability, tranquility, and national security. It is departmentally called the Justice Department of the country that comprises the court systems and the police division.

The Greek word as used for authorities is called *exousia*[13] (Rom 13:1). *Exousia* is the power to act especially with reference to a moral authority. It is the influence derived from the later Judaism of a spiritual or the physical power. It is the power of choice (1 Cor 9:12, 18; 2 Thess 3:9), the physical and mental power (Matt 9:9; Acts 8:19), the power of authority (Matt 21:23; Mark 11:28; Luke 20:2), and the power of the rule of government (Matt 28:18; Jude 1:25; Rev 12:10). *Exousia* is the delegated power given to someone to act on behalf of another person or entity. The policeman uniformed to arrest criminals in the street is the exact example of authority in this category. When a believer casts out evil spirit in the name of Jesus, he or she uses *exousia*; however, the believer should have been clothed in holiness

---

[13] Joseph Henry Thayer, "Thayer's Greek Lexicon," accessed August 27, 2022, https://biblehub.com/greek/1849.htm.

in order to do so (Rom 1:4; Acts 19:11–20). In the passage, Apostle Paul admonishes that every soul be subject to the governing authorities because such authorities are placed to enforce the law (Rom 13:1). The clue is that Apostle Paul wrote this letter to both Jews and Gentiles believers to prepare for his planned visit indicates that Apostle Paul might have heard information regarding the rebelliousness of both Jews and Gentiles believers toward authority figures in Rome. During this era, there were both house and Synagogue churches that Apostle Paul addressed; however, the universality of his address extends his audience beyond these groups.[14]

Apostle Paul used rulers twice in the plural form that reference the executive assembly of elders appointed in the provincial divisions of the country to govern. Rulers are leading men, chiefs, or governors. In the Roman's provincial divisions, they were called kings appointed by the Roman Emperor to lead provinces. Like King Herod, the Great, was appointed by the Roman Emperor, Caesar Augustus, to lead Judaea, the name that derived from the Kingdom of Judah of the 6th century BCE (Matt 2:1–23; 24:1–51; Luke 9:7–9; 1:5). Apostle Paul said, "For rulers hold no terror for those who do right, but for those who do wrong. Do you want to be free from the fear of the one in authority? Then do what is right and you will be commended (Rom 13:3). May writes,

> Some might question, however, the one image that sounds like it originated in a Roman Empire context: "for the authority does not bear the sword in vain!" (13:4b). As Nanos points out, this word for sword can also be used for the knife in circumcision (Joshua 5:2), or it could be used metaphorically as a symbol of the authority of the synagogue rulers to inflict punishment. Paul himself has submitted to such punishment according to his account to the

---

[14] Herman Hendrickx, "The "House Church" in Paul's Letters," *The Theology Annual* 12, no 1 (1990–1991); 154–186.

Corinthians: "Five times I have received from the Jews the forty lashes minus one" (2 Cor 11:24).[15]

The word 'sword' as used in the text is called *machaira* defined as a short sword, a dagger or a slaughter-knife used for stabbing; therefore, figuratively, it is used as the instrument for exacting retribution (punishment). The context used of the word 'sword' is figurative of punishment; therefore, it cannot be used to represent the knife used in circumcision. If it is the symbol of the Synagogue rulers to inflict punishment, what kind of punishment were they to inflict on the believers? 2 Corinthian 11:24 does not fit in the context of Romans 13:4 with reference to the 'sword.' In 2 Corinthians 11: 1–30, Apostle Paul is addressing the subjects on false teaching in the Corinthians church and his persecution with reference to preaching the Gospel; therefore, 2 Corinthians 11:24 does not address punishment for wrong doing; instead, it references persecution he received from both Gentiles and Jews while preaching the Gospel. If the Judean Spiritual authority belongs to God, how will she punish someone who preaches the Gospel? The Judean Spiritual Authority does not fit in the context as advanced by the New Testament Historian. This text references non-believers who have been involved in the persecution of Apostle Paul because he preached the Gospel. Apostle Paul concludes regarding his persecution and writes, "If I must boast, I will boast of the things that show my weakness. The God and Father of the Lord Jesus, who is to be praised forever, know that I am not lying. In Damascus the governor under King Aretas had the city of the Damascenes guarded in order to arrest me. But I was lowered in a basket from a window in the wall and slipped through his hands" (2 Cor 11:30–33 NIV). Apostle Paul is making reference of the provincial kings of the Roman Empire in Romans chapter thirteen verses one to seven as authorities. The kings were small gods of the Roman Empire; therefore, they could execute anyone at any time based on their wishes. Like King Herod, who sought Jesus to kill after his birth; unfortunately, when

---

[15] Ibid.

15

he failed to find Jesus because the Magi did not return to him as instructed; consequently, he got agitated and massacred the children of Bethlehem (Matt 2:16). The Greek word for rulers as used in the text is called *archon* (Rom 13:3). *Archon* is defined as the executive assembly of elders such as leading men, rulers, chiefs or governors (Rev 1:5; Matt 20:25); hence, rulers command authorities to act on their behalves.[16]

Apostle Paul addressed two categories of servants in the text. One category of servants addressed in the text is called *diakonos*[17] in Greek (Rom 13:4). A *diakonos* is a servant, an administrator, a minister, a waiter, or a deacon in the church setting entrusted with the piece of job (Matt 22:3; 1 Tim 3:8; John 2:5, 9). Apostle Paul writes, "For the one in authority is God's servant for your good. But if you do wrong, be afraid, for rulers do not bear the sword for no reason. They are God's servants; agents of wrath to bring punishment on the wrongdoer" (Rom 13:4).[18] *Diakonos* refers to the Roman's rulers or authorities that comprise of magistrates, governors or kings in the judicial system. The second category of servants as mentioned in the text is called public servants known as *leitourgos*[19] in Greek (Rom 13:4). In the Greek New Testament Bible, the servants are categorically indicated; unfortunately, the New Testament Greek translator probably did not have the word equivalence to assign for the English language; therefore, he called both as *diakonos* in the English Bible. *Leitourgos* are public servants that work in civil governments of the particular jurisdiction or servants entrusted to offer religious services in the temple in Judaism. These servants are called Priests and Levites that are placed in the spiritual position in Judaism during the Mosaic Covenant (2 Sam 13:8; Josh 1:1) or public servants in the civil administration of the government. *Leitourgos* and *diakonos* refer to servants outside and inside of the religious circles as used in Romans chapter thirteen verses one to seven in this context. *Diakonos* is

---

[16] Ibid.

[17] Ibid.

[18] Ibid.

[19] Ibid.

the general word that refers to rulers or authorities known as Magistrates or Kings in the Roman's jurisdiction as used in this context. In this light, when Apostle Paul wrote, he was very inclusive regarding the Lord's instruction; therefore, he addressed both Jews and Gentiles alike and asked them to submit to the governing authorities according to the grammatical context of the passage (Rom 13:6–7). Apostle Paul concludes in this manner, "Therefore, it is necessary to submit to the authorities, not only because of possible punishment but also as a matter of conscience. This is also why you pay taxes, for the authorities are God's servants, who give their full time to governing. Give to everyone what you owe them: If you owe taxes, pay taxes; if revenue, then revenue; if respect, then respect; if honor, then honor (Rom 13:6–7). *Phoros* as used in the text is defined as tribute, the annual tax levied on houses, lands, and persons that are used to fund the security and infrastructures development budget of the Roman Empire.[20] The Christian's response to the governing authority on the subjects of respect and taxation in the context of Christian stewardship of treasures (money) is recommended. Good Christians should be good citizens while respecting the boundaries that guide God's attributes and the civil administration (2 Cor 6:14). Hafer writes,

> The interpretation and appropriation of Romans 13:1–7 have been a challenge for generations because this text confuses Christians as to how they should relate and participate in the politics of the day. This article interprets the text in its historical and literary context before appropriating it to the Second Republic of Zimbabwe. The conclusion reached is that the text does not directly speak to church–state relations but rather should be understood in its context in Paul's time. Appropriating the text to the Second Republic requires us to delineate whether the governing authorities of the Second Republic are doing the will of

---

[20] Ibid.

God or whether they are terrorising people into obedience. The article concludes that the text does not forbid people from resisting illegitimate and brutal governments and does not demand passive citizenship.[21]

From the above quotation based on Hafer's exegetical approach to Romans chapter thirteen verses one to seven, he concludes that Apostle Paul indeed addressed governmental authority; however, his address was restricted to the Apostle Paul's day context. He denied the universality of the command's application as defined in the Apostle Paul's context; however, he did not deny that it can be applied to the 21st century Christian church; therefore, government should be obeyed not on terror; instead, she should be obeyed based on good citizenship in order to represent God of order who has called believers to be at peace with all men including governmental authority. Schmanlhofer agrees with Hafer with reference to the restricted universality of the text application based on Apostle Paul's context with reference to the happening in Paul's day; however, he did not root out that the commandments in the text are not applicable to the 21st century Christian church.[22] Hanc adds,

Paul writes to the church in Rome not as a political activist, but rather in terms that resonate with the Isaianic features of the servant of God. His self-understanding as the Servant of the Lord, who seeks for a way of salvation not an escape from society, indicates that the original meaning of his theology is rooted in the Old Testament, not in the socio-political realities of first century Rome. The Scripture represents the all-encompassing factor that motivates simultaneously his citizenship of the Roman Empire and of the Kingdom

---

[21] CharletonHafer, "Exegesis of Romans 13:1–7 and Its Appropriation of the Second Republic of Zambawe," *Eleutheria* 5, no. 2 (2021): 234–257.

[22] Travis Schmanlhofer, "Romans 13:1–7: An Historical and Exegetical Analysis," *Presbyterion* 45, no. 2 (2019): 187–188.

of God. Paul commands the Church not to subvert the Empire, but to serve it in a Christ-like sacrificial manner. He is not a revolutionary figure but a servant who is willing to submit to civil authority as a servant of Christ.[23]

Some scholars of the Bible have said that the texts recorded in Romans chapter thirteen verses one to seven are interpolations; however, looking at the structure of the book of Romans, Apostle Paul made mention of the Old Testament Law most often in his deliberations throughout the book. Being a Pharisee, he had interest in the study of laws that governed the nation Israel; therefore, Apostle Paul was acquainted with the Mosaic Law that references the moral, the ceremonial, and the civil law. Taking into consideration his Pharisaic background, it is not a coincidence that Apostle Paul admonished the believers in Rome to submit to governing authority based on his background and also as the Roman citizen. Apostle Paul had not been in Rome before writing the book; however, he was well informed about tax payment to the government. Hanc's statement in the above quotation resonates with this injection regarding Apostle Paul's address in Romans chapter thirteen verses one to seven to submit to governmental authority; therefore, these texts cannot be interpolations. The governing authorities referenced in Romans chapter thirteen verses one to seven constitute magistrates and governors in the Roman provincial jurisdictions.[24]

Exegesis versus Eisegesis

In the introductory section of this monograph, it is learned that Romans chapter thirteen verses one to seven has been misinterpreted as the result of context's problem; therefore, it has been helpful to introduce exegesis in order to solve the hermeneutical controversy that the New Testament Historian had created since the context scriptural thesis for the discourse

---

[23] Ovidiu Hanc, "Paul and Empire: A Reframing of Romans 13:1–7 in the Context of the New Exodus," *Tyndale Bulletin* 65, no. 2 (2014): 313–316.

[24] Ibid.

on the government has been chosen to be Romans chapter thirteen verses one to seven. This book cannot be written using this Scripture unless the problem is resolved through exegesis. The problem the New Testament Historian might have encountered to be exclusive in his argument is the lack of proper exegesis of Romans chapter thirteen verses one to seven; therefore, he concluded that the authority referenced in Romans chapter thirteen verses one to seven referenced the Judean spiritual authority only. He is right on one axis of the polarity because the second category of servants Apostle Paul referenced in the text refers to the Priests and the Levites who might be members of the Judean spiritual authority; however, he failed to find out that the first category of servants Apostle Paul mentioned in the text called *diakonos* who are also servants refer to the Roman's authority comprising of Magistrates and Kings in the Roman's context. His problem might have been the lack of the understanding of the Greek language; therefore, he conducted eisegesis instead of exegesis. To eisegete is to misinterpret the biblical text out of the context by reading into the text without using proper exegesis. The failure to contextualize Scripture using proper exegesis such as history, literary, and grammar can lead to misinterpretation of the Scripture.

Exegesis is the interpretation methodology employed in which the biblical interpreter speaks into the context of what the original author of the biblical text meant to convey to the biblical and the contemporary audience. In simplicity, it is the legitimate interpretation methodology in which the biblical interpreter reads out of the text what the original author meant to convey to both the biblical and the contemporary audience. On the contrary, eisegesis is the opposite in which the interpreter reads into the text what he or she wishes to find there. Such interpreter speaks out of the context in order to establish a misleading theological doctrine without biblical evidence. On average today, many ministers who preach are found in this category. Only few, one will hear preaching from the context of the Scripture. The lack of study of God's word, theological training, coupled with limited resources had made preachers to eisegete Scriptures on average. There are preachers who look through the Bible on Sunday morning to find something that favors their theological appetites; therefore, such subject chosen and introduced on Sunday morning to the congregation may not have a goal of preaching; therefore, one will see a sensational theological preaching wherein the preacher moves with high tone of voice on top of the congregation; unfortunately, the message is misleading to the congregation because the preacher is reading into the text without getting the understanding of what the biblical author meant; nevertheless, the Holy Spirit still uses the message to get people saved. God does not depend on one's theological analysis before He saves anyone; however, God recommends and supports studiousness in the Scriptures (2 Tim 2:15). Apostle Paul writes, "I plant, Apollo waters, and God gives the increase" (1 Cor 3:6). Preachers are able to plant and water well when they study the Scriptures.

Scripture Interprets Scripture

The statement "scripture interprets scripture" defines that Scripture can be used to interpret another Scripture; therefore, to validate the proof text, the scripture used to validate, should agree with the proposition. A proof text is used to establish a proposition based on the biblical evidence when exegesis is considered using history, literary, and grammatical contexts; then, the statement 'scripture interprets scripture' is adopted in such situation. Preachers who exegete and eisegete scriptures use the methodology of proof texting in order to establish their truth or misleading proposition. Proof texting is the practice of using a proposition or quotation from a document, either for the purpose of exegesis in order to establish a proposition in eisegisis. To exegete is to read out of the text in context while to eisegete is to read into the text out of the context. Example of the proposition in the Bible is Romans 3:23. It reads, "For all have sinned and fall short of the glory of God." This is the number one verse Catholics hear to refute Immaculate Conception of Mary. If all have sinned, does that mean Jesus, too sinned? Apostle Paul is saying in this verse that Jews are not superior to Gentiles because all are sinners as the result of the Adamic nature (Gen 1:1–15). Second example of the proposition is Matthew 23:9. It reads, "Call no man your father on earth, for you have one Father, who is in heaven."

Some Protestants have said that Catholics have violated this verse by having fathers in their churches. If that is true; then, it will be wrong to call our biological fathers "fathers." Jesus made this statement to refer to the Pharisees who sought seats of honor in the public places to be called teachers; on the contrary, they did not have the humility to be called fathers. Taking either of the above quotations and establishing it as the theological doctrine is called proof texting. Using cross references with historical and grammatical contexts to prove the proposition exegetically to become a theological doctrine is called exegesis; on the other hand, the failure to prove that it is wrong to call someone "father"; instead, establishing it as the theological doctrine without proof is called eisegesis. A proof text becomes wrong when it cannot be proven exegetically; similarly, it becomes true when it can be proven exegetically. A proof text can be a Bible verse or a statement made by someone. A proof text is a guess answer; therefore, it must be proven to stand as the theological doctrine. If it is wrong to call someone "Father" it must be proven using cross references or else it will become a proposition in eisegesis. When the New Testament Historian said that Romans chapter thirteen verses one to seven is being interpreted out of context, his statement becomes a proposition; therefore, unless, his statement is proven false, it could serve as the theological doctrine and made others to believe him. Proposition or proof texting elected as the theological doctrine and not proven biblically as evidence is the ground for false teachings in Christendom. It is evidenced that cross references are being adopted to prove the New Testament Historian's statement false with reference to his exclusive arguments regarding submitting to authority figures. Matthew writes,

> They sent their disciples to him along with the Herodians. "Teacher," they said, "we know that you are a man of integrity and that you teach the way of God in accordance with the truth. You aren't swayed by others, because you pay no attention to who they are. Tell us

then, what is your opinion? Is it right to pay the imperial tax to Caesar or not?" But Jesus, knowing their evil intent, said, "You hypocrites, why are you trying to trap me? Show me the coin used for paying the tax." They brought him a denarius, and he asked them, "Whose image is this? And whose inscription?" "Caesar's," they replied. Then he said to them, "So give back to Caesar what is Caesar's, and to God what is God's." When they heard this, they were amazed. So they left him and went away (Matt 22:16–22 NIV).

In the above passage, Jesus knowing their evil intent discovered that the group wanted to trap him. Why? The Herodians were members of the Herodian dynasty who ruled one of the provincial territories in the Roman Empire; therefore, this group was a royalist to the Roman government while the Pharisees were members of the Jewish community who were under the Roman's oppression (Matt 22:15–22; Luke 20:19–26). This group which included the Jewish community did not want to pay taxes to the Roman's government. With reference to the question posed to Jesus, if Jesus answers 'yes,' the Pharisees will accuse him of being a traitor to the Jewish community. If Jesus answers 'no,' the Romans will accuse him of treason. In Jesus' response, he said, "Give to Caesar what is Caesar's and to God what is God's" (Matt 22:21). Jesus' answer to the group is full of wisdom that speaks volume of the demarcation between the divinity and the humanity when it comes to submitting to secular authorities. Jesus said, "Give to Caesar what belongs to Caesar" since the coin you are holding bears the inscription of Caesar; however, don't give to Caesar what does not belong to Caesar. The things that belong to Caesar are honor and tributes (taxes); therefore, if Caesar deviates from these boundaries and attempts to set himself up as the god to be worshipped, don't obey him because he has taken the thing that belongs to God. God is the only person that should be worshipped instead of Caesar. During this era, Tiberius was the Emperor of Rome while the Emperor's worship was still enforced. The Emperor was the god of Rome; therefore, the refusal to worship him was death. You can pay honor and taxes to Caesar; however, you must not do anything for Caesar that becomes a disobedience to God. It tells us that our obedience to secular governments does not infringe on our biblical tradition how we live as believers. Paying respect and taxes to secular authorities is not sinful; instead, it is a biblical mandate because God is the One who has placed these authorities in power to put restraint on evil doers and to provide security for all.

Apostle Paul writes, "The Son is the image of the invisible God, the firstborn over all creation. For in him all things were created: things in heaven and on earth, visible and invisible, whether thrones or powers or rulers or authorities; all things have been created through him and for him" (Col 1:15–16 NIV). No one was born a Christian; therefore, humanity was conceived in sin as the result of the federally committed sin Adam and Eve committed in the Garden of Eden (Rom 5:12; Gen 3:1–15); therefore, leadership in the secular world, salvation is not the requirement. This is the reason, both Christian and secular leaderships are endorsed by God for the reasons to restraining evil doers in society and providing stability, and tranquility for all (Rom 13:1–7). Apostle Paul in his address said that everything created visible or invisible including thrones or powers or rulers or authorities were created by God for the purpose of stewardship. Stewardship fundamentally teaches that God owns all; therefore, humanity is the manager of God's creation. Thrones, powers, rulers or authorities are placed in the position of stewardship to manage people in the world; therefore, stewardship has universal position.

Apostle Paul writes, "I urge, then, first of all, that petitions, prayers, intercession and thanksgiving be made for all people—for kings and all those in authority, that we may live peaceful and quiet lives in all godliness and holiness. This is good, and pleases God our Savior, who wants all people to be saved and to come to a knowledge of the truth" (1 Tim 2:1–4 NIV). God has interest in universal stewardship; therefore, He urges believers to pray for authorities in secular leaderships; hence, the authorities are stewards of God placed in various positions to manage human beings. Having discussed the exegetical analysis of Romans chapter thirteen verses one to seven with reference to history, textual analysis of the biblical words, using the proof texts, the below bulleted have been considered as conclusive:

- Apostle Paul addressed both Jews and Gentiles Christians to submit to the God's ordained authorities;

- The subjects to be obeyed included both spiritual and secular authorities (Priests, Levites, and Roman's rulers);

- God ordained secular authorities to provide national security for all;

- Authorities are ordained of God no matter whether such authorities operate within the guidelines of God's ethics;

- Salvation is not a pre-requisite for God's ordained leadership;

- Christians are required to submit to secular authorities within the confine of God's boundaries and not violate God's ordinance;

- God is the ruler of all because He ordains both secular and spiritual leaderships;

- Humanity is the manager of God's creation in regardless of religions, creeds, histories, geographies, cultures, races, and salvation; therefore, God endorses universal stewardship.

Ethical Reflection

Apostle Paul's instruction to the Roman Christians to submit to civil authority seems situational and specific; however, the instruction to submit to the civil authority is universal and inclusive; therefore, the New Testament historian's claim that the letter was addressed to the Judean spiritual authority only is unauthentic. Based on the research with reference to the Greek grammar, historical context, and the proof texts, it can be deduced that Apostle Paul's address was universal and inclusive to the Roman Christians of his days. The universality of the text with reference to what kind of governments to obey does not signify that all governments should be obeyed due to the flawed nature of governments and laws enacted by them that do not dictate the ethics of God; therefore, the Scripture allows civil disobedience where laws become flawed that question integrity. All governments in the world despite of their kinds, God has ordained them to restrain evil and to keep national peace and stability for all.

CHAPTER III
THE PRIMARY HOLISTICITY

Chapter Overview

This segment of the discourse introduces the eleven major world religions and forms of government in synopsis, biblically defines the roles of civil authority and citizens in the community of nations; hence, it delineates taxation, the biblical view of wealth, wealth redistribution, and the dichotomy between social and biblical justices; however, biblical view of justice tends to conflict with the social justice system as delineated in this segment. At the conclusion, the author has developed a reflection on the chapter to redress the subject in order to pin a mental picture in the mind of the reader for personal subjective reflection.

The Forms of Religion

The influence of religion on God's established institution warrants their synopsis that resonates with religious commonalities based on rituals and practices; therefore, the commonalities seen in all religions of the world constitute solidarity, compassion, and respect for the human person; hence, additionally, all religions usually have rituals or special patterns of actions. In this light, religion is the relationship that exists between the deity and the followers based on worship.[25] These elements

---

[25] Dale Tuggy, "Theories of Religious Diversity," *A Peer-Reviewed Academic Resource,* accessed June 19, 2022, https://iep.utm.edu/reli-div/.

are present in all religions of the world; therefore, they are the commonalities that should be seen by virtue as religion is concerned. The birth of religions is the ideology that someone or something is supreme that needs respect, submission, and worship from the followers. Categorically, there are eleven world religions that are monotheistic or poly-theistic; hence, amongst these religions, Judaism, Christianity, and Islam worship one God; unless, the rest, they are polytheistic religions. These polytheistic religions include Hinduism, Buddhism, Sikhism, Zoroastrianism, Shinto, Jainism, Taoism, and Confucianism.[26] The followers of the polytheistic religions named above practice idolatry; therefore, they worship nature; for this reason, these religions practice zoolatry or animism based on worship classification. Based on the commonalities with reference to respect, submission, and worship, it is obvious that the religious books guiding the behaviors and practices of the membership of these religions-should be able to support submission to governmental authorities since they form part of the nation by virtues of their placements. All religions should have norms that endorse submission and worship in regardless of their orientations and theologies.[27]

In the context of this discourse, Christianity is the focal subject influencing God's established institution that constitutes the government; therefore, the message presented in this discourse is grounded on the teachings of the Bible. While the use of secondary sources other than the Bible to cement the argument is employed, it remains grounded to the ethics and philosophies of the Christian religion. The Bible is hundred percent adequate; however, it remains fragmentary to our understanding in the absent use of the secondary sources to substantiate the argument.

Religion is the relationship that exists between the adherences and the deity and requires that respect, submission, and worship be ascribed. These elements must be present and executed between the deity and the worshippers in order to keep the relationship solidified. In the Christian

[26] Andrew Gardner, "Students and the Study of Religion: The Extra-curricular Origins of the World Religions Paradigm," *Implicit Religion* 23, no. 1 (2020): 54–62.

[27] Ibid.

religion, the ritual of daily prayers, reading of the Scripture, meditations, devotional worships, and the observance of the Christian norms with reference to morality should be kept by the believer to qualify him or her approach the holy God. On the contrary, government is to be respected, obeyed, and tribute paid to her based on the biblical stance as dictated in the Bible. In the context of submitting to governmental authority, it should be understood that the Christian's submission excludes worshiping the authority. The believer might not literally bow down to the authority; however, any activity conducted by the believer toward the authority that crosses the biblical boundaries is the form of worship to the authority. When Jesus was asked by the Pharisees if it was necessary to pay taxes to Caesar, Jesus responded by saying, "Give to Caesar what is Caesar's and to God what is God's" (Matt 22:21). What Jesus meant in the text is that, one can pay taxes to Caesar; however, if Caesar sets himself up to be worshiped, one is not required to submit to him because worship belongs to God and Caesar is not God; therefore, the Christian's submission to secular authority excludes worshipping the authority.

The Forms of Government

Government is defined as the political direction and control exercised over the actions of the members, citizens, societies, and States; therefore, government is the instrument of the States.[28] In the democratic society, the separation of government and church is obvious like the United States of America and other countries that value democratic values. The separation of government and church as enacted in the Amendment Clause of the United States of America's constitutionality advocates that government has no jurisdiction nationally to impose States' religion on her people; as such, individual citizen has the right to choose which religion he or she wants to belong to; therefore, it advocates for the freedom of

---

[28] William Collin Son & CO. LTD, "Dictionary.com, accessed June 19, 2022, https://www.dictionary.com/browse/government.

religions.[29] In essence, realistically, one cannot separate government from the church because by social contract and association people who are part of the government might be part of the church also; therefore, the separation of government from the church has to do with influence instead of social contract of association. Similarly, one cannot separate politics from the church because people who make up the church are political beings; therefore, they have the right to exercise their political franchise. In discussing the influence of religions on God's established institutions, the terminology politics is unavoidable; therefore, it is being adopted throughout this monograph since religion and government are intertwined; therefore, they co-exist. It is not surprising why God has laid emphasis on the governing authorities because He is the One who has established all that resonate with the universality of stewardship. Streater writes to substantiate the above statement regarding government and people who made up the church. He writes,

> Any reasonable acquaintance with Church history will confirm the fact that secular thought has played a large part in fashioning the manner in which the Church works. The 'Turnbull Report', at present being debated by the General Synod of the Church of England, is a case in point. What is less well known, or understood, is the way in which the Reformed Church has influenced the Western world in the gradual adoption of democracy. Douglas F Kelly in this work examines the development of the idea that the governing of society should be based on the consent of the people.[30]

---

[29] Brett G. Scharffs, "the (Not So) Exceptional Establishment Clause of the United States," *Journal of Law and Religion* 33, no. 2 (20218): 137–154.

[30] David Streater, "The Emergence of Liberty in the Modern World: The Influence of Calvin on Five Governments from the 16th through the 18th Centuries," *Churchman* 110, no. 1 (1996): 90–92.

Namely, the systems of government of the world include democracy, monarchy, dictatorship, oligarchy, communism, autocracy, aristocracy, socialism, republic, and theocracy.[31] Besides these major systems of governments, there are thirteen hybrids of the systems of governments giving the total of twenty-three. The thirteen that are not named in this monograph are hybrids of the ten listed above. The multiplicities of the systems of governments indicate the evolving complications of the human beings in the political arenas. Man by nature is the political being and likes to be seen in the political arenas as the result of fame, power, and the love for money. This is the reason world leaders who suppose to be role models to democracy like Russia and China have taken the back seat and supported totalitarianism in the world.

The Functions of Government

The biblical functions of the government to restrain evil and to provide security to the nation resonate with the responsibilities of citizens to respect and to pay taxes to their governments. Reciprocally and fiduciary, this obligates the government also to provide services such as education, healthcare, and infrastructures developments to her citizens as the tertiary responsibilities in addition to the biblical functions (restraining of evil). The issue of security provision to the citizens underscores the above mentioned services government is obligated to provide by virtues of her fiduciary duty to the nation. The roles of the government to her citizens are delineated as the following:

The Restraining of Evil

Apostle Paul writes, "For rulers hold no terror for those who do right, but for those who do wrong. Do you want to be free from fear of the one in authority? Then do what is right and you will be commended. For

---

[31] Evan Thompson, "Cheat Sheet: 10 Common Forms of Government," accessed June 19, 2022, https://thebestschools.org/magazine/common-forms-of-government-study-starters/.

the one in authority is God's servant for your good. But if you do wrong, be afraid, for rulers do not bear the sword for no reason. They are God's servants, agents of wrath to bring punishment on the wrongdoer (Rom 13:3–4 NIV). One of the functions of the governing authorities is summarized in the above quotation. It makes sense that the endorsement of secular governments by God is necessary due to the proliferation of the agents of evil in the world; therefore, government exists to restrain evil in society, which is the primary biblical function of the government. Apostle Paul inspired by the Holy Spirit instructs believers to submit to the governing authorities (Rom 13:1–7). In his address, Apostle Paul primarily mentioned authorities four times in sets as plural and singular that indicates immediate attentions to the Roman Christians for compliance. From the Greek context, authority refers to law enforcement division and the department of justice in the nation. This is the reason police are deployed strategically in the nation to crack down on criminals who pose threats to peaceful citizens. When criminals are arrested by law enforcement division, they are taken to custody to face the court systems. If they are convicted during the court proceeding, they are sent to jail to serve the sentence. This serves as the deterrence to discourage others from doing similar things in the community of nations. The proliferation of terrorisms both domestic and internationally calls for law enforcement to exist in order to provide national security. The deployment of the police force and the judging of cases to acquit peaceful citizens and to punish evil doers is the function of the government to restrain evil. Citizens of nations have the moral and reciprocal obligation to submit to the governing authorities because authorities are ordained by God. This has moved Borggren to examine the inadequacy of the unimaginative and binary categories of assimilation or resistance and cooperation or disobedience regarding submission; then, the author re-examines Romans 13:1–7 and Philippians 3:17–21 through the lens of Japanese American internment in American concentration camps and finds a fresh reading of Romans 13:1–7 and Philippians 3:17–21 in which citizenship in heaven enables submission on Earth that empowers hope-filled resistance rooted in the love of neighbors.[32]

Laboring

The subject of security with reference to the nature of the job cannot be underestimated regarding the labor involved. Security job in law enforcement is both physical and mental work to keep criminals out of the street for the safety of all. These officers are placed in the street to guard community members while community members lie in beds. Law enforcement is the difficult job; nevertheless, God has ordained people with the passion and placed them strategically within the various communities of the country to keep security for all. People who do such job should be respected; unfortunately, some authorities in some parts of the globe had abandoned the security apparatuses of those countries. The stronger the nation is security wise is the result of how well the government has taken care of the country's police force and the military. Law enforcement division and the military should be paid as scheduled. It releases them of stress related issues full of traumas and makes them maintain security in the country as their families are maintained economically. This is one of the strengths of the United States because she takes care of her security by paying regular salary to members as scheduled. Across all federal and States governments, workers are paid with incentives. The quick fall of Afghanistan's democracy in 2021 is the result of the corrupt government; as the result, the military and police who had not been paid as scheduled despite of foreign aids from America refused to fight the dissidents resulting into the Taliban's take over.

---

[32] Erik Borggren, "Romans 13:1–7 and Philippians 3:17–21: Paul's Call to True Citizenship and to Gaman," *The Covenant Quarterly (Online)*, no. 1 (2015): 1–16.

Ordination

Understanding that authorities are ordained of God gives informed decision to citizens that authorities are placed by God for their safety. This is the reason Apostle Paul said that people who refuse to submit to the governing authorities are affront with God with reference to what God has instituted. Rebelliousness against governing authorities is the direct rebelliousness against God. This is the reason Apostle Paul said that citizens obey governing authorities not because of the fear they will be punished, but it is the matter of conscience. It should be understood that submission to the governing authorities should be in agreement with one's Christian ethics. Any submission that infringes on the biblical stance how Christians live in conformity with biblical doctrine is not a biblical submission to the authorities; therefore, no Christian should submit to the governing authorities in the situation wherein he or she commits sin against God. The Lord Jesus summarizes it in Matthew 22:21 and said, "Give to Caesar what is Caesar's and to God what is God's. Any action carried out by the Christian to obey the governing authorities must not violate the boundaries against Christian living or else it is not a biblical submission; instead, it is sin against God; therefore, such submission is not supported by the Scripture.

Morality

Morality is the Christian virtue that sets the boundary between the governing authorities and how Christian relates to the authorities. In society at large, Christians are categorically classified as the light and the salt of the Earth; for this reason, Christians should be role models that others can emulate (Matt 5:13–16). Christians support governing authorities morally when they are law abiding; in this light, Apostle Paul said that if it is taxes, pay taxes, if it is revenue, then, revenue, and if it is respect; then, give respect due to the governing authorities. It should be understood that these wordings were addressed to Christians in Rome that resonate with the present Christian community of the 21ˢᵗ century. This principle doctrine is timeless that extends to the present generation and beyond; though, it might have been addressed to the Christians of Rome based on the prevailing situations [33]; however, Apostle Paul wrote this letter when there was relative peace in the Roman Empire. The function of government interconnects and intersects with the Christian's responsibility and morality. Government restrains evil in society; therefore, Christians including non-Christians are obligated to submit to the governing authorities understanding that God has chosen them to labor for the good of all (Rom 13:1–7).

Provision of National Security

The secondary function of government is to guarantee national security. To guarantee national security is the direct approach to restraining evil doers in the nation. Restraining evil doers through systematic arrests followed by punishments is the means to the end. This security strategy is the best approach to lasting national stability and tranquility. The failure to restrain evil through effective law enforcement activities will cause criminals to show up because they will have felt secured in the absence of impunity and will have miscalculated the strengths of law enforcement division and the judicial system of the nation to be weak. To set deterrence is to punish evil doers in the society- without compromise. By doing so, government discourages potential criminals who want to become members of any gang movement in the nation. The failure for the governing authorities to arrest and to punish evil doers is the open door to national instability, in-tranquility, and insecurity.

Instability

The other side of the coin is the failure for the government to arrest and to punish criminals in the society that resonates with instability. Most

---

[33] Ibid.

of the countries where violence and drugs have become the order of the days have been the failure of law enforcement divisions to arrest criminals.[34] The dilemma exists when people who are in law enforcement division become the architects of these evils taking place daily; therefore, such system becomes dangerous to national stability, tranquility, and security; consequently, government finds it difficult to stabilize national peace because the enemies are within the camp where truth should be preached and practiced. If the leader of the law enforcement division becomes drugs addict; the issue of drugs law enforcement in the country is dead. This is one of the reasons, Apostle Paul wrote the Christians of Ephesus asking them to offer prayers for kings and all those in authority so that they can live peacefully in all godliness and holiness (1 Tim 2:2). To maintain national stability, tranquility, and security, God has called the church to an intercessory ministry in regardless of denomination, creed, and faith tradition. The stability, tranquility, and security of communities can be maintained through prayers as law enforcement division plays her roles in the nation through systematic arrests of criminals. Physicality and spirituality should co-exist in order to mitigate system's failure in the human's society where physical and spiritual agents exist that pose dangers to national peace.

In-Tranquility

In-tranquility is the absence of domestic and national peace as the result of instability in the nation due to government's failure to restrain evil. One gives renaissance to the other due to the failure for one to perform security wise; therefore, law enforcement division is advised to take proactive notice with reference to intelligence followed by action. When the leadership of America under looked the essence of security threats posed by potential terrorists to the nation, over three thousand Americans

---

[34] Avinash Singh, "State and Criminality: The Colonial Campaign against Thugee and the Suppression of Sikh Militancy in Postcolonial India," *Sikh Formations* 8, no. 1 (2012): 37–58.

died at the Trade Center due to terrorists' attack on September 11, 2001. The signal coupled with threat was talked about by the intelligent agencies of America; unfortunately, the White House and law enforcement division took it for granted, miscalculated the threats posed, and slept. This incidence led America to Afghanistan for two decades war that cost American lives coupled with billions of dollars in cash excluding military hardware and among others. When government allows criminals to thrive as the result of the lack of arrest and punishment of evil doers, evil doers will thrive in society; consequently, government becomes incapacitated to crack down on criminals leading to the detrimental security situation posed in the nation.

Insecurity

Government's failure to maintain stability through inconsistent law enforcement leads to the lack of domestic peace that threatens national security. The establishment of the police department and the military is the goal of keeping national peace in the nation. Apostle Paul admonishes believers to pay taxes to the governing authorities because they have given their lives as sacrifices to save the nation.[35] The taxes paid by citizens go to subsidize the budget for national security. This budget is allocated for salary payments and the purchasing of police and military hardware. Paying taxes to the governing authorities is the collaborative act aimed at maintaining national sovereignty whenever the enemy attacks the nation from the outside and inside. In most instances in some countries where taxes are paid by citizens are never allocated for its intended purpose as the result of corrupt practices. This is bad governance that can undermine peace and threatens national security. Since religion plays roles in national peace and security; therefore, Apostle Paul admonishes believers to pay taxes to the government in order to contribute to this process. Lucius in her article underscores Apostle Paul's position and explores how President

---

[35] Dave Kroeker, "What Belongs to Caesar: A Discussion on the Christian Response to Payment of Wars Taxes," *The Mennonite Quarterly Review* 46, no. 1 (1972): 91–92.

Barack Obama views the role of religion in relation to national security interests[36]

Provision of Social Services

Health Care System

Social services are ranges of public services intended to provide support and assistance towards particular groups, which commonly include the disadvantaged. They may be provided by individuals, private and independent organizations, or administered by a government agency.[37] In this context, citizens of nations are inclusive in this program that references health care, education, and development projects. In the context of religion, Apostle John understands the expediencies of social services as he deliberates with reference to health care. He writes, "Dear friend, I pray that you may enjoy good health and that all may go well with you, even as your soul is getting along well" (3 John 1:2 NIV). God who is Spirit has holistic interest when it comes to the dimension of humanity with reference to well-being. John the Beloved, inspired by the Holy Spirit prays for believers to experience good health on every level. The word "good health" as used in the text is called *hugiaino* in Greek that comes from the English word "hygiene." *Hugiaino* is defined as being freed from physical illness that incapacitates the human being to function. Such freedom has to do with being freed from debilitating sickness.

Since government governs citizens and obligates them to pay taxes, government has the moral responsibilities to her citizens. The health well-being of citizens is being down played by some governments in the world; paradoxically, event some developed nations in the west where government has many resources to help citizens, had politicized the health

---

[36] Casey Lucius, "Religion and the National Security Strategy," *Journal of Church and State* 55, no. 1 (2013): 50–70.

[37] NC Department of Health and Human Services, "Social Services," accessed June 20, 2022, https://www.ncdhhs.gov/divisions/social-services.

care system and ignored the suffering masses of the middle class. Health care delivery system like the United States of America has capitalistic ideology; therefore, health services have become too expensive for capital gain; consequently, the issued governmental health insurances like the Medicaid and Medicare including the Affordable Care Act adopted during the Obama's administration do suffer losses in term of spending the Federal government rendered for the re-imbursement of health services rendered to citizens in cash payment to the private health institutions.[38] Such incidence can discourage members of congress to continue to endorse programs relative to health services when citizens are over charged for services rendered them when services received do not qualify for the amount spent during the hospital or doctor's visit. People, who do not have health insurance, find it difficult to obtaining health insurance due to underlying medical condition, the lack of funds to fund the insurance, and among others; consequently, maintaining optimal health becomes impossible. The lack of money or health insurance to pay for medical services for citizens can accelerate morbidity rate in the country and reduce population density due to early mortality.

Prior to the introduction of the Affordable Care Act in America, the number of uninsured Americans in 2010 was 50 million people. After the approval of the Affordable Care Act, the number of uninsured Americans has dropped to 30 million people from 2010 to 2020 respectively.[39] The difference of the 30 million people still remained uninsured. The uninsured population is vulnerable to morbidity and is likely die from diseases. The evidence has been seen during the Pandemic at which people who die the most are people who have underlying medical conditions due to lack of health insurance coverage. The subject of preventive medicine is in utopia because such population never visits the hospital or doctor's office until the sickness has affected the entire body. The probability of

---

[38] Adam Gaffney and Danny McCormick, "The Affordable Care Act: Implication for the Health Care Equity," accessed June 20, 2022, https://pubmed.ncbi.nlm.nih.gov/28402826/.

[39] Ibid.

life expectancy can be minimal for survival because the disease will have already metastasized and body organs will have become affected greatly. The lack of money or health insurance can lead to early death because the illness will have spread to body organs before being detected. Based on the kind of food one eats and some risk practices some people are involved with reference to drugs used and illicit sexual activities, it is recommended that people do regular physical exam annually even if one feels healthy. It is impossible to carry out such in the absence of money or health insurance.

With reference to the third world countries, the issues of healthcare are never the priority subject on the agenda for governments. The budget allocated for health care for third world countries can resemble pocket change as compared to government official's salary. Liberia seems to be the perfect example for such statement. The nature of greed and lack of concerns for the masses matched with wickedness is the description of law makers, senators, and the executives in third world countries on the average. Governments in most of the third world countries have considered healthcare as private issues when it should be the concern of governments. Unlike the United States of America, has the Medicaid and Medicare programs for children age one week old to 21 years old and for the aging populations, and food stamp for people in the poverty gap do qualify when they apply for it. The adoption of the Affordable Care Act has been able to offer free health insurance to people who are considered middle class in America based on income levels; however, much still need to be done in order to address the morbidity crisis.

Education

The author of Proverbs writes, "The wise prevail through great power, and those who have knowledge muster their strength "(Prov 24:5 NIV). The author reveals that those who have knowledge are stronger than those who have physical power; therefore, as the individual continues to grow in knowledge, the individual will have become the leader of those who have physical power because it operates differently than intellectual knowledge based on its application (wisdom). God is speaking through King Solomon, the wisest King that ever lived on planet Earth. The proliferation of technological advancements and space exploration is the result of knowledge gained through learning. God is interested that humanity attains knowledge to know Him better and His created acts. Astronaut has gone to the moon, developed the International Space Station, and launched a rover and a helicopter called Perseverance and Ingenuity to Mars. The invention of these spacecrafts and the continued scientific research is the result of education.

One of the most important roles of government is to provide public education for the masses because every child deserves to be educated. It is one of the most significant investments that government can contribute to national developments. National development with reference to early childhood education is the bedrock to secondary and university education that imparts the child's mind leading to the production of the human resources that give renaissance to scientists, technocrats, nurses, medical doctors, teachers, and among others. These expertises are necessary to national development; unfortunately, some governments tend to under look the paramount of these personnel. The above mentioned personnel would be trained in these disciplines provided government had provided public education from kindergarten to university levels. The issue of education in some third world countries has been privatized; unfortunately, parents don't have the means financially to send their children to private schools due to poverty. Unlike the United States of America, she provides free education from kindergarten to secondary education level coupled with the subsidization of the bachelor degree for college students who qualified for financial aid. Understanding that college education in the United States from the master to the doctorate seems expensive, some members of Congress are advocating that government provides free education to all levels as student loan proliferates while graduates receive huge students' debts. Student loan debt in the United States is the issue that stresses graduates beyond the limit and leads them to default regarding payment. With reference to educational stories in third world countries, the educational stories with reference to governments subsidizing education is the downside of the coin because most governments have not come to the realization that educating the minds of the children is the direct act of national building. The greed for money and property is on the accelerated levels because some government officials are uneducated despite of the positions they are holding in the nation. This is one of the reasons wickedness is on its elevated levels because when cruel and uneducated people are placed in offices, they are always afraid to be removed from such position; as the result, they feel threaten by those who are educated; therefore, losing the position becomes the eternal loss to them due to the lack of educational capacity to obtain another job based on the merit systems. This is one of the reasons ritualistic killing is seen in Liberia and educated people have been killed who can contribute to national development. The killing of the auditors in Liberia and justice not being played out is one of the reasons of having cruel and uneducated people in offices who are the perpetrators.

Development Projects

Moses writes, "And God blessed them. And God said to them, "Be fruitful and multiply and fill the earth and subdue it and have dominion over the fish of the sea and over the birds of the heavens and over every living thing that moves on the earth" (Gen 1:28 ESV). The genesis of development is clearly seen in the above text. Humanity was given dominion over God's creation to subdue it including everything that moves upon the earth. The developments seen in countries that are developmentally oriented like the United States of America is the gift God had given to humanity from the beginning; unfortunately, this gift has not been actualized in most of the nations across the globe. The gift has been given to all. Why others are still behind is the big question that remained unanswered until there is a self-discovery. The construction of roads, repairs of old roads, the construction of health and educational institutions, technological advancements, and transportation networks on seas, air, and on land are amongst the infrastructures developments that government should undertake and consolidate for the use of her citizens. These are basic needs in addition to healthcare delivery provided by the government for her citizens. The execution of the above mentioned areas are the direct approach to distributing the wealth to the national population. Wealth should be decentralized to be properly allocated to the masses based on their constituencies when developments are undertaken to affect the above mentioned areas. The issue of wealth decentralization for equal distribution to the masses is the problem that needs to be addressed in third world countries as rampant corruption in governments proliferates. Government by virtue has moral and fiduciary responsibility to her citizens; paradoxically, fiduciary responsibility does not exist in some governments based on bad governance that is cancerous to equity; therefore, disparities are seen across governments because national wealth has not been decentralized.[40] Decentralization of wealth is the act of distributing the country's resources to the various constituents of the nation by electors. Development budgets should be allocated annually based on constituencies to make sure that development goes on periodically and constituently; unfortunately, when money that should have been allocated for such project is put into private pockets due to corrupt practices; such development becomes stagnated. Corrupt practices in third world nations are cancerous to national development. Self-discovery is never actualized until government officials have vision, die from selfishness, are honest, and are ready to make changes in the present corrupt system.

The Functions of Citizen

Understanding that government and citizens owe one another in reciprocity with reference to service delivery systems, citizens are likewise obligated to honor and to pay taxes to government in reciprocal to the services

---

[40] John Alexander Mackay, "Religion and Government, Their Separate Spheres and Reciprocal Responsibilities," *Theology Today* 9, no. 2 (1952): 204–222.

offered by the governing authorities in the embodiments of national security, health care delivery systems, education, and development projects; meanwhile, the reciprocities to the services offered.[41]

Apostle Paul writes, "Let everyone be subject to the governing authorities, for there is no authority except that which God has established. The authorities that exist have been established by God; therefore, whoever rebels against the authority is rebelling against what God has instituted, and those who do so will bring judgment on themselves" (Rom 13:1–2 NIV). God is not a totalitarian; however, He is the God of order and the rule of laws; therefore, He has given a command for the stability, tranquility, and security of communities of nations. Living in the vacuum without the rule of laws is not healthy for the well-being of humanity understanding that we live in the evil world where Satan is the god (2 Cor 4:4). The response to the above command is summed up in honoring and paying tribute to the governing authorities. Apostle Paul concludes that this is the reason humanity pays taxes; therefore, give to everyone what you owe them: If you owe taxes, pay taxes; if revenue, then revenue; if respect, then respect; if honor, then honor" (Rom 13:6–7 NIV); therefore, the biblical roles of citizens to government are honoring, obeying, and paying taxes. These three functions are tied to the moral and financial responsibilities that citizens owe to their governments; therefore, they are required contributing to national development. The three roles are biblically recommended to both Christians and non-Christians; in this light, the above functions fit for all members and non-members of the eleven world religions including Christianity.[42]

Honoring

Primarily, honoring connotes submission to an authority; therefore, biblically, citizens are mandated to honor governing authorities. Honoring

---

[41] Ibid.

[42] Ibid.

is the act of paying respect to someone whom one appreciates based on the services the individual has rendered to humanity or the individual's achievement obtained distinct in life that requires endorsing. When citizens honor the governing authorities, they show gratitude to them. Apostle Paul said that, if it is respect; then, give respect. Respect is due to superior; however, to command respect as the superior, it is also necessary to show respect to the subordinate because the person who may be one's house boy today can become one's president tomorrow; therefore, reciprocity should be adopted as the constant in submission. This is the reason, it is expedient never to look down on people because they are poor than what you are. It is just the matter of time because such individual will resurrect to become one's leader worthy of your honor. Apostle Paul wrote to the Christians in Rome; hence, it reads, "For by the grace given me I say to every one of you: Do not think of yourself more highly than you ought, but rather think of yourself with sober judgment, in accordance with the faith God has distributed to each of you" (Rom 12:3 NIV). In the above passage, Apostle Paul is saying that the success of an individual is tied to another person's success; therefore, humility is the constant factor that determines the levels of an individual with reference to success; paradoxically, the approach to success by some people appears to be relative; therefore, it should be defined in the individual's context when it comes to success. This is the reason wherever one finds oneself presently with reference to status; one should appreciate God for such status because it is God who has placed one in such position in order to prepare him or her for another level; hence, life comes in phases and takes on faces. The reason success takes distance from some people is because they lack patience and consistency in their dealing with God; therefore, they take the escape route and run away from reality. The theme of the above Scriptural text is humility in the service to one another. Apostle Paul said that, if it is honor; then, honor. He uses the transition word "then" followed by the imperative mood. Such statement is called the "Statement of Situation Necessity." It is a command; therefore, the failure to honor one's boss or superior is a sin that takes on another repercussion. He or she can fire the individual from the job due to insubordination the individual has shown at work. It goes against the individual's professional code of conduct at the workplace and violates professionalism; consequently, it goes against one's conscience as the Christian if one is found in such category. Apostle Paul said, "Submit to authority not because of the fear of the punishment, but of conscience's sake." The Christian's attitude should be guided by the conscience because the Holy Spirit speaks through the conscience that gives believers directions. This is the reason the Scripture has said that if believers are led by the Holy Spirit, they are not under the law because the Holy Spirit will never direct the believer to break the law that He has given him or her (Gal 5:18). The honor one gives to one's superior, one's governmental authorities, one's spouse, and one's children is the platform for one's elevation in the workplace, in the nation, in the family, and in the church. Honoring is the virtue used to promote one to another level; therefore, one does not disobey one's superior because God has placed him or her over the individual to train him or her for life contingency. Honoring someone does not mean that the person is better than who the individual is; however, it is tied to one's maturity disconnect from spirituality. Have you seen people in the church who speak in tongues, fast and pray for twenty one days, and even preach; paradoxically, what they speak and do is contrary to the nature of these activities. They might be spiritual; however, they lack maturity; therefore, one's lack of maturity affects one's spirituality.

Honoring is not limited to one's superior; instead, it extends to people who are part of the organization one belongs. Leaders are required to honor people who are rendering services in the ministry. One honors one's church workers when one allows their opinions to be heard in the organizational meeting that indicates inclusiveness in organizational leadership; therefore, people should be allowed to contribute to organizational discussion. Decision taken should show inclusiveness instead of being autocratic; in this light, one honors those who are working in the organization. What one does in the church can be translated to the governing authorities; therefore, it is impossible to honor someone when one has refused to submit to them.

Obedience

Secondarily, the function of citizens to the governing authorities is to obey. Obedience is the voluntary action of an individual; therefore, it must be learned daily in child training, in the workplace, and in the church's ministry due to its voluntary nature. It takes the voluntary effort of the obedient individual to obey due to the involuntary nature. Obedience requires allowing someone to violate one's rights even when one is right before raising objections. This is the reason people who do not have the spirit of humility cannot obey because obedience and humility are twin. The lack of humility is the lack of obedient spirit to submit to authority. Disobedient people are pride people. Women who are disobedient lack the spirit of humility; therefore, they cannot keep husband because they lack the spirit of submission; similarly, men who lack humility, cannot keep wife because they lack love in their lives. Humble Christian husband has the tendency to love his wife because humility is tied to forgiveness; similarly, unloved husband lacks the spirit of forgiveness. Husband who has the spirit of humility has the tendency to love on average especially God fearing husband. Such husband forgives his wife even when the wife has gone wrong several times. This is how true love and humility that come from God behave.

Citizens including Christians are commanded in the Scriptures to obey governing authorities. How one relates to law enforcement officers who represent the government determines one's obedience; therefore, it resonates with one's God fearing orientation engrained in the Christian life. Honoring and paying taxes to the government are acts of obedience; on the contrary, refusing to do so is the direct act of disobedience to governing authorities. This is one of the reasons people are charged penalty fees on unpaid taxes because government wants to redirect their disobedience. Such disobedience may not be intentional; however, government treats it as disobedience and places penalty fees. The case story concerning John is an unintentional disobedience because he tries to escape debts legally imposed on him based on the taxes' law of the United States; however, he is still in complete disobedience to the government because he has failed to practice obedience which has repercussion attached to financial debts. He must pay the penalty of his disobedience to be free from arrest and clear conscience before God.

Taxation

Apostle Paul writes, "This is also why you pay taxes, for the authorities are God's servants, who give their full time to governing. Give to everyone what you owe them: If you owe taxes, pay taxes; if revenue, then revenue; if respect, then respect; if honor, then honor" (Rom 13:6–7 NIV). The issue of paying tribute to the governing authorities is spelt-out in the Scripture. Apostle Paul said that tribute should be paid by citizens because the authorities have given their time to public service to labor for the well-being of all. Tribute paid to the governing authorities is used to supplement the national budget allocated to pay salary to government officials, to fund the healthcare system, to educate, to fund infrastructures developments, to fund national security, to fund social services to citizens, and among others. The payment of tributes to government obligates the government to provide the above listed services that are within the functions of the government. In this deliberation, one can extrapolate that government and citizens have reciprocal functions. Author Reuss, in his article, supports this extrapolation regarding the reciprocal functions citizens and governments have toward one another.[43]

---

[43] Henry S. Reuss, "Taxes, Income and the Distribution of Wealth," Christianity and Crisis 35, no. 10 (1975): 139–145.

The Distribution of Wealth

Social Injustice

If citizens pay taxes to the government in addition to what government receives from national resources, government is obligated to distribute the wealth to her citizenries. Taxation misappropriation coupled with misappropriation of the national resources tailored toward national developments in the areas of healthcare, education, infrastructures developments, and social services to citizens are apposite of wealth distributions to the national population. The decision to misappropriate resources to intentionally refuse to distribute the resources to the general public who owns the resources by virtue of her birth in domicile based on her political franchise is called social injustice called corruption. This action defines social injustice in the context of wealth distribution that is very obvious in countries that corruption has become the common norm. The problem of third world countries is the intent to misappropriate the national resources away from their citizens as the result of corrupt practices in governments. Government officials are full of greed, wickedness, and the lack vision for the nation and its people. The budget that should have been allocated for healthcare, education, and development projects is stolen by individuals and banked abroad. The populations in such constituencies will die from diseases, left uneducated, and communities remained underdeveloped due to the lack of service delivery. Can you imagine how many scientists, medical doctors, nurses, or engineers would have been saved from diseases and educated had the national resources been correctly distributed to her populations? Human resources developments achieved through healthcare delivery and education to citizens are bedrocks for national development and sustainability. The national leaders are dying and left uneducated because the national resources are poorly managed, undistributed, and stolen by individuals and banked abroad. One person's greed is used at the expense for the entire population.

Imagine the hospital built in South Africa at the expense of the country's resources during President Ellen Johnson-Sirleaf's administration. Had it been built in Liberia, it would have helped to save lives. This is the perfect example of the national wealth not being distributed to the population; instead, it has been stolen through corrupt practices.

Government will be unable to revitalize the country's economy if the wealth of the country is left in few people's hands because every citizen has gifts to meaningfully contribute to national development; therefore, citizens need empowerment to accomplish it. Citizens can do so when they are empowered. Empowerment comes when the government invests in healthcare, education, social services, and development projects. When citizens get sick, they should have access to treatments. Every child in the nation has the right to be educated and should live in the environment freed from threats. Better housing, free education, and provision of social services to citizens are parcel of the wealth distribution to the public. It is evidential that some third world countries are rich in natural resources; unfortunately, they are poorly managed as the result of greed, wickedness, lack of systems put into placed, misguided ethically, and government officials commit economic crimes with impunity.

When the United States government experienced economic recession in 2008, she had to subsidize big companies like General Motor and among others to revive the stagnated economy. Once these companies were empowered financially, they maximized productivities while hiring workers to do the job. The empowerment the companies received from the government through subsidization opened the door for citizens to obtain employments. This enabled employees to buy basic needs for their families causing the money to circulate from the government's hand to companies, to employees, and to the business communities who are involved in trades nationally and internationally. Someone might say one cannot compare America to third world countries. America was as poor as third world countries before America rose to become world leader economically; so it is China who is competing with America presently on the global economy. Secondly, America had faced economic breakdown; then, resulting citizens to lose their homes. Countries that rise today to become world leaders economically, changed their mindsets how they did things before risen and how they are doing things today to remain in that gap category. The mindsets of corrupt governments in third world countries are the root causes of economic deprivation. The author of Proverbs writes, "Above else, guard your heart, for everything you do flows from it. Keep your mouth free of perversity; keep corrupt talk far from your lips" (Prov 4:23–24 NIV). The heart of the individual will never be bigger than his vision; therefore, guarding the heart is guarding one's vision. The Bible declares that where there is no vision, the people cast off restraint (Prov 29:18). It means people will die intellectually and developmentally with reference to life vitalities when governmental authorities lack vision and intentionally neglect their responsibilities as spelt-out in their job descriptions. Human beings need air, water, food, shelter, sleep, clothing, and reproduction for continuity. These needs are vital to keep human beings alive. They are physiological needs that regulate body metabolic processes to keep human beings going stronger. The second level of needs include personal security, employment, resources, health, and property. These are safety needs that protect human beings from traumas. The third level of needs include friendship, intimacy, family, and sense of connections. These needs when provided for humanity, humanity feels loved and belonged to society. When the above mentioned needs are provided for humanity, individual member of the populations reaches self-actualization.[44] Government can alleviate the human's problem holistically when the wealth of the nation is managed and equally distributed to her citizens. Such approach of wealth distributions will alleviate humans' problems and provide the hierarchies of needs for citizens.

---

[44] Susan Mettes, "Ministry after Maslow: Maslow's Hierarchy of Needs Has Leavened the Teaching in American Churches, That's a Problem, "*Christianity Today* 62, no. 5 (2018): 38–43.

Author Huston, in his article, advocates for wealth distribution and narrowed it to government that it is the fiduciary responsibility of the government to distribute wealth to her citizens.[45]

The Biblical View of Wealth

Having discussed wealth distribution in the political arena, it is necessary to discuss the biblical view of wealth to help the reader understands what wealth is. The biblical explanation of wealth will help the reader understands wealth in the context of the national resources that government is obligated to distribute to all citizens. If government will distribute the wealth, all citizens should be able to live balance lifestyles in the country they belong to. Business professionals are cognizant of revenues and profits procurement because it is coded on their fiscal DNA; therefore, they know how to strike the right balance between risk and recompense while growing the top-line and delivering the end result in order to establish their business enterprises and personal finances. This makes their businesses to pay off more often than let them down and at the end of the day; therefore, they generally create wealth where there was none previously.[46] The word "wealth" is often misunderstood by many based on abundance according to the world's view. This is the reason, one often hears, this individual is the richest person in the world according to statistics based on how much he or she has in the bank. The biblical view of wealth is different from the worldly view; in this light, it is deceiving to define wealth based on abundance. As Christians, it is paramount to understand our material wealth disconnect from God's point of view regarding wealth accumulation. What we consider materially as

---

[45] James L. Huston, "The American Revolutionaries, the Political Economy of Aristocracy, and the American Concept of the Distribution of Wealth, 1965–1900," *The American Historical Review* 98, no. 4 (1993): 1079–1105.

[46] Patrick Layhee, "A Biblical View of Wealth and Riches," *Center for Christianity in Business*," accessed September 27, 2021, https://bbu.edu/center-for-christianity-in-business.

wealth is different from what God considers as wealth from the biblical standpoint. Jesus was tempted by one of his attendees and he replied, "Someone in the crowd said to him, "Teacher, tell my brother to divide the inheritance with me."Jesus replied, "Man, who appointed me a judge or an arbiter between you?"Then he said to them, "Watch out! Be on your guard against all kinds of greed; life does not consist in an abundance of possessions"(Luke 12:13–15 NIV). The worldly view regarding wealth is attached to abundance; for this reason, people who are considered wealthy are always wanting more in order to satisfy the craving for riches; unfortunately, they never reach satisfaction because life does not consist in an abundance of possessions one has according to Jesus; on the contrary, satisfied life is tied to godly fear where the individual considers that it is God who has empowered him or her. In the biblical view, wealth is defined as a suitable accumulation of resources and possession of value; therefore, the Bible defines wealth in the individual's context based on the need according to the Scripture. Life does not consist in the abundance of possession defines wealth biblically in the individual's context with reference to submission to God as the provider. Considering this definition biblically, one is wealthy to the extent that one has sufficient food of good quality, clothing appropriate to keeping one cool or warm, and shelter for protection from the elements.[47] In the modern setting, being wealthy satisfies the access to safe, reliable transportation and communication that enable an individual to work in biblical stance. Considering the biblical definition for wealth, some people who live in the western world are wealthy; on the contrary, they consider themselves to be poor based on their mindset contrary to biblical mindset. Author Williamson, in his article, delineates the biblical view of wealth contemporary to what has been discussed in this monograph.[48]

---

[47] Ibid.

[48] Hugh G. M. Williamson, "A Christian View of Wealth and Possession: An Old Testament Perspective," *Ex auditu* 27, no. 1 (2011): 1–19.

Apostle Paul writes, "But godliness with contentment is great gain; therefore, we brought nothing into the world and we can take nothing out of it. But if we have food and clothing, we will be content with that. Those who want to get rich fall into temptation and a trap and into many foolish and harmful desires that plunge people into ruin and destruction. For the love of money is a root of all kinds of evil. Some people eager for money have wandered from the faith and pierced themselves with many griefs" (1 Tim 6:6–10 NIV). This Scripture gives a complete description of worldly riches and those who follow them. Godliness with contentment is great gain according to biblical wealth. Wealth and riches are used interchangeably in the Bible; on the contrary, there is the difference between wealth and riches based on the attitude tailored toward wealth. The love of money attached to wealth defines wealth as self-indulgent heart attitude. This kind of wealth does not consider God has the giver; instead, it is self-proclaimed empowered by self effort while ignoring God as the Giver of wealth. People, who pursue riches through self-indulgence, will wander away from the faith because money becomes the god in their lives. They can do anything to get money in the isolation of moral values.

Understanding what wealth is biblically, the hierarchies of needs proposed by Abraham Maslow, the child psychologist, should define the basic elements what it means to be wealthy. Having one's daily needs met such as food, clothing, air to breath, shelter, favorable temperature for survival, good health, property, reproduction, sleep, employment, resources, and security are amongst the physiological and safety needs that satisfy what it means to be wealthy. These needs give renaissance to the other three levels of needs. These needs are ladders to get one to love and belonging, esteem and self-actualization. Most of these needs have been provided by God to humanity; however, government needs to subsidize these needs for re-enforcement. Government does so via the provision of education, healthcare, national security for all, and development projects. This should give informed decision to electors how they elect people to national leadership. Electing people into office who have no knowledge of these needs, have no passion, lack vision, unpatriotic, and lack the technical know how to navigate these needs in order to get them to citizens can be disastrous.

John writes, "Dear friend, I pray that you may enjoy good health and that all may go well with you, even as your soul is getting along well" (3 John 1:2 NIV). God is interested in our physical and spiritual health as indicated in the above text. The maintenance of our physical health depends on the provision of the physiological health; since, our spiritual health is also connected to our physical health. The lack of provision for the physicality such as food, shelter, employment, resources, and safety can lead people to experience traumas that can lead to health problem. When people are emotionally disturbed as the result of traumatic events, it negatively impacts the human's spirit. It is called emotional illness; hence, God is interested in the well-being of our emotional health.

During his ministry, Jesus spoke much about the poor with reference to riches and poverty. The question posed by a certain rich ruler with reference to entering heaven and Jesus' response is based on the test of the heart's condition of man toward riches and salvation. In Jesus' conclusive statement, he said, "How hard it is for the rich to enter the kingdom of God! Indeed, it is easier for a camel to go through the eye of a needle than for someone who is rich to enter the kingdom of God "(Luke 18:25 NIV). The scripture concerning these things are being examined in the following paragraphs. Dr. Luke writes,

> A certain ruler asked him, "Good teacher, what must I do to inherit eternal life?" "Why do you call me good?" Jesus answered. "No one is good—except God alone. You know the commandments: 'You shall not commit adultery, you shall not murder, you shall not steal, you shall not give false testimony, honor

your father and mother.' "All these I have kept since I was a boy," he said. When Jesus heard this, he said to him, "You still lack one thing. Sell everything you have and give to the poor, and you will have treasure in heaven. Then come, follow me." When he heard this, he became very sad, because he was very wealthy. Jesus looked at him and said, "How hard it is for the rich to enter the kingdom of God! Indeed, it is easier for a camel to go through the eye of a needle than for someone who is rich to enter the kingdom of God(Luke 18:18–25 NIV).

In the above passage, this rich man had self-indulgent attitude toward God; however, he was still inquisitive about his salvation. He disagreed to give his possessions to the poor with a sad countenance. The Bible says that his countenance fell. Jesus references such attitudes in the Parable of the Sower that people whose hearts are set on the care of this life including riches are choked by the worries of this world (Matt 13:1–23). On another time, Jesus was passing through Jericho when he met another rich man called Zacchaeus. Zacchaeus having the desire to see Jesus went ahead the path Jesus was traveling and climbed into the sycamore-fig tree. Dr. Luke writes,

A man was there by the name of Zacchaeus; he was a chief tax collector and was wealthy. He wanted to see who Jesus was, but because he was short he could not see over the crowd. So he ran ahead and climbed a sycamore-fig tree to see him, since Jesus was coming that way. When Jesus reached the spot, he looked up and said to him, "Zacchaeus, come down immediately. I must stay at your house today." So he came down at once and welcomed him gladly. All the people saw this and began to mutter, "He has gone to be the guest of a sinner." But Zacchaeus stood up and said to the Lord, "Look, Lord! Here and now I give half of my possessions to the poor, and if I have cheated anybody out of anything, I will pay back four times the amount." Jesus said to him, "Today salvation has come to this house, because this man, too, is a son of Abraham. For the Son of Man came to seek and to save the lost" (Luke 19:2–10 NIV).

The second rich man's heart attitude is different from the first Jesus met. Zacchaeus agreed to give half of his possessions to the poor, half of what the first rich man disagreed to deliver. Wealth is defined in the individual's context based on the individual's heart attitude toward wealth. When wealth becomes idolized, it becomes riches and diverts people from serving God. Another third biblical character that defines wealth distinctly based on godly attitude is Lydia. Dr. Luke writes,

On the Sabbath we went outside the city gate to the river, where we expected to find a place of prayer. We sat down and began to speak to the women who had gathered there. One of those listening was a woman from the city of Thyatira named Lydia, a dealer in purple cloth. She was a worshiper of God. The Lord opened her heart to respond to Paul's message. When she and the members of her household were baptized, she invited us to her home. "If you consider me a believer in the Lord," she said, "come and stay at my house." And she persuaded us (Acts 16:13–15 NIV).

Lydia was a wealthy woman before her conversion. After her conversion, she decided to use her wealth to promote the kingdom of God. From the three biblical passages, one can extrapolate that the difference between riches and wealth is that riches exhibit self-indulgent attitude toward God while wealth recognizes God as the giver and glorifies Him. If governments can distribute the wealth of the nation to all, citizens should have balance lifestyles with reference to basic needs. Jesus warns against greed and possession distribution because wealth can become an idol and poverty symptom to the fallen society.[49]

The Biblical View of Wealth Redistribution

Pope Francis of the Vatican called for the legitimate redistribution of economic benefits on Friday 2021, arguing that the Bible demands an economic system that cares for the poorest and those most excluded.[50] Pope Francis made the comments while speaking before the gathering of several United Nations agency leaders, including the United Nation Secretary General, Ban Ki-moon. He is the first Latin American Pope who has asked those present to resist the economy of exclusion and to welcome the mindset regarding the redistribution of wealth to the marginalized communities of nations. His opened statements to the United Nations leaderships have prompted this book to discuss the issues regarding biblical redistribution of wealth after having discussed wealth distribution politically; it is expedient to look at the biblical views of wealth redistribution in the Old Testament. Biblically, understanding the essence of wealth redistribution in the Old Testament gives an idea how it could be related to the present practices regarding distribution of national wealth to citizens. It might not be exact contemporarily to the present practices; however, one should find some practices that are applicable to the present governmental practices since Israel was a theocracy government. In the democratic society, something contemporary might resemble some practices in the Old Testament; however, such practices in the Old

---

[49] David Murchie, "New Testament View of Wealth Accumulation," *Journal of the Evangelical Theological Society* 21, no. 4 (1978): 335–344.

[50] Jane Timm, "Pope Francis Calls for Wealth Redistribution," accessed June 26, 2022, https://www.msnbc.com/pope-call.

Testament, if the Scripture is not taken at fixed values, they could be termed as socialism due to misinterpretation; therefore, the Scripture should be examined.

The idea of wealth redistribution in the Old Testament with reference to the Levitical Law began during the Old Testament dispensation, when God required the Israelites to leave the portion of their crops in the field after harvest so the poor could gather them (lev 19:9–10; Deut 24:21). In this light, one can see Ruth gleaning in the field of Boaz as instituted in the Levitical Law practices wherein the poor was required to work by picking up the leftovers on the agricultural fields. This practice was voluntary as instituted by God; therefore, it did not require the civil government of Israel to enforce such law.

The second practice regarding the redistribution of wealth in Israel was called the Year of Jubilee. The Year of Jubilee was the year that all land bought by previous buyers were to be returned to the owners who sold them. In the Jubilee law, every seven years was a Sabbath year for the Jews to not work the land bought; in this light, they were to live off the produce from the previous years. Every seven Sabbath year also called forty-nine years (49 years) was extended to another year called the Year of Jubilee known as the fifty years (50 years). The Year of Jubilee dealt with land, property, and property rights. According to the Jubilee Law, slaves and prisoners including debts owed could be forgiven and set freed; consequently, the mercies of God would prevail. Under the Jubilee system, an Israelite who owned land could sell the right to farm it until the year of Jubilee with the price based on the value of each year's crop and the number of years remaining until the Jubilee. When the year of Jubilee arrived, the land reverted back to its original owner. The understanding of Jubilee as the lease pay off is common in the Old Testament with respect to Levitical practices. From the legal stand point, Jubilee Law effectively banned the sale of land; therefore, land could be leased for no more than fifty years. Understanding that, the Jubilee Law might not work in the present situation regarding wealth distribution in the present century, and do not exist presently in Israel; however, one can learn from the Jubilee Law and navigate cognitively how Jubilee Law relates to the wealth distribution in the 21st century. The Jubilee Law was instituted to close the wealth gap between the buyer and the seller and to rehabilitate and to re-accommodate prisoners and slaves into society; additionally, the Jubilee Law was put into place to establish economic and social justice equitably for all. When governments of this century behave equitably with reference to economic and social justice for all, they will close the wealth gap between the middle class and the elites. Understanding the Jubilee Law and its application, God is against economic and social injustices in the land. Government will be blessed when government takes care of her citizens; on the contrary, the failure for the government to take care of her citizenries leads to curse initiated by God that affects officials of government. Social injustice is the act of depriving citizens from the distribution of wealth, opportunities, and privileges within a society. Corrupt practices executed in nations to deprive citizens from receiving social justices are the national sins that will hunt past and present leaders and their posterities (families). God is against social injustice in the land and He punishes those who are involved. Salaries given to government officials astronomically is an organized crime; therefore, they are cursed money. Government officials in the United States of America don't take astronomical salaries; unfortunately, a nation which is one of the poorest countries in Africa and whose people are suffering, has developed astronomical salary scales for themselves. One month salary taken by government officials in Liberia is an annual gross income that some people make in the United States annually. This is one of the reasons one sees ritualistic killings in Liberia because people want to remain in those positions to continue to earn astronomical salaries at the expense of people's children lives. Children murdered through ritualistic killings are future scientists, doctors, nurses, teachers, and technocrats. Greed, wickedness, and lack of education are the result of barbarism in Liberia. If one sees several things happening, the first thing that happens does the most harm; therefore, it is the astronomical salary scales.

Ethical Reflection

God has the universal security interest in the human society; therefore, He has sanctioned human government to keep law and order for national security and stability. The ordination of civil authority by God does not require the salvation of leadership; however, civil authority is encouraged or required to align herself with God's standard of ruling; therefore, government has the fiduciary responsibility to restraint evil while citizens have the reciprocal responsibility to honor and to pay taxes to the government as defined by the Scripture (Rom 13:1–7); however, despite of these ordinances prescribed by God, some governments on average have failed to keep security due to the proliferations of evil in the world and the neglects some governments have adopted overtimes as the result of untrained security and criminals in the government who sent third party to accomplish their diabolical deeds in the context of the Liberia's situation with reference to ritualistic killings. The examples are ritual killings in Liberia whereby no one has been arrested for trials; therefore, it can be deduced that there are people in the Liberian government who are involved in this criminality. Ritualistic killings have been in existence since Liberia was founded. The only administration who hunted people involved in ritualistic killing was the deposed President Samuel Kanyon Doe. Ritualistic killers should be hunted and brought to trial to avoid the wrath of God on the nation of Liberia and its leadership.

CHAPTER IV
THE SECOUNDARY HOLISTICITY

Chapter Overview

In this segment of the discourse, the secondary holisticity discusses social, biblical, criminal, and environmental justices while giving the dichotomy between biblical and social view of justice. While giving the difference between the two, the chapter delineates the facets of social, biblical, and criminal justices and concludes with environmental justice laying emphasis on the environmental damage that has been caused by human's activities on the planet. At the conclusion, the author has developed a reflection on the chapter to redress the subject in order to pin a mental picture in the mind of the reader for personal subjective reflection.

The Justices

The subjects of democratization, criminal and social justices connote justice for all; therefore, democratization defines the larger analysis of both social and criminal justice systems; integrally, social justice and criminal justices become the subset of democratization; therefore, with reference to social and criminal justices, even in the democratic society, the subjects of social and criminal justices are still being downplayed institutionally based on systemic racism in the context of the American's scenarios; therefore, the subject of equality for all is still being fought through political advocacy. Disparities are seen with reference to healthcare, education, employment, salary scales, and among others due to systemic racism and sexism seen vividly in institutions on both state and federal levels in the American society; however, America appears to be called the giant of democracy in the world based on the message she preaches; on the contrary, she has psychological wounds she needs to clean up before preaching democracy to the world. The killing of George Floyd, the African American, on May 25, 2020 by Derek Chauvin, the white police officer, after the video had gone virus, triggered agitations across the fifty States of America leading to peaceful protests under the slogan "Black Lives Matter." Prior to the murder of George Floyd, other black people have been murdered annually in like manner with impunity due to systemic racism. Black people in the United States have been demonized based on past history with reference to slavery and being perceived as criminals; therefore, some white police officers in law enforcement see black people as threats; prejudicially, they are in hyper vigilant to shoot at them. America has the history of slavery; therefore, systemic racism is seen in some institutions in America across federal and states' level.[51] The laws that were enacted by those who supported racism in America, these laws are still being used against black people in America. The American Civil Rights Movement, led by Dr. Martin Luther King, Jr. arose and fought against these disparities in the American society; then, things began to change. The movement endeavored to destroy systemic racism in America; unfortunately, the movement could not destroy the ideology; consequently, systemic racism continues in the American society; even though, America preaches democracy. The institution of racism has been gradually eroded; however, America still has much work to be done with reference to institutionalized racism that permeates diabolically in the police force when it comes to racial profiling. The law that was enacted that divide America on racial lines needs to be revisited and amended so that the national wealth can be distributed equitably to all without discrimination. America, who considers herself

---

[51] Samuel L. Perry and Andrew L. Whitehead, "Christian America in Black and White: Racial Identity, Religious-National Group Boundaries, and Explanations of Racial Inequality," *Sociology of Religion* 80, no. 3 (2019): 277–298.

a democratic society, has a rival to deal with. The rival is systemic racism that permeates institutionally through healthcare, education, housing, employment, and criminal justice system. She needs to remove the plank from her eyes in order to see well or else, she will be a hypocrite and will be unable to preach democracy to the world (Matt 7:3–5).

Similarly, all democratic societies need to practice justice on all levels with reference to criminal and social justices because the word "democracy" signifies justice for all; so, it is social justice and criminal justice system, which are the smaller analyses for democracy. Liberia including all third world countries whose citizens have been marginalized economically and socially as the result of corrupt practices in governments must change to the better to represent true democratic society in Africa. The issue of slavery had existed in biblical history; therefore, the repeat of history is neither a coincidence nor a novel subject. Moses writes, "And God spoke all these words: "I am the Lord your God, who brought you out of Egypt, out of the land of slavery" (Exod 20:1–2 NIV). Slavery is the diabolical act of denying someone from his or her inalienable rights; similarly, it is social and criminal justices that citizens are entitled to by virtue of their political franchise. The children of Israel were denied such rights in the land of captivity. The above text is the acid test that God hates injustices. Slavery is an embodiment of social and criminal injustices in which someone is denied the necessities for life. Historically, post-slavery had existed during the 15th century between Europe, Africa, and the Americas termed as the Trans-Atlantic and Tran-angular Slave Trade at which Africans were dehumanized.[52] The slaves' birth rights were taken away by their captors as the result of free capitalistic labor imposed on them and were subjugated and beaten when they refused to work. These Africans worked and built America from free capitalistic labor via slavery. Such vehicle the white men used to deny their neighbors of life necessities are sinister. Today, some of the States in the United States of America, the issue of reparation has

---

[52] Shelton H. Smith, "Am I Not a Man and a Brother: British Missions and Abolition of the Slave Trade and Slavery in West Africa and the West Indies, 1786–1838," *Church History* 42, no. 2 (1973): 290–291.

resonated with them and they have decided to pay restitutions to the children of the African-Americans who were dehumanized by their slave masters; contemporaneously, past leaderships of nations that have denied their citizens from the national wealth as the result of corrupt practices owe the people of such national restitution payment; unfortunately in the African context, the idea of restitution is rarely birthed in leadership. How can people be so wicked and refused to recognize realities due to greed? Zacchaeus understood the gravity of denying someone from their rights when he defrauded them through taxation; as the result, he promised Jesus that he could pay back four times of what he had stolen from the people (Luke 19:1–10). Social and criminal injustices are the national sins that hunt past leadership; unfortunately, they are ignored by leaders who are full of greed no matter the consequences are. Leaderships who are full of greed never learn from past history mistakes despite of the consequences other past leaderships had experienced negatively. Denying someone to possess the national wealth through corrupt practices is the form of slavery. God is against oppression; therefore, He sent Moses to free the children of Israel out of bondage and subsequently visited the Egyptians according to their deeds (Exod 1:1–13:16); similarly, God is against injustices in the land. One of the senators in the Liberian government called Abraham Darius Dillon understands this social injustice in the land; therefore, he has brought it out to the Liberian public regarding the salaries Liberian government officials have been paid monthly and cut his salary to be donated to his constituent.[53] He said that government officials' salaries should be reduced and the reduction should be spread out and used as the budget for development projects. His recommendation has been fought on all levels by government officials who don't care for the people who have elected them into office.

The message recorded in Exodus chapter 20:1–21 is the post-message God delivered to the children of Israel after their captivity in Egypt. It

---

[53] Abdur Rahman Alfa Sshaban, "Liberia Senator Takes Pay Cut, Donates $10,000.00 Monthly Constituency," accessed June 28, 2022, https://www.africanews.com/2019/08/16/liberia-senator-takes-pay-cut-donates-10000-monthly-to-constituency//.

was the time of the Mosaic Covenant establishment in order to adopt the Moral Law of the Creator. True religion that is from God, the Creator, must adopt these value systems; similarly, true democratic society should adopt the Moral Law of God in order to remain obeisance to moral values God has intended. All laws in nature that are intrinsically put into place regarding morality come from the Ten Commandments (Jer 31:33). In the message, God gave the moral law to guide them how they should relate to God and to their neighbors. From verses 3 to 11 of Exodus chapter 20, the moral law explains the duties man has toward God; similarly, from verses 12 to 17, the moral law explains the duties man has toward his neighbors. The two classified groups of laws sum up the Ten Commandments. If humanity can keep her duties toward his Creator, God, humanity should be able to perform well when it comes to how she relates to her neighbors. The constant that lies between how humanity relates to God and her neighbors defines true religion. Apostle James defines true religion as taking care of the widows, the orphans, and being separated from the pollution that comes from the world system (Jas 1:27). Any religion that comes from God cannot be involved in psychological and emotional terrorism; therefore, such religion is not from God if it exhibits such nature; instead, it is a man-made religion that is diabolical. Similarly, any democratic society cannot be involved in act that emits emotional and psychological terrorism to citizens. When a family wakes up in the morning and does not know where to find food for her children, or if one of the family members has gotten missing or killed through ritualistic killing, it can be traumatic. This is psychological and emotional terrorism that can lead to health problems as the result of traumas experienced over time. Most of the sickness human beings have experienced is the result of traumas they have experienced over time. Its root causes began with past and present leadership of the nation. This is one of the reasons that the nation needs God fearing people who can represent their people; hence, Christians and non-Christians alike, who serve in the legislature, judiciary, or the executive branch of government of Liberia, knowing what they were elected for, should be able to speak the truth because God has placed them in such position for such reason. Liberia has a representative democracy; therefore, law makers or senators should represent their constituents according to the will of the people.

The duty humanity has toward God and her neighbor is the acid test that determines what substances humanity is made of. The demonstration of the acid test is seen in Luke 10:25–37 with reference to the Parable of the Good Samaritan. In the parable narrative, the man was beaten by robbers; eventually, the oncoming levite and the priest refused to help the man based on their religious ritual since they were going to the temple for prayers; hence, touching the dead body would made them impure and incapacitated to enter the temple. The Samaritan man who was regarded as the sinner aided the man; on the contrary, the priest and the levite allowed religion to have precedent over righteousness. The priest and the Levite thought they did the right thing; unfortunately, they broke the second commandment in the moral law by refusing to take care of their neighbor who was beaten by robbers. In the Parable of the Good Samaritan, the lawyer, the expert in the law, asked Jesus who was his neighbor? The Parable of the Good Samaritan demonstrated to the expert who his neighbor was. Today, neighbors are killed in Liberia through ritualistic killings. What are the law makers, senators, and the executives in the government are doing about such? If John was ritualistically killed; then, no one is safe in the Liberia. Ritualistic killing in Liberia is cancer and must be addressed by all Liberians. If the people who were elected cannot do anything about what is going on currently, the electors have to decide the leadership the next coming election or force concession through petition to redress these matters in the Liberian society.

The Priest and the Levite knew the right thing to do; on the contrary, ritual took precedent over righteousness. People can sin against God while they are trying to keep rules that God did not sanction. By nature apart from the written commandments, human being knows what is morally right or wrong according to the book (Rom 1:20; 12:12–16; Jer 31:33). Members of the legislature, judiciary, and the executive branch of government know what is morally right or wrong; unfortunately, they have taken the back seat and refused to perform their jobs. They were elected to represent their constituents to the government regarding justice for all. Representation defines the security of the people, the delivery of services to the people in the embodiments of healthcare, education, social services, and among others. When representatives had voiced up and spoken against ritualistic killings in Liberia and spoken for social justice for all; then, it would have indicated true representation of the people who have elected them into office. Primarily, the president of Liberia should be the first to speak out and should layout recommendations to law enforcement ordering the Judiciary to take action. Members of the government of Liberia has fiduciary responsibility toward the Liberian people and should assume the roles of the Good Samaritan(Luke 10:25–37).[54]

The Brief History of Social Justice

What then is democratization and social justice? Democratization is the action of making something accessible to everyone while social justice is the equal access to wealth, opportunities, and privileges within the society. In the democratic society, the issue of social justice should not be a problem because the word "democracy" connotes Justice for all. Justice indicates fairness in society; therefore, the issue of limited justice is not a justice but injustice for all who are victims of the perpetrations. The concept of social justice began early in the 19th century at the onset of the Industrial Revolution and the proliferation of subsequent civil revolutions aimed to creating an egalitarian society in order to remedy capitalistic exploitation of human labor.[55]During this era, social justice advocates primarily focused on capital, property, and the distribution of wealth. By the mid-twentieth century social justice had taken tones based on advocacy; consequently, social justice changed course from being concerned with

---

[54] Matthew Chalmers, "Rethinking Luke 10: The Parable of the Good Samaritan Israelite," *Journal of Biblical Literature* 139, no. 3 (2020): 543–566.

[55] Ruth Chames, "US History Textbooks: Help or Hindrance to Social Justice," *Church and Society* 78, no. 4 (1988): 48–58.

economics to include social life, the environment, race, gender, and other causes of manifestations of inequality in the human society. Currently, social justice has expanded from being measured and enacted by the government to include universal human dimensions. For example, government today measures income inequality by comparing people within the same nation; however, social justice should be applied to a broader scale at the level of humanity as a whole. While social justice had been the focus during the mid-twentieth century, it had taken another embodiment to reflect environmental justice based on its connectivity to the environment. Social and environmental justices are intertwined because destroying the environment through the assumption that the Earth is separate from us and thus exploitable is paralleled by the assumptions that some people are different and inherently disposable.[56] The justice for the Earth with respect to climate change is the justice for all. On the recent discussion on climate change with respect to its effects on people on the globe, it has been figured out by scientists that the marginalized communities on planet Earth are going to experience the manifestations of climate change three times as compared to the non-marginalized communities on the globe. Unfortunately, the marginalized communities on the globe like African nations do not have the advance technology like the west to predict if stormy wind is imminent; therefore, natural disaster like flood, earth quakes, hurricane etc. will have taken people by surprise in these regions. This is scary and it is unfortunate that the marginalized nations which often burn less fossil fuel can be impacted by the climate change drastically and catastrophically. The actions of industrial nations that burn more fossil fuels had led to the irreversible damage of the planet Earth. The manifestations of the damages caused are floods, stormy winds, the rise in heat wave, volcanic fire, and among others. The end result of these manifestations is human's suffering across the globe. The injustice done to the environment through human's actions is the result of the above manifestations that threaten the Earth and its inhabitants. Conservation

---

[56] Ibid.

of the environment is highly recommended and encouraged; therefore, it should be the responsibility of everyone on the globe in regardless of geography since mankind is interconnected geographically. Rendering social justice to humanity across the globe is environmental justice that is interconnected to social justice. Democratic society like the United States of America has realized and taken the lead to cut down carbon gas emission by making all vehicles to run on electricity by the year 2050; similarly, other industrialized nations of the west have promised to cut down carbon gas emission. Based on the prediction, other nations of the Earth have begun to plant trees as the result of the imminent rise in temperature that kills both human beings and animals; unfortunately, some places on the globe like Liberia, individual members in the government have sold these trees to logging companies; consequently, deforestation continues to occur without the measure of reforestations.[57] Trees have been cut down and never planted; eventually, after sometimes, such places on Earth will begin to experience drought. Since trees play major roles for the removing of carbon dioxide from the air, storing carbon in the tress and soil, and releasing oxygen into the atmosphere, the conservation of vegetation is the mitigation to climate change for the better. When all the trees have been cut down without planting new ones, it leads to the destruction of the environment that sets tones to drought occurrence. Individuals in government are destroying Liberia's rain forest with impunity. This is environmental injustice that is directly linked to social injustice carried out in Liberia at the expense of the populations. There should be legislation put into place to preserve trees and wild life in Liberia. This is one of the reasons law makers were elected to make laws that protect the people of Liberia and its natural resources. In the genesis, God commanded humanity to replenish the Earth instead of destroying it; therefore, God is the God of conservation (Gen 1–2). Environmental stewardship is grounded in the

---

[57] Afua Hirsch, "Liberia Has Sold Quarter of Its Land to Logging Companies, Says Report, "*TheGuardian,* accessed June 28, 2022, https://www.theguardian.com/world/2012/sep/04/liberia-sold-quarter-land-logging-companies.

Scripture and humanity will be held accountable for the destruction of the Earth through the burning of fossil fuel and deforestations.

The Facets of Social Justice

Opportunities

One of the facets of social justice is opportunity; hence, opportunities are circumstances available to citizens to do something desirably as per their aspirations according to their capabilities engrained in their capacities. Many people have capabilities; unfortunately, they are incapacitated to achieve them due to the lack of provisions for the elements. Government is required to create an atmosphere of opportunities for all citizens equitably to do something. The creation of opportunities constitutes the creation of schools, jobs opportunities, micro-loan programs, provision of agricultural tools to farmers, scholarship programs and among others. Social justice under opportunities defines the provision of the above services to citizens. Opportunities that define the above mentioned services are components of wealth distributions. The subjects of patriotism as so called, if adopted, government should be able to provide the above mentioned opportunities useful to citizens. The problem of third world countries is not poverty; instead, the problem is the lack of credible leadership to manage the national wealth. Leadership that cares for her people cannot embezzle the wealth that belongs to them; on the other hand, the leadership will put the resources at work transparently and responsibly to make sure the resources are used to the betterment of the people. The Vice President of Liberia, Dr. Howard Taylor, recently said during the inspection of the center that Senator Abraham Darius Dillon has built that all representatives should build rehabilitation centers in their various constituents to help treat people who are on drugs.[58] She is

---

[58] Lennart Dodoo, "V. P Howard Taylor Tours and Inspects The Mother of Light, Liberia Inc. Rehabilitation Center, accessed June 28, 2022, https://frontpageafricaonline.com/news/vp-howard.

right to say so because the money that should have been used to develop these constituents' infrastructures is the money being stolen in the name of salary to pay them. This is social injustice perpetrated to the detriment of the Liberian people in the name of salary payments. Social injustice is the national sin punishable by God; therefore, He spoke through Moses to inform the oppressors of Israel to let Israel go; similarly, God is speaking to the present leadership of Liberia and the world to do the same. The Liberian people are economically, emotionally, and socially oppressed due to social injustice.

Moses writes, "Do not pervert justice; do not show partiality to the poor or favoritism to the great, but judge your neighbor fairly (Lev 19:15 NIV). The government of Liberia faces a national sin with futurity consequences regarding social injustice due to the perversion of justice in the land. This is very clear regarding the astronomical salary that has been developed to ravage the country of its resources and to deny the people of Liberia. In the above text, justice is perverted to show partiality to the poor in order to favor the great. In the text, the great refers to the legislature, the judiciary, and the executive branch of government especially those who are receiving astronomical salary monthly. The wealth belongs to the citizens of Liberia; instead, the wealth is being diverted and given to the selected few leading the masses to suffer. The poor loses opportunities in the land when justice is perverted. In the last verse, Moses admonished the children of Israel to judge their neighbor fairly. The neighbor in the text is assumed to be victim of injustice in the land of Israel; therefore, Moses placed a caution and said, judge your neighbor fairly. Examine the needs of your neighbors and minister to them equitably so that you will be blessed in the land the Lord is going to give you as your inheritance. God will curse the national leadership that steals from the masses and will bless the national leadership that provides for the masses. Poverty is lacking necessity for life as the result of inaccessibility to the national wealth in the context of social injustice as used in the above text (Lev 19:15). One of the reasons the United States of America is blessed; hence, she puts America and her people primarily above personal interests through the provisions of social services and among others to her citizenries. When national leadership practices the Scripture obediently, the Scripture will be fulfilled favorably in her setting; on the other hand, when the Scripture is violated, it will be fulfilled unfavorably. The psalmist writes, "The LORD loves righteousness and justice; the earth is full of his unfailing love" (Ps 33:5 NIV). The wisdom writer concludes, "Let them drink and forget their poverty and remember their misery no more. Speak up for those who cannot speak for themselves, for the rights of all who are destitute. Speak up and judge fairly; defend the rights of the poor and needy" (Prov 31:7–9 NIV). God is describing His attributes as righteous and just through the psalmist and giving His ordinance through the King of Israel, King Solomon, to be applied in the nation of Israel in the favor of the poor; hence, the poor in the nation is the priority of God[59]; therefore, it was one of the reasons that the Jubilee Law was put into place in Israel to close the wealth gap between the buyer and the seller of the land. It was done so to redistribute the national wealth between the elites and the middle class after fifty years in order to alleviate poverty in the land. If government avoided corrupt practices and distributed the national wealth equitably to her citizens, poverty would have been alleviated in the land.

Privileges

The second facet of social justice is called privilege. Privileges are special rights, advantages, or immunities granted to a particular person or group. The status of being a citizen of the country grants the individual the exercise of freedom of speech, freedom of movement, the provision to own property, the right to education, the right to healthcare, to right to peaceful protest, the right to sue the government, the right to protection, the right to freedom of assembly, and the right to vote; hence, these are citizens' entitlements. In the democratic society these non-materials under no circumstances should they be infringed on by the government

---

[59] Robert B. Chisholm, "Rizpah's Torment: When God Punishes the Children for the Sin of the Father," *Bibliotheca* 175, no. 697 (2018): 50–66.

or a group. The denial of privileges to the people is the direct denial of social justice. Any act exhibited by the government that inhibits the above mentioned privileges is the direct denial of social justice. The psalmist recognizes the divine privilege being accorded him by God and he writes,

> When I consider your heavens, the work of your fingers, the moon and the stars, which you have set in place, what is mankind that you are mindful of them, human beings that you care for them? You have made them a little lower than the angels and crowned them with glory and honor. You made them rulers over the works of your hands; you put everything under their feet" (Ps 8:3–6 NIV).

The privileges mentioned such as the freedom to protection, the freedom of speech, the freedom of movement, the freedom of religion and among others are replicas of God's privileges to humanity. The psalmist said, "What are human beings that you care for them?" What an individual often sees in the democratic society are replicas of God that resonate with humanity to choose between rights or wrongs. When the government undermines the privileges of the people through physical, psychological, and economical oppression, the government infringes on God's agenda for the people.

Wealth

It would be a good idea that those who aspire presidential position prior to general election, write a proposed platform, how, when, where, and to what extent he or she would govern the nation if elected. Such proposed plan to govern the nation should be defended before the panel of judges that served as the blueprint how the nation would be run by the individual after the win. It is necessary to do so because the proposed plan to govern the nation could serve as the road map to navigate the slippery slope of presidential expedition with complex decision to make in the midst of the storm. Leadership such as presidential has asymmetrical challenges contingent; therefore, the leader must be prepared and ready to fight the asymmetrical warfare. What does this tell the leader concerning the challenges that lie ahead? The leader must be well capacitated to solve the asymmetric problems; therefore, capability is needed to solve the problem in the school of presidential leadership. Capability requires formal education in the classroom while capacity requires hand-on-experience based on analytical thinking because check list can fail in the asymmetric situation. This is one of the reasons the American troop in Iraq suffered the first casualty when the woman dressed in suicide mission approached the gate with her children while pretending to be helpless. In the event, the soldiers tried to help her; suddenly, the soldiers were in flame and dozens of American soldiers died that day. The bomb was mounted on her vehicle while the woman drove slowly to the Rangers' gate. After this incidence, the American troop had to changed course asymmetrically. American soldiers are trained according to check list; however, this incidence made the American troop in Iraq to change course because standardized check list could not work in asymmetrical warfare; so, it is presidential leadership.

Presidential leadership is characterized with asymmetrical situations; therefore, only the prepared leader is able to govern well in the midst of challenges with reference to fix economic recession, to fix national insecurity, to buttress wealth creations, to expand wealth distributions, to deliver social services, and among others. To deliver these opportunities and privileges owed to citizens, the national leadership needs to exhibit tolerance, be educated, and experienced in leadership. How, when, where, and to what extent does the government deliver opportunities, privileges, and the wealth to the citizens? How does the Minister of Health, Education, Justice, and Defense administer health, education, justice, and security to all? They should be educated, tolerant, and honest to deliver these services accorded the citizens. Understanding that wealth is the third facet of social justice, the distribution of opportunities and privileges to citizens through education, tolerance, and honesty are the sum total of wealth distribution that significantly contributes to the well-being of the masses. Education, tolerance, and honesty are key factors for the government's ability to distribute the wealth to the citizens understanding that wealth cannot be distributed unless it is created; therefore, it requires education to create wealth. When it comes to honesty, education, and tolerance, does one see these elements in the national leadership of Liberia? A neighbor in Liberia applied for the passport and the police clearance and paid the required fees. After having gone to the office several times, the office could not deliver his documents to him; hence, he got frustrated. He had to bribe the office before his documents could be delivered. Such government is the problem to citizens because it lacks integrity. These guys are asking for money because some have not been paid; as the result, citizens become the victims of bad governance.

Leadership cannot minister social justice equitably to her people if she lacks the education, the tolerance, and the honesty. Why? Since social justice entails delivering opportunities, privileges, and wealth equitably to citizens, the services can be offered provided the above mentioned non-material elements are exhibited. One does not deliver what one has not created. The technical know-how and the personalities involved in creating and delivering wealth is tied to education, tolerance, and honesty. Business professionals are trained in the business world with reference to how they can navigate the top-line of the business in order to produce the base-line of the business coupled with ethics adopted resulting into profiteering leading to the production of wealth; similarly, people who hold public service positions in government should be educated and held ethically responsible according to the position assignment. The Minister of Education should have learned the discipline to deliver the services to the people; similarly, the Minister of Health and Social Welfare should do as well. Each of these ministries is in the industry that is involved in the production and delivery of wealth to citizens. Every ministry in the nation is the potential producer and deliverer of wealth to the citizens. If unqualified people are given position in the government not based on merits, they will be unable to produce and deliver the wealth in their department because they lack the knowledge and the skills. A government that does well will invest in education while laying emphasis on justice. Government with untrained personnel will be the consumer instead of the producer; as the result, the individual is unable to contribute to national development. In the African settings, government's ministries are often ghost ministries created with names on the salary with no meaningful contribution to development. This has been very common in the Liberian's government in previous years; hence, the Liberian's norm had been characterized with dishonesty in government over 132 years of rules. The freed African slaves being oppressed in the United States of America arrived in Liberia on February 6, 1820 and also became the oppressors of the indigenous. During their rules from Joseph J. Roberts to William R. Tolbert, taxes collected coupled with natural resources proceeds were distributed in their circles as family business. People who could not afford to pay the hut tax were beaten mercilessly.[60]Liberia remained undeveloped for over 132 years and the trend continues until Samuel Kanyon Doe became the first president to build governmental buildings. Government's buildings have been housed by individual's building; therefore, government will have to rent those buildings endlessly. These are obstacles to equitable wealth distribution to the population of Liberia because the country's resources are going into individual's pockets.[61]Another ghost ministry camouflaged is astronomical salary payment to government's officials with no reasonable explanation why such salary can be allocated and given to the selected few. Liberia has a bad foundation; unfortunately, the trend continues because the present generation of Liberia had adopted the past and refused to make changes to the system due to greed. Liberia has systemic corrupt practices over time; consequently, every politician who aspires to get into power is coming with the same mindset.

---

[60] Alfred P.B. Kiadii, "The Rice and Rights Riot: Social Struggle and the Quest for An Alternative Society in Liberia, Part II, The Perspective, accessed June 28, 2022, https://www.theperspective.org/2019/0507201901.php.

[61] The Analyst, "Liberia: Reform Lease Policy," *Editorial*, accessed June 28, 2022, https://allafrica.com/stories/200408260378.html.

Primarily, national leadership should be educated and patriotic in order to equitably distribute wealth because wealth needs to be created before it can be distributed. Leaderships placed in various governmental sectors should be educated according to the job assignment area; then, will they be able to create wealth based on their expertise. People should be placed in leadership based on qualification and not on party or tribal lines. The failure to place qualified individual in the office to do the job is the failure to distribute wealth. Secondarily, national leaderships should be tolerant in order to deliver social justice to all. Privileges accorded citizens such as the right to peaceful assembly to protest; national leaderships should be tolerant towards protesters. One of the reasons security forces crack down on protesters is the lack of education, democratic values, and tolerance. In the democratic society, national leadership is required by law to allow citizens to exercise their political franchise. Depriving citizens by using force is undemocratic; therefore, it undermines social justice and subsequently subjugates citizens to exercise their democratic rights.

Thirdly, national leaderships should exhibit honesty in order to deliver social justice to all. There is no school for honesty; therefore, honesty is in the heart; in this light, honesty is learned in the school of wisdom; on the contrary, honest can be avoided by the dishonest person in the school of reluctant behavior. Many dishonest people don't learn from past failures or the downfalls of those who failed their people. Most politicians on average are found in the school of reluctant behavior because they have refused to practice honesty. No one could imagine that the former President Ellen Johnson-Sirleaf's administration would become corrupt when she accused William R. Tolbert for corruption. She fought against it; on the contrary, she practiced it after she had the opportunity to the presidency; similarly, President George Manneh Weah's administration has become corrupt as though corruption has become a generational trend.

When Solomon, the wisest King said that everything is vanity and the vexation of spirit, it speaks volume of the revelation that lies between worldly wealth and true riches (Eccl 1:1–2). He writes,

The word of the Teacher son of David, King in Jerusalem: "Meaningless! Meaningless!" says the Teacher. "Utterly is meaningless! Everything is meaningless." What do people gain from all their labors at which they toil under the sun? Generations come and generations go, but the earth remains forever. The sun rises and the sun sets, and hurries back to where it rises "(Eccl 1:1–5 NV).

King Solomon's statement with reference to the vanity of life and the description of nature defines the unquenchable greed of humanity and the unending natural phenomena under the sun. No matter how many frequencies generations come and go and the sun rises and sets in its original position, the phenomenon goes to circular direction; similarly, no matter how much wealth a man obtains in life, there is never satisfaction gained to compensate the craving of the human's nature. This is the reason worldly leaders who embezzle the national wealth never get tired embezzling. King Solomon said that despite of the wealth accumulated by the individual overtime, it has no significant impact to end the embezzlements. Based on the revelation regarding wealth, Dr. Luke has a revelation concerning worldly wealth and true riches. He writes,

Whoever can be trusted with very little can also be trusted with much, and whoever is dishonest with very little will also be dishonest with much. So if you have not been trustworthy in handling worldly wealth, who will trust you with true riches? And if you have not been trustworthy with someone else's property, who will give you property of your own?" (Luke 16:10–12 NIV).

In the above text, under the inspiration of the Holy Spirit, Dr. Luke said that whoever can be trusted with little can also be trusted with much; similarly, whoever is dishonest with little, can also be dishonest with much. The statement defines the proportionality between trust and dishonesty. A trusted person has developed the personality of being trusted in the midst of competing temptations; therefore, he or she has resisted temptations overtime and has developed spiritual resilience to keep integrity into place; similarly, the dishonest person has failed to resist competing temptations overtime and has been engulfed timely as temptations approach his or her door; therefore, he or she has developed dishonesty overtime and engulfed by it. Jesus said in the Matthew's gospel that a good tree cannot bear bad fruit, and bad tree cannot bear good fruit (Matt 7:18). His statement supports Dr. Luke's statement regarding trust and distrust. In most democratic societies, like the United States of America, integrity is the factor to ascend into public office; therefore, it is necessary to examine the candidate's life before voting him or her into office. Primarily, one wants to examine the sexual and financial life of the person who desires public office.

A trusted person might likely not fail the test of integrity no matter how much money is given to his or her trust; similarly, a dishonest person will fail the test of integrity regardless of how much is being given to his or her trust. Number does not have influence on the individual's response to the test of integrity, but character does. He said that if one has not been trustworthy in handling worldly wealth, who will trust him with true riches? The limit set between worldly wealth and true riches is trustworthiness. This is the reason people who are involved in embezzling public wealth never achieve true riches because they have been dishonest of handling wealth that does not belong to them. True riches are characterized with God's revelation and blessing; on the contrary, people who embezzle national wealth are cursed along with their materials possessions. The Bible has warned humanity not to pursue riches because it brings problems and flies away quickly especially when it becomes god in the individual's life (Prov 23:4–5). Worldly wealth that corrupt people obtained as the result of defrauding others becomes cursed money because the intended people did not use the wealth when some died from diseases as the result of lack of medical care, some remained uneducated as the result of lack of public education, some died from hunger, or some remained unsheltered. Dr Luke concludes that if one has not been trusted with someone's property, who will give him property of his own? People who are dishonest in handling someone's property never achieve true riches; therefore, the property in their possession actually belongs to people they had defrauded when they were in power. When people get into power in an environment that is unregulated, like Liberia, they use their place of power to defraud others because they feel that there are not consequences of their criminalities. Unregulated power in an unregulated society in the hand of the executive like Liberia is the broken society unless someone changes the system and begins to bring to justice past leaderships and sending them into prisons. The George Manneh Weah's administration refused the Economic and Criminal Court to be set up in Liberia because the administration came with the same mindset of past leadership and would be guilty had the administration accepted it. The administration failed the acid test of integrity; therefore, she cannot be trusted with the wealth of the nation according to the above Scripture; so, are the past leaderships of Liberia who had been involved in defrauding of the Liberian people in the past.

The word *mamonas* in Greek as used in Luke 16:10–13 defines worldly riches that resonate with money, possession, or property that belongs to an unspecified individual.[62] In the Semitic term, it is used as *mammonas* that defines the treasure a person trusts in. It is also an Aramaic term that is related to the Hebrew term *aman* that defines to trust in. Matthew writes, "No man can serve two masters: for either he will hate the one, and love the other; or else he will hold to the one, and despise the other. Ye cannot serve God and mammon"(Matt 6:24 KJV). The King James Version uses *mammom* that references *mamonas* in Greek and *mammonas* in Semitic or Aramaic language as used in the Hebrew term '*aman*.' When Christians pray in the name of Jesus, they usually conclude with 'Amen." The term "aman" is the Hebrew language that is being transliterated as "Amen' in English. Corrupt people cannot serve God because they are chasing after

---

[62] Ibid.

worldly riches while defrauding people of resources; as the result, they are saying "Amen" to money (*mommon*) instead of saying "Amen" to God; contrary, they cannot serve money and God simultaneously. Zacchaeus understood the consequences of defrauding people as tax collector and promised to pay restitutions to the people four times he had defrauded (Luke 19:1–10). *Mamonas* is the worldly riches associated with corrupt practices that divert leadership from doing the righteous things. It is sin to deprive the poor from the immunities that accord them because the ruler is in power. Power is being misused in the context of the presidency in countries that are guilty of human rights abuses and corruption practices. The primary reason God places people in the place of authority is to become blessings to them; on the contrary, power is being abused by leaders who are corrupt.

The second word known as "true riches" as used in the text is called *alethinos* in Greek. *Alethinos* emphasizes the integrity of what is true and down to it in the inner make-up. Such truth is full of revelations of God's faithfulness expressed in the leadership who does the right things for the benefits of the people. Such leadership that goes after *alethinos* is not selfish, self-contained, and egoistic; instead, the leadership does care about the welfare of the people; therefore, the leadership does not defraud the people of resources; instead, the leaders go after true riches that belong to themselves; hence, democratic society needs legislations put into place to stop criminals from defrauding the people.

Wealth is an abundance of value possessions; on the contrary, wealth is the accumulated value necessary for the daily needs and has no connection to abundance according to biblical stand point.[63] Wealth comes in the embodiments of capital, property, money, and natural resources. Such natural resources include oil, rubber, gold, iron ore, trees, land, water, wild life, and among others. By virtues of being the citizens, one owns these things. Most natural resources of third world countries have been owned

---

[63] Russell St. John, "Exploring Prosperity Preaching: Biblical Health, Wealth, and Wisdom," *Journal of the Evangelical Homiletics Society* 14, no. 2 (2014): 90–91.

by individual as the private entity when it should have been used for the benefits of the general populations.

According to two years of field research conducted by the International Consortium of Investigative Journalist, the document entitled, "The Pandora Papers," with reference to the offshore havens and hidden riches of world leaders and billionaires exposed in an unprecedented leak, reveals the inner workings of a shadow of economy that benefits the wealthy and well-connected at the expense of everyone else in the world.[64] The field research conducted by the team of more than 600 journalists from 150 news outlets, obtained the trove of more than 11.9 million confidential files, sifting through them, tracking down hard-to-find sources and digging into court records and other public documents from dozens of countries around the globe, discovered a widening authoritarianism and inequality with reference to the unequaled perspective on how money and power operate in the 21st century—and how the rule of law has been bent and broken around the world by a system of financial secrecy enabled by the U.S and other wealthy nations around the globe. The research uncovered the financial secrets of 35 current and former world leaders, more than 330 politicians and public officials in 91 countries and territories, and the global lineup of fugitives, con artists, and murderers.[65] The Pandora Papers exposed the offshore dealings of the King of Jordan, the presidents of Ukraine, Kenya and Ecuador, the Prime Minister of the Czech Republic and former British Prime Minister Tony Blair. The files also detailed the financial activities of the Russian President Vladimir Putin's "unofficial minister of propaganda" and more than 130 billionaires from Russia, the United States, Turkey, and other nations. The leaked records reveal that many of the power players who could help to bring an end to the offshore system instead benefit from it—stashing assets in

---

[64]Dean Starkman, Fergus Shiel, Emilia Díaz-Struck **and** Hamish Boland-Rudder, "Frequently Asked Questions about the Pandora Papers and ICIJ," accessed June 29, 2022, https://www.icij.org/investigations/pandora-papers/frequently-asked-questions-about-the-pandora-pape.

[65] Ibid.

convert companies and trusts while their governments do little to slow a global stream of illicit money that enriches criminals and impoverishes nations around the globe leading the citizens of these nations to suffer poverty.

The world is the broken and deprived society without God; hence, the Pandora Papers substantiates this statement. Power players and wealthy nations such as the United States and other wealthy nations, who legislate laws and enforce them, can take the back seat and allow criminals to prevail is hypocritical. They make the laws and break them because the big guys are benefiting from the offshore banks hosted by companies in secrecy. Unregulated and unsubstantiated banks they support in secrecy; on the other hand, they force regulations on banks to play by the rules; on the contrary, they pretend that they are playing by the rules when they are doing the opposite. This is the nature of the fallen humanity that refuses to recognize her fallen nature, repents from them, and turns to her Creator, God.

The Controversy between Biblical and Social View of Justice

Generally, justice defines fairness that reflects the universal ethical code of moral goodness toward humanity; however, this definition is limited with reference to how humanity views justice under the umbrella of self-contained and egoistic attitude relatively especially in the democratic society that defines justice in contrast to God's view of justice. Like the United States of America where LGBTQ and pro-abortion's rights are advocated for based on self-contained and egoistic attitude contrary to the righteousness of God, justice is defined contrary to God's view of justice. Such Self-contained and egoistic mindset regarding justice reflects the fallen human's philosophy disguised under what is called social justice in the context of the American's politics; consequently, such social justice system as preached reflects relativism across the human's cultures. What may be right in America in the context of social justice based on democratic values may not be right in other countries based on cultural context. Social justice and biblical justice advocates vary in ideologies and practices in some degrees; however, they agree in some areas with reference to wealth redistribution. For examples, citizens have the right to health care, education, protection, the exercise of the right to vote in provincial and general elections, the right to freedom of speech, the right to freedom of movement and among others; hence, the both agree on these values; on the other hand, biblically, citizens don't have the right to commit abortion and to have homosexual relations with one another. In some democratic societies like the United States of America, these things are allowed and social justice advocates preach the rights of these marginalized communities called the homosexuals coupled with abortion's right and take them to legislation.[66] In the biblical stand point, this is not justice; instead, it is sinful to do so; therefore, it is punishable in the court of the divine. In social justice, punishing homosexuals and abortionists is the direct infringement on their constitutional rights in the American context; therefore, social justice is relative based on culture, history, society, and truth accepted by some societies across the globe. From the above statements, the biblical view of justice reflects God's character; on the contrary, social justice reflects a fallen human's philosophy. In biblical justice, the concept of the truth and the divine is rated in His character (Ps 82:3–4; 89:14). The psalmist writes, "Righteousness and justice are the foundation of your throne; love and faithfulness go before you. Defend the weak and the fatherless; uphold the cause of the poor and the oppressed. Rescue the weak and the needy; deliver them from the hand of the wicked "(Ps 89: 14; 8:3–4 NIV). Biblical justice is pure, always upholding good and denouncing evil; on the contrary, modern social justice is often the opposite of biblical justice. Biblical justice defines justice in two ways. They include retributive justice, the justice that demands that someone who commits sin being punished and restorative justice, the justice that demands that those who are unrightfully hurt should be

---

[66] Robert M. Pennoyer, "No Surrender: To Defend Reproductive Rights, First Protect Church-State Separation," *Church & State* 74, no. 2 (2021), accessed June 29, 2022, https://www.au.org/church-state.

restored and given back what has been taken from them. The core value of social justice is the redistribution of wealth which biblical justice also concords with this core value.

The Facets of Biblical Justice

The dissimilarities that exist between social and biblical justices are engrained in the divine justice in the context of retribution and restoration. Biblical justice defines God as the transcendent being sets apart from human's identity and philosophy. The justice of God is the complete opposite of the philosophical understanding of justices advocated for in the secular world in the context of social justice in some degrees. Some of the justices advocated in social and criminal justices in the human's court systems, some do agree with the biblical justice; therefore, majority of the justices are not in compliance with the biblical kind of justice. Most of the justices preached from the human's point of views rooted in various constitutional laws disconnect from the moral law are in opposition to biblical kind of justices (Exod 20:1–21). Justice being one of the moral attributes of God defines Him as just or righteous. It separates Him from humanity because humanity is not just or righteous as the result of the fallen nature obtained in the Garden of Eden due to disobedience (Gen 3:1–15). Humanity can obtain righteousness only in Jesus Christ through faith. Because God is just, He is qualified to judge and to condemn wrong doing. This is indicative of the woman caught in the act of adultery (John 7:53–8:11). The Pharisees could not condemn her because they were guilty of wrong doing. On the other hand, God is the only one who is qualified to judge and to condemn wrong doing based on His guiltlessness; nevertheless, the human's court system that is being set up with judges has been instituted by God in order to restrain evil and to maintain security in society for all. God has ordained human judges to judge cases and to settle disputes between and among parties involved in the conflicts (Rom 13:1–7). Dissimilarly, biblical justice is different from social justice in some degrees based on the definition and application of retributive and restorative justices which contain no human's philosophy.[67]

Retributive Justice

Retributive justice is the act of rendering punishment to the sinner who has broken the law of God. Retributive justice is obvious in the Old Testament era. In the Old Testament era, if a woman were caught in the act of adultery, she would be stoned to death according to the Mosaic Law. This system of justice changed when Christ died to change the Old Order and to bring in the New Order called the New Testament through his death on the Calvary cross (Rom 5:12–17). The provision has been made to make mankind to escape the retribution; however, those who will refuse the provision, retribution awaits them for the Second Advent when Christ returns to Earth to judge the dead and the living (Rev 20:11–15). When the woman was caught in the act of adultery, she should have been stoned to death; on the contrary, she was set freed by the mercy of God. Jesus told her to go and sin no more. In the social justice system, committing adultery could not be considered as wrong doing based on some cultures. In some cultures, women are allowed to have sexual activities with multiple men without facing punishment because such is accepted in the society based on cultural relativism. In biblical justice, it is unacceptable; however, in the selective society, it is the social right of people who form part of such society; therefore, such act is not considered wrong doing because society has accepted it as acceptable standard based on her value system. This makes biblical justice to be in opposition to social justice in some degrees because mankind by nature hates righteousness; therefore, social justice in some degrees is relative based on culture, society, and history as the result of the human nature of sin.

---

[67] Mariam KamellKovalishyn, "A Biblical Theology of Social Justice," *Crux* 55, no. 3 (2019): 30–39.

Restorative Justice

Restorative justice is the act of paying back to people whose immunities in the form of divine privileges, opportunities, and wealth have been stolen or taken away from them. The restorative act of God is to restore humanity back to Himself based on the lost fellowship due to disobedience as explained. Apostle Paul writes,

> Therefore, if anyone is in Christ, the new creation has come: The old has gone, the new is here! All this is from God, who reconciled us to himself through Christ and gave us the ministry of reconciliation: that God was reconciling the world to himself in Christ, not counting people's sins against them. And he has committed to us the message of reconciliation. We are therefore Christ's ambassadors, as though God were making his appeal through us. We implore you on Christ's behalf: Be reconciled to God. God made him who had no sin to be sin for us, so that in him we might become the righteousness of God" (2 Cor 5:17–21 NIV).

The restorative justice of God as stated in the above text required that Christ died for sinful humanity in order to restore humanity to God's fellowship as the result of the conflict that divided mankind from the holy God due to disobedience. The restorative justice restores divine privileges mentioned in above text once someone is born of God. This is the reason Christians need to know the privileges accorded them so that they can claim them retroactively. If one is wearing the covenant attire (holiness), there is no reason that the devil should rob him or her of his or her God's giving privileges. Jesus died to remove the Old Order in order to establish the New Order (Jer 31:31–34). The covenant is fully established with better promises because it is sealed with Christ's shed blood (Heb 10:1–18). In the social justice system, restorative justice is allowed when government gives back to citizens what has been stolen from them. It is called privilege, wealth, or opportunity restoration. Privileges are rights owed to citizens with reference to wealth distribution, which is the core value for social justice. The right to privileges is attached to birth rights; similarly, in the kingdom of God, a believer via the virtue of spiritual birth rights is entitled to privileges in the embodiments of healing, materials possessions, deliverance, and among others. It is necessary as the believer to know his or her rights in the kingdom. Failure to know them is the failure to claim them. Believers have the right to claim the privileges, opportunities, and the wealth in the embodiments of material possessions and spiritual blessings. Believers have the right to be delivered and healed. Knowing their privileges in the kingdom enables them to claim their birth rights via deliverance and healing. Misunderstanding of their privileges gives the devil the edges to interfere with their blessings. Leaders who use their power to corrupt citizens have the notion that citizens don't know what belongs to them; therefore, they will claim ownership of the wealth of the country that belongs to citizens because no one is advocating for his or her rights. In the democratic society is less fearful to advocate for rights through protest; on the contrary, it is fearful to advocate for rights in the autocratic societies like Russia, China, Iran, and among others. Among countries in the world, America should be given credit when it comes to citizens advocating for their rights through protest. The reason is that America has grown and become mature to democratic values despite of the fragility of democratic values that has tested America in previous times; however, America remained the free society in the world.

Criminal Justice

Criminal justice is the delivery of justice to those who have committed crimes. It is the series of government agencies and institutions that comprises the police department and the court systems. Its goal is to rehabilitate offenders, prevent future crimes, and to render moral support to victims of the crimes.[68]Criminologists have developed theories over-time based on the theoretical and field studies conducted on the types of crimes and their punishments. Criminologists developed them objectively to ensure appropriate punishment for criminals in order to ensure the security for society. The theoretical development of the types of criminal punishment in criminology with reference to restorative justice is newer; however, criminologists see it as option for criminal punishment besides the four that are described in this monograph as the facet for criminal justice system. People who judge the types of crimes use one of these punishment types to guide them how they handle criminals in the justice system. Among the types of criminal punishment include incapacitation, deterrence, retribution, rehabilitation, and restoration.[69]Apostle Paul writes,

> For rulers hold no terror for those who do right, but for those who do wrong. Do you want to be free from fear of the one in authority? Then do what is right and you will be commended. For the one in authority is God's servant for your good. But if you do wrong, be afraid, for rulers do not bear the sword for no reason. They are God's servants, agents of wrath to bring punishment on the wrong-doer; therefore, it is necessary to submit to the authorities, not only because of possible punishment but also as a matter of conscience" (Rom 13:3–5 NIV).

In the above text, Apostle Paul via the inspiration of the Holy Spirit writes the Christians in Rome to submit to the civil authority. He uses the plural for the authority for individual member in the group and the singular for collectivism to indicate inclusiveness and universality of the command. The clue is from the use of the word "servant' in two categories.

---

[68] William H. Manz, "Encyclopedia of DNA and the United States Criminal Justice System," *The Catholic Library World* 74, no. 4 (2004): 279–280.

[69] Point Park University Online, "The Types of Criminal Punishment," accessed June 29, 2022, https://online.pointpark.edu/criminal-justice/types-of-criminal-punishment/.

Primarily, the first servant called servant, known as "*diakonos*' as used in Greek refers to the servant authority of the Roman Empire while the second servant called the public servant, known as "*leitougos*" as used in Greek refers to the servants priests and levites and the civil authority of the government (Rom 13:3–5). The letter was addressed to believers; however, the authority addressed is universal and timeless based on God's providence regarding governance in the world. The above scriptural passage defines and approves criminal justice system with relative to biblical justice in some degrees. In the criminal justice system, the punishments of retributive and restorative justices are being adopted by criminologists in the secular judicial system to compensate for rehabilitation and incapacitation of criminals. This is done to restrain evil in society. God is the One who has instituted criminal justice system in the world; therefore, God is commanding Christians and non-Christians alike to submit to all governing authorities tasked with the maintenance of societal peace and stability.

The Facets of Criminal Justice

Retributive Punishment

Retribution had been common in the Old Testament era used as the type of punishment executed under the Mosaic Covenant (Exod 21:12; Num 35:16–17). This justice is the idea of "an eye for an eye." Sometimes retributive justice may play out well for society as the deterrence; on the contrary, it might not play out well as true justice in the interest of the perpetrator of the crime based on some underlying problems in the context of biopsychosocio spiritual dimensions of the human beings; therefore, it is necessary to take a breath in order to conduct some psychiatric examinations on the criminal to determine what has been the motivation behind the behavior before sentencing the criminal; therefore, retribution should not be the last resort of the punishment levied against the potential criminal.[70] Miss X was arrested and imprisoned when she set the house on fire and fled while her family members occupied the premises. She was arrested and charged with felony and was scheduled to be sentenced for 15 years of incarceration. During the day of her sentence, the judge forgot to pronounce her sentence during the court proceeding after which Miss X was acquitted. After her acquitting, she was taken to a psychiatric hospital for examination and was diagnosed with bipolar disorder. Miss X explained her experience with the bipolar disorder after she was treated for the condition. According to her, she was under intense hallucination while being instructed to set the house on fire. She said that she could not control it because the voice was telling her to do so. Miss X was interviewed on BBC regarding her incarceration fall off and her experience with the mental illness. Retribution could have been wrong if Miss X had been sentenced for 15 years of incarceration. It could have added to her condition; therefore, it was not the rightful criminal punishment for Miss X and some people in society.

Juvenile, who commits crime like murder, retribution should not be the primary approach punishment based on children brain development with respect to individual child, the past experience of the child with respect to trauma or brain damaged, and the environment the child had lived previously or the child is living presently. All these factors influence the child's brain developmentally with reference to the cognitive, social, emotional, and physical developments that impact behavior.[71] At certain ages, children's behavior can change dramatically based on age and the individual child's characteristics. If the child committed murder at age 16 years old, when the child had grown to manhood or womanhood between 25 and 30 years old, the child would have regretted why he or she did such. The stored memory will resurface to remind the present brain development; therefore, the brain being well developed at this time will recognize the error some years ago when the child committed the crime.

---

[70] Ibid.

[71] KateriniGouli& Nicholas Karellos, "Children Behind Bars: A Voice for Greece's Juvenile Offenders," *Road to Emmaus* 7, no. 1 (2006): 39–49.

This is one of the reasons incapacitation or incarceration is not the best punishment for the juvenile who committed crime some years ago. The death penalty or incarceration is wrong for the juvenile based on the above factors. It will be wrong to kill the person once the person is no longer the threat to society after the person has served the prison sentence and had had some underlying brain development issues that influenced the past behavior. People who committed crimes during the juvenile years and are on death roll; hence, most are found in such category. Those who favor retribution believe it gives the victims of the crime a sense of satisfaction knowing a criminal received the appropriate level of punishment for the crime committed.[72] Do the Old and the New Testament support retribution? The Old Testament does support retribution; however, the idea of retribution in the New Testament has not been strictly mentioned; hence, in Jesus' messages, he preached forgiveness instead of retribution. In the Old Testament, sin such as homosexuality, witchcraft, adultery, homicide, hitting one's parents, kidnapping, cursing one's parents, idolatry, violating the Sabbath, child sacrifice, and incest received the death penalty (Exod 21:12; Deut 32:35). The Old Testament does endorse the death penalty of criminals who committed murder. Moses writes, "Anyone who strikes a person with a fatal blow is to be put to death (Exod 21:12 NIV). Christians generally believe that the New Testament does not support retribution on the ground that Jesus paid the price for the retribution of sinners when he died on the Cross in order to negate the regulations of the Old Testament that have been opposed to sinners. This is true; however, Apostle Paul mentioned the punishment of evil doers in Romans Chapter thirteen verses one to seven; though, he is not explicit of what kinds of crimes and the corresponding punishments; however, the retribution is generalized to all crimes. It depends on the authority to prescribe the punishment according to the types of crimes committed. By inference, Apostle Paul is referring to both civil and criminal cases judged in the judicial systems. The phrase "evil doers' indicates criminalities in this

---

[72] Ibid.

context despite of implicit indicator. It is implied to all evils. If the crime committed requires the death penalty in the criminal justice systems, the authority stands in the position by law to render judgment to the perpetrator of the crimes. According to Romans chapter thirteen verses one to seven, the authority is working for God in order to restrain evil and to maintain national security for all (Rom 13:1–7). Killing someone is wrong; however, if the criminal has killed someone; eventually, he or she becomes a threat to public safety; therefore, scripture recommends the death penalty for the individual in order to keep others from being killed in like manner. How the Christian who opposes abortion rights advocates will oppose the death penalty of the murderer who is a threat to national security and human's peaceful co-existence? It would be a double standard with no logical and unsubstantiated reasoning in such situation. The unborn child who did not commit a crime was killed in the name of reproductive rights women have based on the constitutionality of the United States. How will a murderer who has gone through the judicial system equitably and unprejudiced declared guilty of the crime; paradoxically, a Christian who would stand and preach that the individual be forgiven to avoid the death penalty; in this regard, he or she would be insensitive to the norms governing the criminal justice system in the land. I am not in favor of someone dying because the individual committed a crime and retribution should be the last resort to determine the person's fate. I am reasoning as an individual in line of justice played out so that the victims of the crime will be fully served as the human being though the person might not be living; however, it will serve as deterrence for others to avoid such aggressive and fatal behaviors in society. Advocating for murderers to avoid the death penalty; hence, one will not be doing justice for children who have been killed through abortion who did not commit a crime; instead, the murderers did. If abortion would be regulated as the capital crime, doctors who do abortion would face execution as the result of homicide according to biblical retributive and criminal justice system.

Abortion falls in the category of homicide if it is regulated as the capital crime and will be punishable by the death penalty.[73]

Incapacitation punishment

In the criminal justice system, incapacitation is the form of drastic judgment rendered by the court to disenable the criminal of functions in society. Such punishment is prescribed for murderers who are dangerous to society at large. Incapacitation is done through incarceration, house arrest, and execution of the criminals. The degree of punishment levied against the criminal determines the gravity of the act committed. Some are placed under imprisonment for life while some are placed in temporal house arrest coupled with the death penalty. Incapacitation is the high degree of retributive punishment that ends the life of the prisoner through life imprisonment, detention, and execution. The flaw in incapacitation is that it does not address rehabilitation or recidivism. This makes law-makers faced the job to determine the appropriate levels of punishment, which ranges from speeding ticket fine to mandatory sentences for certain crimes committed. It is true that the Old Testament has sanctioned incapacitation in the embodiment of the death penalty; however, it is advisable to conduct some psychological examinations on the notorious criminals in order to understand their biopsychosocio spiritual dimensions before the prescription of the death sentence or incarceration. It is necessary to test the balance in the brain chemistry to see if the notorious criminal could be prescribed rehabilitation punishment to have him or her restored to society. Counseling, psychiatric treatment coupled with drugs treatment could rehabilitate murderers to have them restored and re-integrated into society.[74] If the rehabilitation fails; then, the criminals

---

[73] Amanda Kendrix-Komoto, "The Other Crime: Abortion and Contraception in Nineteenth and Twentieth-Century Utah," *Dialogue* 53, no. 1 (2020): 33–45.

[74] Pamela Hayes & Mary Grant, "Spiritual Direction and Counseling Therapy," *The Way Supplement* 69, no. 1 (1990): 61–71.

could be incapacitated through incarceration, detention, or execution for the safety of society (Exod 21:12; Num 35:16–17; Ezra 7:26; Rom 13:4).

Rehabilitation Punishment

The subject of spiritual formation occurs on all levels in the context of initiation, indoctrination, institutionalization, and societal affiliation. Because spiritual formation is real, the movements of societal establishments in the context of churches, mosques, temples, terrorist groups, and their allied affiliates give renaissance to existence of such organizations. In this regard, religious groups such as churches, mosques, temples, and terrorist organizations need rehabilitation in order to convert to another movement. People who are involved in suicide bombing cannot convert to the better when anti-terrorist organizations use the same weapon against them because such weapons are recipes for their thriving; therefore, there should be some modified approach how the world fights against terrorism. Military force should be used along with diplomacy and the technical calculated educational methodology in order to minimize terrorism in the world. The major players in the fight against terrorism in the world need to rethink and to reverse their positions to successfully fight against terrorism in the world; similarly, criminals that are incarcerated need to undergo spiritual formation in the embodiment of rehabilitation programs in order to convert them from their criminalities to the betterment of their usefulness in society.

Rehabilitation seeks to prevent opportunity crimes by changing the criminal's behavior; therefore, therapy of behavioral psychology is necessary in rehabilitation program, which states that in order to change someone's behavior; the person should be taught new doctrine that counter interposes on the former doctrine that controls the person's ideological behavior. This is what behavioral psychologists do in rehabilitation program; similarly, in the spiritual ministry, it is what pastors do using biblical doctrine to convert people from their former way of lives to new paradigm shift of life changes through the power of the Holy Spirit. Based on spiritual formation with respect to spiritual rehabilitation, Apostle Paul wrote to the Christians of Ephesus to remind them that they were taught according to their former way of life to put off the old life of sin and to put on the new life of righteousness in order to be made new in the attitude of their minds to be like God created in true righteousness and holiness (Eph 4:22–24). Apostle Paul was referencing spiritual rehabilitation in behavioral psychology. In conservative Christianity, the subject of psychology is being rejected with the belief that psychology is in opposition to the Bible. This is a falsehood statement that is contrary to what psychology teaches. Psychology is the general word that covers diversity of psychological doctrines and practices; in this light, there are secular psychologies and Christian psychologies as well as there are secular psychological and Christian psychological therapies that cover how mental psychoses are treated in order to alleviate brain disease. It is from psychological and psychiatric practices, there are mental health hospitals or clinics to treat mental diseases that have become epidemic in the world. Know that God is the originator and the brain behind medical and spiritual healing; in this light, not all illnesses are connected to demonic influences; therefore, some illnesses will require both prayer and prescription medication. That does not root out the fact that God does not heal all illnesses. He heals all including both spiritual and medical problems; nevertheless, incorporating and integrating psychological practices in the spiritual ministry enables the pastoral counselor to make sound decision when praying for people. Some might say that integrating psychology with the Bible will cause one to not walk in faith. It is false. It depends on the kind of psychologies one uses in the Christian ministry. There are Christian psychological therapies adopted in the mental health field and the Christian ministry to deal with spiritual issues regarding behavior. It is not the word that matters, but how the individual uses the practices of psychologies matters in the field of psychologies; therefore, integration is encouraged in the Christian ministry using biblical wisdom to make sound decision.

The problem faced by humanity with respect to illnesses is not only spiritual; therefore, some are clinical that need clinicians like psychologies, psychiatrists, and medical doctors to treat those diseases. This is the reason there are health institutions in the world including behavioral health. Rehabilitation is the behavioral health program done through counseling and drug administration; therefore, the needs for psychologists and psychiatrists are needed to have such health institutions in the world.

God, the Creator of the universe is the Psychologist due to the fact that He knows the mind of humanity; for this reason, it is helpful to integrate psychological principles in the Christian ministry using the Bible as the yard stick to make decision. Loving God with our mind, soul, body, and spirit entails adopting and integrating psychological principles in the Christian ministry and practices because God endorses it (Matt 22:37). Psychology is the study of the human's mind known as *Psuche*. Understanding oneself enables one to relate to the Creator well; similarly, to lead humanity successfully before God as the church leader one should understand what humanity is like in practice and theory. To understand the holistic aspect of the human being, leaders need to know the human being holistically. Psychology will get leaders there with respect to human's relations. In the absence of the study of psychology coupled with the Bible, leaders' understanding how they deal with humanity and God is fragmentary when it comes to making sound decision. Human being by nature is the psychological tool used in the hand of his Creator, Cod. One should understand the human beings in order to lead them successfully. Pastors by default, who lead churches, are adopting psychological principles unknown themselves.

In the rehabilitation programs, criminals are offered a host of programs while in prison. They include educational and vocational programs, treatment center placement, and mental health counseling. These programs are designed based on the psychological approach to treatment of criminals to have them revived and placed in society. These approaches give judges the flexibility to mix in rehabilitation programs as part of a criminal's sentencing. If the criminal was sent to a treatment facility, the judges use the reports on the criminal at the treatment facility to make decision. If the criminal has been responding to treatment and his or her behavior has improved to the better, the judge could limit the years of imprisonment or acquit the criminal after the treatment and have the person reintegrated into society on parole. At this time, the person is offered employment while the employer becomes the agent of the government for monitoring. The goal of rehabilitation is to make the person useful to himself or herself to society and to lower the rate of recidivism.

The Facets of Rehabilitation Programs

David writes,

> The LORD is my rock, my fortress and my deliverer; my God is my rock, in whom I take refuge, my shield and the horn of my salvation, my stronghold I called to the LORD, who is worthy of praise,and I have been saved from my enemies. The cords of death entangled me; the torrents of destruction overwhelmed me. The cords of the grave coiled around me;the snares of death confronted me. In my distress I called to the LORD; I cried to my God for help. From his temple he heard my voice;my cry came before him, into his ears (Ps 18:2–6 NIV).

King David addressed the words of his song to the Lord on the day when the Lord delivered him from the hand of his enemies. Imagine the traumas King David experienced when he had encountered these experiences while being under attack at the point of being killed. The indulgence of human beings into criminalities coupled with drug use can lead to traumas which have altering effects on brain function negatively. Most criminals are often involved in drug use which can lead to brain damage and make them disable in society. Most can be dangerous to people and to themselves and suffer from suicidal ideation. This is the reason most often one hears that a prisoner was found dead in the prison. This is common in the world's prison system. Sometimes fight can break out in the prison system and lead many dead in the minutes because these criminals are already suffering from mental illness. Rehabilitation is the program put into place to help them recover from these traumas. King David experienced traumas and sought refuge in God; analogically, rehabilitation program is the refuge for criminals' recovery. Understanding that rehabilitation is the behavioral health program in the criminal justice system that is equated to spiritual formation, there are mechanisms put into place to rehabilitate an individual in order to convert the person to meet the goal of the rehabilitation program. These approaches vary with institutions with respect to the kind of programs and the conditions treated by the facility based on individual's needs. For example, there are rehabilitation programs that deal with notorious criminals, mental health counseling and drug treatments on adults and juveniles with respect to substance abuse problems, family therapy with reference to divorce, domestic violence and among others. These programs designed to rehabilitate victims go through initiation, indoctrination, deinstitutionalization, and allied affiliation; hence, these facets of rehabilitation are delineated in this monograph

Initiation

Initiation is the action of admitting someone into a secret or obscure society or group, typically with a ritual; therefore, in the contextualization of the rehabilitation facility, initiation is the step taken to introduce the patient to the rules that govern the daily behavior of the patient in conformity with the facility's norms, the therapies, and departmental staff that are involved in the treatment of the individual. The rules, the therapies, and the expectations anticipated by the treatment team are rituals. They are rituals in the sense that these things are only made known to patients who are admitted into the rehabilitation facility. The nature of the norms, to which the norms are made known, and the rules governing them define the obscurity of the group and its ritual implications. On the onset of the initiation procedures, the individual is told what to do and what not to do and what the expectations are. The individual is told the various therapies administered that are within his or her reach based on his or her conditions being treated. Such therapy includes recreational therapy that the individual will be involved during the treatment period. Recreational therapy such as sport activity will upgrade the patient's social and emotional health understanding that most criminals are drug users whose emotional and social health have been altered negatively due to the effects of the substance on the nervous system. Recreational therapy such as sport will help the patient to readjust to the coping skills that have been lost over time during the time of his or her drugs use and criminalities. Most notorious criminals who have taken people's lives are vulnerable to hyper vigilant effects; therefore, their experiences during these episodes are stressors that can reinvent and set the stressors into motion and make the person to commit another crime when they are released from the prison system. Most of these crimes committed are connected to mental imbalances because the person is in the different world. Mental health program is needed for the stable society. Most nations that are engulfed with security issues are the result of the lack of the governments to prioritize mental health programs for their youths who are drug users in the nation. Imprisonment is not the last resort to avoid criminalities; instead, rehabilitation program is back up to mitigate them. On the onset of the initiation, the patient is introduced to his or her therapists such as nurses, psychiatrists, psychologists, and among others.

Deinstitutionalization

In clinical and abnormal psychology, institutionalization or institutional syndrome refers to deficits or disabilities in social and life skills, which develop after a person has spent a long period living in mental hospitals, prisons, or other remote institutions. In order to avert institutional syndrome sustained by mental health patients or criminals who have lost social and life skills as the result of long period of institutionalization, the person is admitted to the rehabilitation facility which is the opposite to the above institutions mentioned based on theories and practices. In mental health hospitals or prisons, people are confined and placed under certain restrictions based on the nature of their conditions. In the mental health hospitals, patients who are placed on suicidal watch are confined and monitored daily; therefore, such individual cannot attend recreational therapy such as sporting. The goal of recreational therapy is to restore social and life skills. In the rehabilitation facility, the treatment is holistic in that it includes drug treatments, education, social, and life skills. Some treatment centers in rehabilitation facility have schools from the first grade to the twelve grade levels especially those facilities that treat juveniles who have gone astray via experimenting with drugs. Such facility has the residential and school units. These facilities are very common in the United States across States levels in both public and private owned. Deinstitutionalization is the restoration of social and life skills to criminals via rehabilitation programs who have been institutionalized in prisons after a long period of time. It is done via schooling, recreational activities, vocational trainings, and university education so that when the individual is released from prison, he or she will be useful to himself or herself and to society at large.

Indoctrination

Indoctrination is the process of teaching a person or a group to accept a set of beliefs uncritically. Mental health or pastoral counselors are involved in indoctrination on the daily basis as they interact with mental health patients in rehabilitation facility. One must have the passion for humanity and being trained well to deal with mental health patients because there are risks involved. In indoctrination, mental health or residential counselors teach patients coping skills. Coping skills are defense mechanisms used by patients when the stressors show up. If the patient gets angry and his or her breathing system changes, what coping skills do you employ to calm him or her down as pastoral or mental health counselor? What will you do as the residential or pastoral counselor when the resident takes a chair and begins to hit the wall? What will you do to deescalate the situation to avoid fatal incidence? Know that most of the people that come from prison systems into the rehabilitation facility have killed people; therefore, hurting you is not a problem to them because they have emotional reflexes that are sociopathic or psychopathic. What you say to them, how you say it, how you approach them, and how you do it timely, can save you and change the situation.

Allied Affiliation

Working with patients from diverse backgrounds with respect to age, social, and cultural characteristics requires cultural competence understanding that one as the nurse, psychiatrist, psychologist, therapist, pastoral counselor, or residential counselor, one is the helper to the resident; therefore, one serves in the supervisory capacity to direct and to redirect the individual during transitions. Know that the person has acquired some spiritual formations from previous affiliates; therefore, the individual has copied practices from the previous affiliations with peers during his or her criminalities; in this light, it takes time for the individual to amend changes from the previously learned behavior. The rehabilitation facility should know these issues with the admittance individual; for this reason, people who are employed to work in such facility have to be trained during job orientation in regardless of the previously obtained degrees in such field of disciplines. Understanding these issues, it indicates that staff members are not trainers to the individual like parents do in child training; instead, staff members are there to cleverly enforce the rules of the facility in order to help the individual amend the changes from the previously learned behavior. Resident patients that are in compliance with the rules of the facility that are designed according to their treatment goal can recover sooner and be discharged quickly based on the reports as indicated in their files that correspond to indicators referencing their daily interactions with peers, family members, and facility staff. Allied affiliation signifies that the person has copied approximately fifty percents of behavioral characteristics from previously affiliated individuals socially and emotionally which can interfere with the individual's comportment while being rehabilitated. Understanding these things indicate that, the resident can insult staff and throw objects at them. Know that patients of such have mood swim due to various psychiatric issues as the result of previous traumas experienced; in this light, they have brain problems and staff should understand what their problems are before taking care of such people. Understanding the age, the social, and the cultural context of the resident patient will help employees work with such individual coupled with interpersonal and intrapersonal skills.

Deterrence

Apostle Paul's message to the Christians in the context of the actions of rulers toward criminals is to deter criminals from criminalities and to serve as the deterrence to the general public. The proactive arrest of criminals by law enforcement divisions is the methodology of deterrence executed to stop potential criminals to become criminals in the future. Deterrence restrains evil and provides confirmed security for citizens and minimizes security threats posed by potential criminals in the land. Criminals will always test the strengths of the government before they maximize their criminalities. The reason why past and present presidents of nations become criminals is because no past presidents have been tried for corrupt practices; therefore, other politicians who are aspiring for government jobs are coming with the same mindset to steal because there has not been deterrence set into place to stop others. When retributive and incapacitation punishments are executed on criminals, they serve as deterrence to deter others from practicing such risky behaviors. Behaviors that threaten public safety with respect to social and economic injustices with impunity encourage criminals to thrive in society and pose national insecurity socially and economically to the populations.

No one including the president of the land should be above the law in the stable democratic society. Behaviors that pose national insecurity should be investigated and prosecuted according to the law. If justice is played out on ordinary criminals that have been incriminated and made them faced the prison sentence; similarly, government officials who are involved in corrupt practices in the land should be prosecuted for their criminalities. The Justice Department's failure to persecute government level criminals is the direct failure of the justice system to fully represent the people and the constitution. Justice maintained in the democratic society is the maintenance of national security for all. Apostle Paul having been inspired by the Holy Spirit had deterrence in his mind as he wrote to the Christians of Rome. He writes,

> For rulers hold no terror for those who do right, but for those who do wrong. Do you want to be free from fear of the one in authority? Then do what is right and you will be commended. For the one in authority is God's servant for your good. But if you do wrong, be afraid, for rulers do not bear the sword for no reason. They are God's servants; agents of wrath to bring punishment on the wrongdoer (Rom 13:3–4 NIV).

Deterrence aims to prevent future crime and can focus on specific and general deterrence. Specific deterrence deals with an individual less likely to commit a future crime because of fear of getting a similar or worse punishment. General deterrence refers to the impact on members of the public who become less likely to commit a crime after learning of the punishment another person experienced.[75]

---

[75] Ibid.

Restoration

I was driving on Wednesday to work at 2:00 PM 2022 news, I heard the judge convicting a juvenile who was involved in school shooting two years ago. The 17 years old killed 14 of his school mates and wounded dozens of students including faculty. The family members of the victims were present during his conviction for life imprisonment or face the death penalty. I heard him apologizing to the victims' families to forgive him. He promised them that when he is reinstated into the society, he will meaningfully contribute to society success. Whether the family victims will forgive him or not, he had made direct amends verbally to the victims of his crime as well as the community where the crime occurred. Restorative punishment is the new approach to criminal justice for the offender to make direct amends to the victims of the crime and the community where the crime occurred. Judges use this criminal justice punishment with juvenile offenders. In such approach, the criminal and the victim meet so that the offender can hear what the victim says about his or her experience with the crime committed. The goal of the meeting is for the offender to make changes to his or her behavior and to seek forgiveness from the victim and the community where the crime occurred. In some instances, the victims might forgive or not before the session closes. The tendency of forgiveness is tied to the religious background of the victim or the victim's family. Someone who is from the Christian's background might likely forgive the person and tell the judge to acquit him or her. It is left to the court system to run the final decision. The criminal has verbally made amendments and the victim has restored the offender affirmatively. This is the punishment of restoration in criminal justice system.

Environmental Justice

In the genesis, God instructed his creation to render justice to the earth and everything in it (Gen 2:1–31). He gave mankind every creeping thing, plants, animals, and their affiliated nature. He told mankind to subdue and to replenish the earth. He instructed mankind to be caretaker of His creations. Mankind by assignment from the beginning is the manager of God's creations; unfortunately, the nuclear man has become the destroyer of God's creation instead of the caretaker via the burning of fossil fuels, the deposal of industrial wastes, the destruction of rain forests via deforestation, the use of bad technological devices, and among others. The issue of global warming that has given birth to climate change with its various manifestations with respect to the change in wind velocity, the rise in temperature, volcanic fire, and among others is the result of injustice being played out by industrial nations via the burning of fossil fuels. Despite of the warning being aired by scientists two decades ago, industrial nations have paid deaf ears to its catastrophic outcomes in the name of economic development stabilization. They are using fire to put off another fire which is temporal; unlike; the former has contingent lasing disastrous effects on the planet and its people. Justice played out to the environment is the justice played out for all because humanity is geographically connected with no boundary when it comes to climate change and its disastrous effects. The use of industrial wastes that contain dangerous chemicals and the burning of fossil fuels has brought pollution and damaged the air quality are direct environmental injustice that cause illness to the human populations and perpetual sufferings. The action of nuclear man through the use bad technology is the result of environmental damage leading to environmental injustice. The cutting of trees on land without planting new ones is the lack of good stewardship that leads to environmental injustice. Governments of nations are guilty of environmental injustice; catastrophically, everyone is inclusive as the victim of environmental injustice; on the other hand, not everyone is the creator of environmental injustice especially third world nations who lack industrialization output.

Ethical Reflection

The terminology "democratization" is synonymous to justice for all; therefore, the society that lacks justice lacks democratic values. Liberia is engulfed with the problems of injustices contributed by the young democracy, camouflaged democracy, and corruptions in the government. The existence of these problems undefined Liberia as the democratic society and therefore undermines democracy. Unless these problems are eradicated, Liberia does not exist as democratic society due to these disparities seen in the Liberian society. The governments that have existed in Liberia from 1847 to the present have been corrupt; therefore, corruption has become the common practice in Liberia with impunity and has become cancerous causing Liberia to be poor. In Liberia, when someone is being elected to the presidency, he or she becomes like the *demi* god; therefore, he or she owns everything in Liberia psychologically; for this reason, former and present presidents of Liberia have stolen the country's resources with impunity. This must change in Liberia when justice is played out holding present and past presidents accountable for their embezzlements.

CHAPTER V
JURISPRODUCE

Chapter Overview

Jurisprudence is the study of the philosophy of ethics and law. While it is true that ethics and law reflect values and guide behavior; however, the two are difference based on human's behavior with reference to how laws are enacted that do not dictate the ethics of God that question integrity. While this is true, in the context of jurisprudence, this section of the monograph discusses the branches of ethics, the principles of ethics, civil disobedience, the just war theory, Christian enlistment into the military, and the principles of absolutism and relativism in the just war conflict situations. At the conclusion, the author has developed a reflection on the chapter to redress the subject in order to pin a mental picture in the mind of the reader for personal subjective reflection.

The Branches of Ethics

Ethics defines the moral principle that governs a person's behavior or the conducting of an activity; therefore, the word "ethics" has given birth to diversities with reference to societal norms, people groups, cultures, customs, and laws enacted in such contexts. The nature of ethics based on the above mentioned core values, has resulted into hybridization of twenty-one sub-branches of ethics that had emerged from descriptive, normative, applied and meta-ethics. The emergence of the twenty one branches of ethics is the result of laws or customs that changed based on changing dynamics of times and societies; consequently, societies structure their moral principles as per changing times and expect people to conduct themselves accordingly. Primarily, this gave birth to descriptive ethics. In descriptive ethics, people hold onto the human actions acceptable or not acceptable under a custom or law; therefore, people are made to believe what is right or wrong. In descriptive ethics, people look at the past and present and make ethical decision based how people conducted themselves in the past according to the norms and then make adjustment to align themselves with the acceptable norms morally acceptable in that culture; for this reason, descriptive ethics is also called comparative ethics because it compares the ethics of the past of one society to the other society; therefore, descriptive ethics seeks inputs from other disciplines of studies such as anthropology, psychology, sociology, and history.

There is the Golden Rule in ethics that says, "Do to others as you would have them do to you." Based on this Golden Rule, no one in his or her right mind will want to hurt himself or herself; therefore, throwing a stone to the neighbor's glass door to break it or hurt him or her is morally wrong; in this regard, such act is universally unacceptable across all societies; consequently, this gave birth to normative ethics. In normative ethics, there is a set of norms or considerations one should act based on the rightness of the actions. Normative ethics is the study of ethical action and it is prescriptive because it rests on the principles which determine whether an action is right or wrong. In normative ethics, justification is provided for punishing a person who disturbs social and moral order of society. Normative ethics constitutes Aristotle's Virtue Ethics[76], Kant's Deontological Ethics, and Mill's Consequentialism (Utilitarianism).

The focus of virtue ethics is character that evaluates ethical behavior; referentially, Plato, Aristotle, and Thomas Aquinas were major advocates for virtue ethics. As the major proponents of virtue ethics, Plato gave the system that defines prudence, justice, temperance, and fortitude

---

[76] May Sim, "Rethinking Virtue Ethics and Social Justice with Aristotle and Confucius," *Asian Philosophy*, no. 2 (2010): 195–213.

while his disciple, Aristotle categorized the virtues as the morality and intellectualism.

Another category of normative ethics is called deontological or duty ethics that focuses on the rightness and wrongness of the actions rather than the consequences of those actions; categorically, theories that constitute deontological ethics include Categorical Imperative, Absolute Morality, and Divine Command Theory. Categorical Imperative is the central philosophical concept in the deontological moral philosophy of Immanuel Kant which states that commands or moral laws are applicable to all persons in regardless of their desires to obey them. These duties laws are found in the Ten Commandments or laws that support ethical behavior in society; hence, such includes, "You shall not murder." Another duty ethics theory called Absolute Morality defines that the ethical view of some actions are intrinsically right or wrong or the position that there are universal ethical standards that apply to actions regardless of context while the Divine Command Theory is the meta-ethical theory which proposes that an action's status as morally good is equivalent to whether it is commanded by God. This theory asserts that what is moral is determined by God's commands and that for a person to be moral, he or she is to follow God's commands in regardless of whether the outcome will be good or bad. The example of this Divine Command Theory in the Scripture is when God commanded King Saul to exterminate the *Amalekites* (1 Sam 15:3). The third category of deontological ethics is called Categorical Imperative Theory. In this theory, Immanuel Kant said that human beings occupy special place in creation and there is an ultimate commandment from which all duties and obligations derived. In an effort to support and to apply this theory, he proposed two principles called Universality and Reciprocity. By Universality, Immanuel Kant said that moral action should be possible to apply to all people disregarding cultural relativism and by the Principle of Reciprocity; he stated that it is necessary to do to others as you would like them do to you; hence, such premise of morality is found in all religious systems, including Hinduism, Islam, Christianity, Judaism, and Buddhism and list goes on. The third normative category of ethics advanced by John Stuart Mill is called consequentialism or teleological ethics which defines that the morality of an action is contingent with the outcome of each; therefore, what an individual sows is what he or she harvests proportionally; similarly, the morally right action would produce good outcome while the morally wrong action would produce bad outcome. Based on the outcome, there are social theories that support consequentialism; namely, these theories include utilitarianism, hedonism, egoism, asceticism, and altruism. Utilitarianism defines that right action that leads to most happiness of greater number of people is acceptable ethical standard. Example of utilitarianism include: "If you are choosing chocolate for yourself, the utilitarian view is that you should choose the flavor that will give you the most pleasure." Hedonism defines that anything that maximizes pleasure is right action; hence, the example of hedonism include the constant pursuit for enjoyment and satisfaction. Psychologically, it is the doctrine that behavior is motivated by the desire for enjoyment and the avoidance of pain. Egoism defines that anything that is good for self is right action. Example of egoism psychologically is when a person always acts in his or her self-interest, even when it appears as though it is not. Asceticism defines that abstinence from egoistic pleasure to achieve spiritual goals is right action of ethical standard. Example of asceticism is when the celibate individual refuses to have sexual intercourse in this life only to be devoted to the service of God. Altruism defines that living for others and not caring for self is right action; hence, the example of altruism is when someone gives his or her belonging or lunch away to someone that needs it; though, he or she desires it; however, he or she denies self.

The third main branch of ethics is called meta-ethics or analytical ethics that deals with the study of origin of ethical concepts themselves. This ethics is the abstract way of thinking; therefore, it does not consider whether an action is good or bad, right or wrong. It questions what goodness or rightness an action itself is. The key theories in meta-ethics include naturalism, non-naturalism, emotivism, and prescriptivism.[77] Naturalism is the philosophical belief that everything arises from natural properties and causes; therefore, the supernatural explanation is excluded. Naturalists and non-naturalists believe that moral language is cognitive; therefore, it can be known to be true or false. Emotivism is a meta-ethical view that claims that ethical sentences do not express propositions; instead, they express emotional attitudes. Example, "Murder is wrong"; therefore, it indicates the disapproval of murder that is expressed in the wrongness of murder to be wrong; hence, influenced by the growth of analytical philosophy and logical positivism in the 20th century is the ethical theory of emotivism.[78] Emotivists deny that moral utterance are cognitive, holding that they consist of emotional expressions of approval or disapproval and that the nature of moral reasoning and justification must be reinterpreted in order to take this essential characteristic of moral utterance into account.[79] Prescriptivism is the ethical theory that moral utterances have no truth value but prescribe attitudes to others and express the conviction of the speaker. Example, "Murder is wrong." Prescriptivists argue that moral judgments are prescriptions or prohibitions of action rather than statements of fact about the world.

The fourth main branch of ethics is called applied ethics. It deals with the philosophical examination of moral standpoint of particular issues in private and public life that pertains to moral judgment.[80] This ethics is significant for professionals such as doctors, teachers, administrators, and rulers. There are six key domains of applied ethics. They include decision ethics, professional ethics, clinical ethics, business ethics, organizational ethics, and social ethics.

Decision ethics is defined as the one that engenders trust and thus indicates responsibility, fairness, and caring to an individual. To be ethical,

---

[77] GK Today, "Four Branches of Ethics," accessed August 28, 2022, https://www.gktoday. in/topic/four-branches-of-ethics/.

[78] Ibid.

[79] Ibid.

[80] Ibid.

one has to demonstrate respect and responsibility. Professional ethics are principles that govern the behavior of a person or group in a business environment. Clinical ethics is an applied branch of ethics which analyzes the practice of clinical medicine and related scientific research. Business ethics is the form of applied ethics or professional ethics that examines ethical principles and moral or ethical problems that can arise in a business environment. Organizational ethics is the ethics of an organization; therefore, it is how an organization responds to internal or external stimulus. Social ethics is the systematic reflection on the dimensions of social structures, systems, issues, and communities. In simplicity applied ethics deals with the rightness or wrongness of an action that references social, economical, cultural, and religious issues. For example, euthanasia, child labor, abortion, homosexuality etc.

The Fundamental Principles of Ethics

Law and ethics are related in that both reflect values systems and guide behavior; on the contrary, they are not homogenous based on the question of integrity with reference to the flawed nature of laws. The reason why ethics and law are not homogenous is that ethics is absolute while law is relative based on cultures and changing dynamics of societal norms. Occasionally, law seems to permit unethical behavior in the societal setting; therefore, flawed laws are imminent and can raise the question of whether humanity should comply with the law. For example, the law the federal government of the United States passed some fifty years ago allowing abortion as the constitutional right called Roe V. Wade, is a flawed law that is unethical. The law is flawed and harmful because it permits women to murder the unborn child while the inalienable right of the child to live is violated. This law raises the question of integrity and poses further questions on such law allowing women to kill babies because it is their constitutional right. Making law in disregard to ethics and integrity is the open door flawed law in society; for this reason, man-made law often lacks the ethics that conforms to the moral law of God. Ethics is

114

understood to be a system of principles that guide how people make decisions and lead their lives while integrity is understood as the consistent application of ethical principles that reflect honesty. Ethics, integrity, and honesty when considered in making law, the law will become consistent with moral or conservative values. While it is true that ethics, integrity, and honesty guide how people make decision and live worthily according to universal morality, there are four fundamental principles of ethics that guide behaviors in the application of ethics in various fields of disciplines when it comes to applied ethics. These principles constitute beneficence, nonmaleficence, autonomy, and distributive justice. Understanding that autonomy has to do with self-determination, the issues of truth-telling, confidentiality, and informed consent are inclusive to guide autonomy. Ethics is a broad word that covers variety of disciplines in the embodiments of medical ethics, business ethics, Christian ethics, professional ethics, social ethics, organizational ethics, and decision ethics. All these ethics named reflect values and guide behaviors in these fields of disciplines. In the context of this monograph as the four ethical principles are concerned, they serve as the guides between man-made law and the divine law that reflect values and guide human's behaviors since man by nature is polarized on two axes to do good or evil; therefore, the issue of avoidance of atrocities during warfare is not guaranteed based on the fragility of the combatant's activities. Adopting these ethical principles in the daily lives of governments, citizens, and military situation during arm conflict in the context of societal socialization is substantiated.

Principle defines the system of reasoning that guides behaviors and reflects values; similarly, ethics guides behaviors and reflects values systems that are consistent with objective and intrinsic moral act across all cultures with reference to Absolute Morality (Exod 20:1–20); contemporaneously, law guides behaviors and reflects values; on the contrary, law is not always consistent with objective and intrinsic moral acts that resonate with universal morality across all culture as the Ten Commandments dictate. It tells the audience that not all laws should be obeyed due to the flawed nature of laws. Such flawed law is the constitutional law given to women to abort unborn children termed as the reproductive rights in the United States. Women who are using their constitutional rights to kill the unborn children are violating the children's inalienable rights to live. This law is flawed; therefore, it is inconsistent with absolute morality. As this section of the monograph discusses the four fundamental principles of ethics, it informs the audience what ethical decisions are necessary when it comes to obeying governing authority. Taking the context of Romans chapter thirteen verses one to seven into consideration, Apostle Paul speaks universally in the passage regarding submitting to governing authority; however, ethical principles should guide the reader to filter what ordinance should be obeyed as laws enacted by civil authority could question integrity due to flawed nature of laws that does not dictate the ethics of God.

The fundamental principles of ethics constitute beneficence, non-maleficence, autonomy, and justice. The former sprang from Hippocrates[81] while the latter emerged later after Percival's book was published in the 1800's. From autonomy, derived truth-telling, confidentiality, and informed consent. Beneficence is the ethical principle that defines doing goodness to all; hence, it is the positive aspect of ethics. This ethics is used in medical practices when it comes to the physician's relationship with the patient. Whatever decision taken by the physician regarding medical interventions according to this principle should benefit the patient and release the physician from medical liability. Similarly, in the government's relationship to citizen's relationship, government has the fiduciary responsibility to provide citizens security, health care, education, and necessities for life as dictated in the functions of the government; similarly, citizens are required to pay taxes and to honor civil authority. Both citizens and government have ethical responsibilities toward one another as dictated in the functions of government and citizens. Corruption in government will undermine the provision of security, health care, education, and necessities for life and eventually violate the ethical principle of beneficence and nonmaleficence toward the citizens.

---

[81] Jean-Marie Gueullette, "Hippocrate, Jesus, Freud, Still: Fondateursd' UneActiviteTherapeutique,?" *Theophilyon* 20, no. 2 (2015): 353–368.

Nonmaleficence is the ethical principle that defines doing no evil to anyone. This ethical principle is the negation of beneficence discussed previously based on function; hence, such ethical principle constitutes, for example, "That shall not kill, steal, or bear false witness against your neighbors at any time." When government restraints evil, provides security for all and distributes wealth equitably to citizens, government fulfills this ethical responsibility toward her citizens; disadvantageously, corruption will undermine equitable distribution of wealth and security to citizens. Autonomy is the ethical principle that defines self-determination; therefore, every individual should be allowed to decide for self when it comes to decision-making provided the person is mentally and physically capable to do so. In the absence of mental incapability, the individual has the right to self-determination; therefore, no governments should impose on citizens those laws that are not consistent with moral goodness of society; unfortunately, these manifestations are common in autocratic regimes like China, Russia, Afghanistan, Iran, and among others.

The principle of ethics in the context of the moral law defines morality objectively and intrinsically in the societal setting across all cultures that necessitates acceptance; on the contrary, most man-made laws do not dictate the ethics of God; therefore, the question of integrity is imminent. Most man-made laws enacted in non-democratic and non theocratic settings are made to favor the elites and may go against the moral goodness of society. In some cultural settings across the globe, morality can also vary with paradoxical truth in respective of cultures, historical orientations, religions, and truth understood in such context. In paradoxical truth where truth becomes relative in such context; then, the people walk paradoxically contrary to universal morality; consequently, they become dangerous to society at large. The practical ramification seen in the world today is the existence of terrorism. People who are involved in suicide bombing on the globe feel that they are doing the right things in the name of religion; therefore, everything becomes relative to them. The doctrine of relativism is dangerous to human society because it ignores reality and restricts its thinking repertoire to its own context in disregard to human well-being. It is egoistic, selfish and does not care about others. The institution of the Atlantic and Triangular Slave Trade, the execution of the Holocaust where the Nazi massacred six million Jews, the institution of the Apartheid in South Africa, and the institutionalized racism in the United States is the sum total of relative thinking. Relative thinking is the vacuum created psychologically whereby people are left to think and to do according to their own desires without observing human rights and moral goodness of society.

Civil Disobedience

The Mahatma Gandhi Salt March in 1930[82], the Transvaal of South Africa in 1906, the American Civil Rights Movement in 1950's which sought to end racial segregation in the United States, led by Dr. Martin Luther King, Jr, using the vehicles of the North Carolina Sit-In in 1960 and the Freedom Rides in 1961 are described in two words called "Civil Disobedience." Civil disobedience lies deeply in the western thought that references Cicero, Thomas Aquinas, John Locke, Thomas Jefferson, and Henry David Thoreau. The concept of civil disobedience was formulated by Mahatma Gandhi, who developed the philosophy of Satyagraha, the philosophy that emphasized the non-violence resistance to evil.[83] Mahatma Gandhi of India sought to obtain equal rights and freedom for all through Satyagraha campaign. These are manifestations of the controversy that exists between universal ethics based on the moral laws contrary to what men have created called man-made laws (Exod 20:1–21); therefore, most man-made laws do not dictate the ethics of God due to their flawed nature. The renaissance and resurgence of these movements in history is the result of injustice played out in society that goes against the God's giving rights of humanity. The man-made laws are made to

---

[82] Douglas Allen, "The Philosophy of Mahatma Gandhi for the Twenty-first Century" (Lanthan: Boulder: New York: Toronto: Plymouth, UK: Lexington Books, 2008), 1869–1948.

[83] Ibid.

favor certain classes in society; hence, such man-made laws include the Jim Crow Law in the United States and the Sharia law in Afghanistan, do not dictate the ethics of God because they are laws enacted to suppress humanity.[84] They were enacted to ignore the moral goodness of society; therefore, can humanity submit to such law? The answer is no. Can Christians be involved in civil disobedience when Scripture has said that everyone should submit to the governing authority? What is civil disobedience? Civil disobedience is the refusal to obey the demands or the commands of a government without resorting to violence or active measure of opposition.[85] The purpose of civil disobedience is to force concessions on the government in keeping with human rights. Civil disobedience is the passive resistance conducted during peaceful protest; however, it is obvious that during peaceful protest laws are broken that might have violated the law when the authorities had verbally forbidden the protest to take place. Sometimes peaceful protest can end into violence when there is counter response from security forces. Democratically constitutional government should allow peaceful protest to go on because protests are facets of democracy; on the contrary, governments that are totalitarian usually will oppose protest and protesting in such environment, will lead to the breaking of the law that could lead to arrest or death of the protesters. This monograph examines instances in the Bible that are related to moderate civil disobedience involving breaking rules enacted by the authority figures. These civil disobediences include the case of King Saul's unjust decree (1 Sam 14), the case of the Hebrew Midwives (Exod 15), the case of Vashti and her refusal to be objectified (Esth 1:15), the case of Esther and her *kairos* moment (Esth 4:16), the case of the golden sculpture (Dan 3), the case of the forbidden prayer (Dan 6), the case of the foreigners who did not comply (Matt 2:1–12), the case of the banned speech (Acts

---

[84] Fair Fight Initiative, "Jim Crow Laws," accessed July 7, 2022, htts://www.fairfightini-tiative.org/jim-crow-laws/.

[85] David Koyzis, "[Consider] Civil Disobedience: Christians Should Submit to the Governing Authority Except When They Shouldn't," *Christianity Today* 60, no. 3 (2016): 38–45.

4), and the case of the ultimate guide and the rolereplica, Jesus Christ (Luke 2:10–11). These cases are vividly spread throughout the biblical text; however, this monograph investigates only one case; nevertheless, the reader is encouraged to read these cases for personal biblical growth.

The Case of King Saul's Unjust Decree
(1 Sam 14)

The children of Israel were at war with the Philistines; eventually, Jonathan and his armor-bearer encountered the Philistines; retroactively, Jonathan and his armor-bearer moved toward the Philistines to war as they were instigated into the conflict by the Philistines. Upon their arrival proximal to the Philistines, they initiated the war and killed twenty members of the Philistines; eventually, the Philistines took off. In response, the entire Israel joined the war and pursued the Philistines. During this era, Jonathan happened to have licked the honey he took at the war site which was forbidden; therefore, the Lord could no longer speak to Israel what direction to take concerning the war. Israel fought holy war; therefore, it was God who fought for Israel during warfare; for this reason, Israel needed to hear from God during the battle before making the next move or else it could become a disobedience to God with bad repercussions. At the onset of the war, King Saul ordered that the men of Israel pursue the Philistines and do them whatever evil each has decided; in opposition to the order, the priest objected to the order and said that it was wrong to do so because they have not heard the order from God. Then, King Saul prayed to the Lord to inquire why the Lord has not spoken and he decided that a lot be taken to figure out the reason why the Lord has not spoken. A lot was cast between King Saul and the men of Israel; then, King Saul and the men of Israel were cleared. Jonathan was taken after the lot was cast; in response, Jonathan admitted that he has taken and licked the honey during the war which was forbidden. The penalty for such an act was death; however, the men of Israel opposed King Saul's order for Jonathan's death. The men of Israel said that Jonathan could not be killed because he was the one who has initiated the war leading to the defeat of the Philistines. The men of Israel and the priest dismissed the king's decrees in two proportions. This is civil disobedience. From this incidence, it can be learned that not all commandments that come from the governing authority should be obeyed because someone's decision can be wrong that does not agree with the universal ethics of God (Exod 20:1–21). According to the Mosaic Law concerning warfare, anyone who took something that did not belong to him during holy warfare could be killed as dictated in the civil law; however, in the moral law of God, God said that murder is wrong; hence, the second part of the Commandments talk about loving our neighbor as we love God. The elders of Israel considered the greater good that Jonathan brought to Israel and consequently used the second section of the Moral Law and opposed his death. Did they oppose God when they opposed the King's decrees? If you were a military Christian soldier, would you take a command from your superior officer to murder the civilian population during civil insurrections? If you did not, did you disobey authority? Obeying authority also comes with responsibilities; therefore, there are ethics involved during warfare according to the military codes of ethics. One is, the civilian populations are never the target for militarization; therefore, Jonathan could not be the target for Israel because he was not the enemy against Israel. Was the Old Testament law concerning the death of someone who took the honey and licked, a flawed law did not agree with universal moral law? Do laws enacted by government agree with normative law?

The Holy and Just War

The ordinance recorded in Romans chapter thirteen in the context of submission to the governing authorities prompts every subject concerned especially those who are listed in the military to defend national sovereignty during warfare. Is there a just or holy war? If so, does either of them exist biblically in the 21st century? How the Christian who is listed in the military responds to the instructions from the superior during warfare? These questions are answered in this monograph.

The just war theory is a Christian philosophy that strives to reconcile that taking human's life during warfare is wrong, that States have the responsibility to defend their citizens and sovereignty, and that protecting innocent human life and defending moral values sometimes involved using violence. In this light, the theory provides guidelines to nations the procedural approach how nations act in potential conflict situation. The theory does not apply to individuals; however, individuals can use the theory to decide whether it is morally right to be involved in the conflict. The principle of the just war theory originated with the classical Greek and the Roman philosophers, Plato, Cicero, and Thomas Aquinas. The elements of the just war theory define the condition under which the use of force is justifiable and how a war can be conducted in an ethical manner. If there is a just war, there should be also an unjust war. The just or unjust war theory was developed by Michael Walzer in 1977 publication using historical illustrations in the context of the bombing of Nagasaki and Hiroshima during World War II, the 1967 Arab-Jews Six-Day War and the nuclear deterrence.[86] In his book, Michael tends to resuscitate the tradition of the just war theory; however, he rejected both amoral realism and pacifism; advantageously, his book has won popularity and praise by world leaders and made them to go to wars to defend the vulnerable populations who have been attacked by their neighbors. Referentially, his book has influenced America to go to war with totalitarian regimes that have treated their neighbors with upheavals. In his book, he did not discuss the significance of the individual who dies in the conflict that is unarmed. In ethics, his theory supports the lesser evil at the expense of the greater good since in armed conflict, it is impossible to avoid the death of the civilian populations because militants can use the civilian populations as human's shield. America dropped a bomb on Nagasaki and

---

[86] David Moszkowicz, "Michael Walzer's Justification of Humanitarian Intervention: Communitarian? Cosmopolitan?Adequate?"*Political Theology* 8, no. 3 (2007): 281–297.

Hiroshima to kill about 210,000 people in the cities to bring World War II to swift end with minimal casualties.[87]Allowing the war to continue, it would have lasted longer and killed more people than the people who died in Nagasaki and Hiroshima. It is called the lesser evil at the expense of the greater good in humanistic ethics; similarly, for the whole world to die and to go to hell eternally, God sacrificed His Son at the expense of sinful humanity in order to save the whole world from the penalty of sin (Rom 5:12).

Ethically, in the just war situation, the civilian population should be protected during armed conflict; unfortunately, the complexity of the human being is unpredictable to reconstruct based on several psychological factors. Such factors influenced by psychosis with reference to sociopathic and psychopathic personalities of the human beings are probable during arm conflicts. In simplicity, the human's brain is wired differently influenced by genetic, social, and self-initiated destructive effort by the use of drugs. People who are holding guns should die instead of the unarmed populations; unfortunately, there are diverse brains that manifest different behaviors during warfare.

Historically, the just war theory tradition began in the Middle Ages as the way of thinking about the use of the military force as a manifestation of the sovereign responsibility; hence, tt emerged from the philosophical patrimony of both ancient Israel and the Greco-Roman worlds.[88]In coordination to ancient Israel and the Greco-Roman worlds, the Christian's expression of the just war theory originated with Augustine of Hippo and attained a theological maturity through Thomas Aquinas over the 800 years period.[89] Biblically, according to the Old Testament, there is

---

[87] Universal History Archive/UIG via Getty Images, "American Bomber Drops Atomic Bomb on Hiroshima," accessed July 13, 2022, https://www.google.com/amp/s/www.history.com/.amp/this-day-in-hist.

[88] Michael Payne, "What Can Church History Tell Us about the Debate between Just War Theory and Pacifism and What Does This Mean for the Church Today," Eleutheria 5, no. 2 (2021): 2017–233.

[89] Ibid.

nothing called the just war. The wars in the Old Testament dispensation were called holy wars fought by God himself. The children of Israel were instructed to obey according to God's instruction during holy warfare. Such examples, include the children of Israel with the battle at Jericho (Josh 5:13–6:27) the war King Hezekiah fought with the Arams (2 Chron 32:8) and King Amaziah of Judah retributive justice rendered to his officials (2 Chron 25:1–28). There is not holy war today as dispensation is concerned in the New Testament era. In the holy war, God fights the war. Any prototype called the holy war carried out especially in the name of religion is the war of the flesh; however, the name of the god is used to justify atrocities on those who refused to submit to the god. The wars in the Old Testament characterized with violence cannot be used for the justification for Christians to be involved in armed conflict with the governing authorities. The Old Testament dispensation regarding holy warfare cannot be applied to the New Testament to allow Christians to be involved in rebelliousness in the name of the just war theory. It is illegitimate and unbiblical to do so because the Old Testament has nothing called the just wars to allow believers to be involved in physical warfare if the just war theory could be used as the ground for such. The just war theory is developed based on humanistic ethics; on the contrary, it is not biblical and does not support any positions for Christians to be involved in rebelliousness against authority. The children of Israel did not fight any just war; instead, they fought those they perceived that God had told them to fight (1 Sam 15:1–25).

Based on the New Testament biblical stand point, Jesus was a pacifist; therefore, he chose to love; in this regard, he negated the Old Testament type of violence and forbid any Christian to engage in violence (1 John 2:6). Jesus' ideology regarding retaliation mediation influences the Christian religion with respect to forgiveness in the favor of the perpetrator of the crimes. He chose to love, to serve, and to die for the enemies; therefore, he does not endorse Christians to take up arms against those they think are their enemies (1 Pet 2:18–23; 3:15–16; Heb 12:2–3). Does that mean Christians are not allowed to join the military or defend themselves when they are attacked? No, Christians can join the military to defend their country against invasions for national sovereignty if they think that God is leading them to serve their country through the military; however, Christians are advised to follow ethical standards how war is fought. People who are involved in the combats are the enemies on both sides; therefore, those are the people who should suffer casualties instead of the innocent. Christians listed in the military can be engaged in combat lawfully and must follow the ethical rules of the military codes of conduct. Killing is wrong; however, it happens during armed conflicts; on the other hand, intentional killing with reference to atrocities is morally and biblically wrong and no Christians listed in the military including non-Christians should be involved in atrocities. The military should be an organized, disciplined, and law abiding organization put into place to keep national security for the benefits all citizens. The military is inaugurated by God to protect life, property, and national sovereignty; therefore, the military is the ordained of God and should respect the universal codes of ethics with reference to warfare as dictated in the universal human rights laws pertaining to armed conflicts situation in the world (Rom 13:1–7).

Christian Military Enlistment

The Bible contains several incidences with reference to serving in the military; therefore, military service has its origin in the Bible. It is evidenced that many of the Bible references with relative to the military service in the New Testament Bible are analogies; however, several verses in the Bible that qualify believers to serve are directly posed to the question if Christians do serve in the military; on the other hand, the Bible is not specific whether or not Christians should serve in the military; however, Christians can be cognizant that being in the military is the respected position; biblically, military position is highly endorsed and respected throughout the Bible. The first military situation in the Bible is found in Genesis chapter four. It references when Lot, Abraham's nephew, was kidnapped by Chedorlaomer, the King of Elam and his allies. Abraham mobilized to Lot's aid and recruited 318 trained men of his household; proactively on rescued mission, they defeated the Elamites. Here, the armed forces are engaged in noble task to rescuing and protecting the innocent.

In the genesis of Israel's history, the fact that God is the warrior who fought Israel's war, made Israel to slow down in developing the standing military; nevertheless, lately, the development of the standing military in Israel emerged during the administrations of King Saul, King David, and King Solomon' rules. Prior to David and Solomon's rules, King Saul was the first to organize a permanent military (1 Sam 13:2; 24:2; 26:2). King David continued with what King Saul had initiated; eventually, King David brought troops from the other regions that were loyal to him and turned over the leadership of the military to the Commander-In-Chief of the military, Joah (2 Sam 15:19–22). Under King David's leadership, the military of Israel became more aggressive in its offensive military policies and over took the neighboring States of Ammon (2 Sam 11:1; 1 Chron 20:1–3). In his leadership proactive approach, King David established the rotating troops with twelve groups of 24,000 men serving one month annually on rotational basis (1 Chron 27). Despite of King Solomon's reign being peaceful; however, he being militarily cautioned, he expanded the military, adding chariots and horsemen to the military he met after King David's reign (1 Kgs 10:26). The standing military continued until 586 B.C after which Israel came to an end as the political entity.

The Centurions mentioned in the New Testament were military officers in charge of one hundred soldiers; retroactively, Jesus did not deny their careers; authentically, the New Testament Bible qualified them as Christians, God's fearers, and men of good character. The Centurions were members of the Roman's military that Jesus endorsed according to the New Testament Bible narratives (Matt 8:5–13; 27:54; Mark 15:39–45; Luke 7:2; 23:47; Acts 10:1; 21:32; 28:10). Based on the biblical evidences from the Old and New Testaments, Christians can serve in the military (Rom 13:1–7).

The Acid Test

Chemically, the test of an acid in solutions is determined by its PH level when it ionizes in water as the hydrogen ion. Empirically, any number that falls below 7 PH level in solution is considered acidic. The nature of the production of abnormal acid in the human body can lead to health problem such as acid reflux disease, necessary hypertension, and among others; therefore, controlling the body's acid level or PH is necessary to the health well-being of the individual to avoid health relative issues; therefore, it is recommended to keep the body alkaline. The lifestyle changes to do with such behavioral change call for the kind of food to eat especially if the individual has been diagnosed with acidosis.

Ethically, the decision an individual takes daily with reference to morality influences the relationship that exists between the individual and God on two axes; therefore, the individual is polarized either to be good or to be bad based on the choices he or she takes daily in life. As the good health well-being level of the human body depends on the level of alkalinity in order to avoid acidosis to prevent future health problems; similarly, the acid test in ethics examines which practice is morally acceptable before God (Exod 20:1–21). In the Ten Commandments, the law has two divisions with reference to the duties humanity has toward God and her neighbor. Apostle Matthew summarizes the Ten Commandments in this manner. He writes, "Jesus replied: "Love the Lord your God with all your heart and with all your soul and with all your mind. 'This is the first and greatest commandment. And the second is like it: 'Love your neighbor as yourself.' All the Law and the Prophets hang on these two commandments" (Matt 22:37–40 NIV). In the summarized Ten Commandments, humanity is commanded to love God with her heart, soul, and mind and to love her neighbor as herself. No one hates himself or herself naturally under a normal condition; therefore, loving oneself should be translated and reflected in loving one's neighbor since the individual is incapacitated to do evil to himself or herself; therefore, the individual should be incapacitated to do evil against his or her neighbor. This is the reason humanity needs to know the God of morality in order to do well morally. The Acid Test in ethics is related to on the Ten Commandments. All intrinsically and objective moral values with reference to universal ethics hang on the Ten Commandments (Exod 20:1–21).

On the other hand, God is the Creator of all laws in nature, including natural, spiritual, and scientific laws. Scientific law such as the Law of Gravitation exists because it has existed in nature before it was discovered by scientists; therefore, it is the natural law that gives birth to scientific law and then to spiritual law. That's being said, the law enacted by humanity ethically should be the hybrids of the law that comes from God; therefore, governing laws should hang on the law of morality; on the contrary, it is not always so because man by nature loves to choose evil.

Ethical Relativism versus Ethical Absolutism

Ethics is defined as the branch of knowledge that deals with principles, morality, honesty, right, fairness, responsibility, conscience, choice, honor, value, and integrity.[90] These facets of ethics cover ethical behaviors across all fields of knowledge in judging the right between the wrong. Individual, who is walking ethically, is guided by these virtues mentioned above; however, the divides arise when the issues of relativism and absolutism surface in applied ethics that dictates how humanity responds to moral languages in order to remain true to her belief in the exercise of ethical behavior based on relativism and absolutism.

According to the just war theory, every nation has the right to defend herself in the time of arm conflicts especially when enemy forces have infringed on national sovereignty; therefore, the issue of infringement is the conscience right that every citizen has the responsibility to defend his or her nation against aggression. The issue of the just war is the philosophical ideology that emerged contrary to the biblical stance. What

---

[90] Kayla Armstead, "Branches of Ethical Philosophy," accessed August 24, 2022, https://study.com/learn/lesson/ethics-philosophy-overview-branches.html.

makes the just war theory to be a philosophical ideology instead of the biblical perspective is that the Bible has not mentioned anything regarding the just war; instead, the Bible does mention the holy war in the Old Testament; on the contrary, the New Testament does not mention the holy war nor support it. In Jesus' messages to the children of Israel, he defined his mission to the Earth that was contrary to what the Jews nation thought; therefore, they became frustrated on the account of Jesus' declared mission as the spiritual deliverer and consequently rejected Jesus as the Messiah (Acts 1:1–8; John 1:1–5). The mindset of the children of Israel was that Jesus actually came to deliver them politically and militarily from the Roman's rule when the Jews were being placed under the imposition of taxes by the Caesars (Augustus to Hadrian) of Rome. Based on these events, the Jews anticipated political redemption instead of what Jesus taught and preached. Jesus came for the spiritual redemption of mankind from sin to victory via his death on the Cross. From the historical and biblical standpoint, Jesus' statement and actions don't support physical warfare neither does he encourage believers to take up arm against any sitting government despite the nature of the government. Understanding that Jesus does not support the just war or the holy war theory, it is necessary to be guided by ethics as the Christian soldier listed legally in the military.

In the field of disciplines of ethics, various terminologies have been adopted to define human's behaviors; therefore, two have been adopted in this monograph as introduced formerly in this section. The terminology "ethical relativism" as defined is the doctrine that teaches that there is no absolute truth in ethics. It teaches that what is morally right or wrong varies from person to person and from society to society. In ethical relativism, humanity decides what is right or wrong based on individual preferences; therefore, ethical relativism is unbiblical and usually goes against universal morality as revealed in the Ten Commandments (Exod 20:1–21). Humanity knows intrinsically what are objective values and moral acts; therefore, killing innocent human being is wrong according to the moral law of God. Killing innocent human being is the transgression of the law (Exod20:1–21). In ethical relativistic philosophy, killing innocent human being could be right because what is morally wrong in some cultures is also what is morally right for some people especially those who are involved in terrorism in the name of religion. The religion of those who are involved in terrorism has taught them that it is religiously right based on their religious tradition to carry out suicide bombing by which they can have their placement in heaven as martyr; therefore, the terminology called "anti-absolutism" is introduced. Anti-absolutism is the doctrine that is against absolute truth and justifiably supports atrocities; therefore, it is morally corrupting and enslaving. People who operate according to anti-absolutism are relative thinkers when it comes to intrinsic and objective moral values practices. Terrorists are relative thinkers; therefore, they support the philosophy of anti-absolutism. Ethical relativism gives renaissance to anti-absolutism; ideologically, crimes committed by relative thinkers are always premeditated before giving renaissance to existence; in this light ideologically, relativism and anti-absolutism are processes of spiritual formation in false religion. The proliferation of false and true religions on planet Earth is the result of the birth of ideologies birthed through the proponents of religions. For example, Christianity is the religion that teaches relationship, forgiveness, love, and self-sacrifice toward her neighbor because Jesus taught these things while he was on Earth to reveal the God of relationship, forgiveness, love, and self-sacrifice. Jesus' philosophical ideology with reference to true religion is revealed in his teaching.

What is false or true religion? Apostle James writes, "Religion that God our Father accepts as pure and faultless is this: to look after orphans and widows in their distress and to keep oneself from being polluted by the world" (Jas 1:27 NIV). Based on this Scripture, terrorists who kill people in the name of religion do not know the Creator of the heaven and the Earth. The elements mentioned in the text are opposite of atrocities; therefore, false religion are religions that commit atrocities against humanity in the name of the god who leads them. The Taliban's takeover in Afghanistan in the name of religion has led to systematic summary execution of people whom they perceived as enemies. They have forbidden girl's education and women from holding public office in the government under the disguised of *Sherea*'s law. In their former rule in Afghanistan from 1996 to 2001 prior to their overthrow by the Americans, they executed women in the public square who did not dress as Muslim in the name of religion. The Taliban commits atrocities and has no respect for human rights, the rule of laws, and universal morality; however, they are people who lead prayers in the mosques.

The upside of the coin with reference to ethical relativism is called ethical absolutism. Ethical absolutism is the doctrine that teaches that there is an existence of objective values and intrinsically moral acts. This doctrine teaches that there is universal moral truth that is generally accepted across all cultures based on the moral law of God (Exod 20:1–21). This law is absolute because it comes from God, the Creator of the heaven and the earth. Being cognizant intrinsically that killing innocent human beings is absolutely and morally wrong; therefore, committing such act is going against what God has forbidden fundamentally. In the time of arm conflicts, fundamental morality can be ignored and these three ethical values (relativism, anti-absolutism, and absolutism) can be tested how combatants behave on the battlefield. During arm conflict, the categories of soldiers seen on the battlefield psychologically with respect to behaviorism are ethical absolute and ethical relative thinkers. The word 'absolute' indicates universal truth while the word "relative" indicates truth limited by individual or societal preferences. Ethical relative thinkers are susceptible to committing atrocities against humanity during arm conflicts because such individuals are never opened to universal moral truth that are associated with moral goodness of society (Exod 20:1–21). Those who are ethical absolute thinkers psychologically are soldiers who play by the rules according to the universal human rights on conflict situation coupled with the military code of ethics. It is morally wrong to kill according to universal morality based on the Ten Commandments; however, during arm conflict it is inevitable to keep this morality because Satan is active at this time to undermine God's moral law.

In arm conflicts, it is legally unlawful to kill the civilian populations; on the contrary, atrocities are committed against the civilian populations where there are relative and anti-absolute thinkers. Anti-absolutists, ethical relativists, and ethical absolutists are categories of people that exist during arm conflicts among the militaries; therefore, atrocities are unavoidable. Sometimes atrocities are committed by mistakes; as the result, this makes war evil; unfortunately, people who are involved in arm conflicts delay to come to resolution regarding reconciliation after they have committed atrocities against their own people. War is never recommended in the human society because it is diabolical; however, warfare has existed in the human history since the fall of mankind in the Garden of Eden (Gen 3:1–15; 4). Christians who are listed in the military are admonished according to the Scripture to be ethical absolutists during arm conflict in order to represent God during their services to humanity. Christian soldiers who fight enemy forces to protect national sovereignty are offering services to their nation. God honors such obedience exhibited by the soldiers to the government; therefore, such soldier is not forbidden to kill; however, the soldier should kill the enemy forces during warfare. It is called the lesser evil for the greater good when the Christian soldiers kill enemy forces to protect national sovereignty. He or she is freed to do so and does not break the law because it is God who ordains authority to protect the nation and its people during arm conflict when invaders have entered the land (Rom 13:1–7; 1 Sam 15). God is the moral absolutist; therefore, Christian soldiers should be moral absolutists during arm conflict. Ironically, God told King Saul to eliminate the *Amalekites* including men, women, children, and livestock; contradictorily, how can God be considered as the moral absolutist when He sanctioned the killing of such generation (1 Sam 15)? This incidence in the Bible has made some believers to think that the God of the Old Testament is different from the God of the New Testament. Understanding that God changes with respect to dispensations and covenants; the Christian can assure that the God of the Old

Testament is the God of the New Testament in regardless of such harsh command from God to have this generation exterminated. His decision to have this generation exterminated was to fulfill the promise He made to Abraham regarding inheritance with reference to the Promised Land. The extermination campaign was the continuation of the war to have the children of Israel entered the Promised Land (Gen 15:16; Exod 17:14; Deut 25:17–19). God's command to King Saul to exterminate the *Amalekites* was not genocide; instead, it was a divine judgment on this generation due to her unprovoked attack on Israel that could hinder Israel from entering the Promised Land; therefore, ethically, the Divine Command Theory, according to Kant's ontological ethics became imminent. Moses substantiates, "Remember what the Amalekites did to you along the way when you came out of Egypt. When you were weary and worn out, they met you on your journey and attacked all who were lagging behind; they had no fear of God. When the LORD your God gives you rest from all the enemies around you in the land he is giving you to possess as an inheritance, you shall blot out the name of Amalek from under heaven. Do not forget! (Deut 25:17–19 NIV). The decision to have the *Amalekites* exterminated was retributive justice rendered to set deterrence for the surrounding nations. God is just, holy, and does not do any wrong or else He would cease to exist as God which is impossible. God's communicable attributes transcend his incommunicable attributes; therefore, God can never do wrong. This was a holy war that is contemporary to the just war situation in the modern warfare of the 21st century era.

In the sixth commandment as recorded in Exodus chapter 2o verse 13, the word "kill" as used in the King James Version is translated as "murder"in the New International Version. Killing is the general word that references lawful legal act or unlawful legal act carried out by individual based on societal preferences or an act legally allowed according to the law based on retributive justice in order to set deterrence in the legal system or the divine court; therefore, the Hebrew and Greek Bible are very specific to what kind of killings that is mentioned in the Moral Law (Exod 20:13). The Greek and Hebrew word for "murder" as used in the biblical texts is *dolofonía* or *retzach*. *Dolofonía* or *retzach* is defined as the murder or the unlawful killing of human beings which is forbidden and punishable according to the Scripture (Gen 9:6); similarly, there are lawful killings of human beings sanctioned according to the divine law. Moses writes, "Whoever sheds human blood by humans shall their blood be shed; for in the image of God has God made mankind" (Gen 9:6 NIV). *Dolofonía* or *retzach* is the capital crime which is punishable by the death penalty according to the Scripture. The sixth commandment references the unlawful killing of human beings known as *dolofonía* or *retzach*; therefore, it does not include all killings because God himself has sanctioned the killing of human beings lawfully in the Scripture. In biblical history, there are two kinds of killings that are sanctioned in the Bible; hence, the first is the punishment of capital crime and the second is during the holy war situation; therefore, these killings are not forbidden according to the Scripture (Gen 9:6; 1 Sam 15:1–15). Throughout the Bible, the children of Israel were at war with their enemies and subsequently killed them in warfare because God sanctioned that those who attacked them should be killed. The Bible supports self-defense during arm conflict; in this light, the sixth commandment does not fit in the category of all killings. The sixth commandment does not prohibit Christians from serving their country in the time of war, nor does it prohibit them from killing their fellow human beings in battle once those human being were enemies(1 Sam 15:1–15; Deut 25:17–19). The New Testament does not talk much about war and capital punishment; however, this is what Apostle Paul had to say about punishment though he is not specific; however, the wordings used in the text are implied to punishment involving general crimes. He writes, "For the one in authority is God's servant for your good. But if you do wrong, be afraid, for rulers do not bear the sword for no reason. They are God's servants, agents of wrath to bring punishment on the wrongdoer "(Rom 13:4 NIV). If the wrong doing is defined according to the context of Romans 13:4, punishment that compensates rebelliousness against authority and the death penalty are inclusive according to Romans 13:4.

Ethical Reflection

The subject of submitting to civil authority as commanded in the Scripture should be guided by ethics taking into consideration that not all laws enacted by governments dictate the ethics of God; similarly, not all governments in the world work according to the norms of God; unfortunately, one rarely sees a theocratic government in the world today. Since man-made laws sometimes can become flawed; therefore, integrity should be used as the metrics to examine man-made laws in order to be in alignment with God; for this reason, civil disobedience is allowed when man-made laws fail the acid test. Ethics and laws reflect values and guide human's decision; however, ethics and laws are not homogenous due to the flawed nature of laws that evoke relative thinking; therefore, in practicing universal moral truth, one must become absolute in decision in order to disregard relativism knowing that the military personnel in the country's military is guided by the military code of ethics according to international laws that guide conflicts; similarly, citizens of nations should obey laws that are in consistent with universal moral acts and that do not infringe on their individual's conscience.

CHAPTER VI
LIBERIANIZATION

Chapter Overview

L iberianization is defined as the characterization of what makes up the character of Liberian or nationality. In the context of Liberianization, this segment of the monograph delineates the Liberia's political history, body politics, and the Liberia's dilemmas with reference to injustice, young democracy, camouflaged democracy, and corruption. Meanwhile, it discusses the subject of responsive actions, solution recommendations, and the analogical approach to the Liberia's elephant meat. At the conclusion, the author has developed a reflection on the chapter to redress the subject in order to pin a mental picture in the mind of the reader for personal subjective reflection.

The Liberia's Political History

The influence of religion on the government cannot be fully studied and understood in the absence of the nation's political history; therefore, it is expedient to give the synopsis of the Liberian history in conjunction with the American revolution from 1815 to 1997 while developing the periscopes of the biblical and theological foundation in connectivity with the past and present governmental leaderships of Liberia.[91] It has been said that Liberia was built on Christian principle; hence, this could be true based on the history of the freed people of color that arrived in Liberia in 1822 due to their connection to Christianity. Having been emancipated from slavery after the Emancipation Proclamation by Abraham Lincoln on January 1, 1863, the freed people of color settled in Liberia; therefore, it is necessary to answer these questions. Was Liberia actually built on Christian principle? Did Liberia exist as the aristocratic-oligarchy nation under the camouflaged democracy over the past 133 years of rules from Joseph Jenkins Roberts to William R. Tolbert? Since the cote d'état in 1980 under the People Redemption Council's government following the era of dictatorship followed by the 16 years of civil insurrection in Liberia, has Liberia achieved democracy? Is Liberia a Christian nation? What is God saying about the nation, Liberia? What decision can the people of Liberia take to change the status quo? These questions are answered in this monograph.

Apostle Paul writes, "For everything that was written in the past was written to teach us, so that through the endurance taught in the Scriptures and the encouragement they provide we might have the hope (Rom 15:4 NIV). Apostle Paul inspired via the Holy Spirit makes reference of the past. The word "past" as used in the Greek Bible is called *prographó*.*Prographó* is the event that has occurred in the past that serves as the analogy to remind people of past history and gives them informed decision how they make decision with reference to the present situation. Apostle Paul said that humans learn from *prographó*; therefore, it enables them to endure in order to face the present reality that leads them to make sound decision in leadership that provides them hope. He said that *prographó* provides humanity practical teaching and makes them apply this teaching in the real life context; therefore, past history of cultures is the blueprint for effective leadership when it comes to decision making in asymmetric

---

[91] Library of Congress, "History of Liberia: A Time Line," accessed August 24, 2022, https://www.loc.gov/collections/maps-of-liberia-1830-to-1870/articles-and-essays/history-of-liberia/.

situations. Most leadership fail their people due to the lack of consideration of the past and their inability to keep current with information coupled with the lack of humility. People who aspire to enter into national politics should learn from the past of their nation they desire to serve politically. The failure to learn from the past is the failure to make good judgment regarding the present national issues predictable to dilemmas that is detrimental to the well-being of the people. *Prographó* (the past) is polarized on two axes; in this light, what an individual learns from past history gives him or her informed decision what he or she needs to adopt or to discard. What *prographó* can the politicians of this era learn from the past political history of Liberia and move them to make sound decision to give hope to Liberia? If you are reading this document that does not belong to Liberia, put the name of your country where Liberia is in this monograph.

Based on the theological and biblical stand point, an individual learns from past history to have informed decision how he or she makes choices in domestic and national leadership; therefore, it is necessary to study the entity that he or she could affect based on contingent decision politically especially when it comes to national politics. God has a universal interest for ruling; similarly, He has a universal interest in stewardship; for this reason, He has ordained governments of nations to lead because He cares about human kinds. Taking *prographó* into consideration and the universal stewardship that God has ordained with reference to religious-politico humanistic politics, it is necessary to adopt the Liberian political history in this monograph to help the reader researches Liberia *prographónostically*. Researching Liberia *prographónostically* from 1815 to 1997 serves as the periscope to help the reader sees further using different lenses to put forth recommendations that could alleviate the present problems and gradually brings systemic changes to the betterment of the Liberian society. Why a country that was never colonized in Africa and happens to be the oldest independent country in Africa remained one of the poorest countries in Africa?

Liberia was founded by the freed people of color of the United States of America on January 7, 1822. Thomas Buchanan, the white governor, one of the proponents of the American Colonization Society, led Liberia under the commonwealth period from 1839 until his death on September 3, 1841; then, he was succeeded by Joseph Jenkins Roberts as governor in 1841, the first African-American to serve as governor of the commonwealth of Liberia.[92] While Joseph Jenkins Roberts served as the governor of the commonwealth, he proposed to the Legislature Assembly in 1846 that it was necessary for Liberia to be declared as the independent nation in Africa; then, the Independence Proclamation was made on July 26, 1847 making Liberia as the sovereign nation in Africa. Liberia was declared as the democratic society; ironically, from 1847 to 1980 until the assassination of president Williams Richard Tolbert, Liberia was ruled under the aristocratic-oligarchy leadership for 133 years. After the overthrow of the Tolbert's government, the nation of Liberia under the People Redemption Council's government descended into dictatorial regime condescendingly for ten years. The dictatorial nature of the People Redemption Council's government coupled with ethnic reprisal against the *Mano* and *Gio* ethnicities in Liberia from the People Redemption Council's government, fueled the Liberia civil insurrection led by Charles Ghankay Taylor from December 24, 1989 to August 2, 1997; then, Charles Ghankay Taylor was elected as the 22nd President of the Republic of Liberia and later resigned on August 11, 2003 as the result of the second Liberia civil war and the growing international pressure placed on him. Based on these timelines from 1847 to the present, Liberia has existed as the First, the Second, and Third Republic. The First Republic began 1847 to 1980 followed by the Second Republic from 1980 to 1990; then, the Third Republic emerged in 1990 and continues after the assassination of President Samuel Kanyon Doe. The events that had occurred during the period of the First and the Second Republic in the Liberian history are *prographós* that develop *prographónosticism,* the doctrine that teaches that past events are references

---

[92] Ibid.

one can use to make sound decision on current affairs of humanity societal problems based on the theological, political, and philosophical basis in the leadership platform.[93]

From 1815 to 1817, the freed people of colors struggled for liberty after the American Revolution as they faced hardship and inequality in the American society; consequently, a number of white Americans who were against slavery joined them to resolve the complex problem that had existed. As the issue of assimilation of the blacks amongst the white became impossible due to systemic racism, some white voiced the need to repatriate the freed people of colors back to Africa; therefore, Paul Cuffee's African venture encouraged white proponents of the colonization to repatriate those freed Africans who were willing to settle in Africa; therefore, the American Colonization Society (ACS) was founded under the leadership of Henry Clay, John Randolph, and Bushrod Washington. Unfortunately, freed African-Americans who supported Paul Cuffee's effort became wary of the organization due to its dominating nature of the Southerners and slave holders who excluded black people from the organization. Despite of the effort to repatriate African-Americans to Africa, some decided to stay in the new nation they had helped to build in order to continue the struggle for justice.

As the American Colonization Society sent its first group of immigrants to the Sherbro Island in Sierra Leone between 1820 and 1847, they faced an unhealthy condition that resulted into death rate among the settlers. This led to the relocation of the settlers from the Sherbro Island to the coastal waters west of Grand Bassa County for the colony relocation. Dr. Eli Ayres purchased this land as Mr. Stockton took charge of the negotiation with the leaders of the Dey and the Bassa People who lived in the area of Cape Mesurado. Initially, the local leaders were reluctant to surrender their people's land to the strangers; however, they had no alternative but surrender the land because they were put at gun point.

---

[93] Robert L. Thomas, "NAS Exhaustive Concordance of the Bible with Hebrew-Aramaic and Greek Dictionaries", accessed May 22, 2022, https://biblehub.com/greek/4270.htm.

This strip of coastal land for trade goods, supplies, and weapons, costs in price approximately $300.00 United States dollars.

On April 25, 1822, the survivors of Sherbro Island arrived at Cape Mesurado and began to build their new settlement. During this time, Jehudi Ashmun, a Methodist missionary who had replaced Dr. Ayres became the American Colonization Society's governing representative; however, some colonists objected to his leadership due to his authoritarian policies; therefore, tensions within the struggling settlement became imminent. Believing that the colonial agent had allocated town lots and rationed provisions unfairly, few of the settlers armed themselves and forced Ashmun to flee the colony. The American Colonization Society's representative resolved temporarily the disagreement and asked Ashmun to return. Steps were put into place to spell out a system of local administration and to codify the laws; however, sovereign power continued to rest with the American Colonization Society's agent; therefore, the colony had to be operated under the common law until the law was codified. Slavery and participation in slave trade was forbidden. This settlement that was originally named Christopolis was renamed Monrovia after the American President, James Monroe and the colony was formally called Liberia. Slave states in North America that were interested in getting rid of their freed African-Americans, independently established the American Colonization Society in North America for the transplanting of freed African-American slaves in Liberia; consequently, the Maryland, the Virginia, and the Mississippi Colonization Societies were established. The Maryland State Colonization Society established its colony in Cape Palmas, Liberia. The Virginia and the Mississippi Colonization Societies also established Liberian colonies for the former slaves and the freed black in Liberia for the transplanting of freed African-Americans.

In 1838, the colonies established by the Virginia Colonization Society, the Quaker Young Men's Colonization Society of Pennsylvania, and the American Colonization Society merged as the commonwealth of Liberia and claimed control over all the settlements between Cestos River and Cape Mount. The commonwealth adopted a new constitution and a newly-appointed governor in 1839, Joseph Jenkins Roberts, a trade and a successful military commander, was named the first Lieutenant governor and became the first African-American governor of the colony after the appointed governor, Thomas Buchanan, died in office in 1841. After the appointment of Joseph Jenkins Roberts as the governor, the Mississippi settlement of Sinoe River joined the commonwealth of Liberia in 1842. The commonwealth received most of its revenue from custom duties which angered the indigenous traders and British merchants on whom they were levied. The British government advised the Liberian authorities that it did not recognize the right of the American Colonization Society, a private organization to levy these taxes. British's refusal to recognize Liberian sovereignty convinced many colonists that independence was necessary for the survival of the colony and its immigrant populations.

Prographónosticism:
The First and Second Republic
(1847–1980)

On July 26, 1847, the Liberia Declaration of Independence was adopted and signed. In the Declaration of Independence, Liberians charged their mother country, the United States of America, with injustices that made it necessary for them to leave and made new lives for themselves in Africa. They called the international community to recognize the independence and the sovereignty of Liberia. Britain was one of the first nations to recognize the new country; unfortunately, the United States of America did not recognize Liberia as the sovereign nation until after the American Civil war. After the independence, the Liberian Constitution was ratified and the first election was held; then, Joseph Jenkins Roberts was elected Liberia's first president in 1848. After the election, civilization gradually took over Africa and the suppression of the slave trade. Maryland colony declared its independence from the Maryland States Colonization Society, but the colony did not become part of the Republic of Liberia; though, the colony occupied the land along the coast between the Grand Cess and San Pedro Rivers in 1854. The settlers who lived there were relocated by the Grebo and the Kru people who controlled that area and were at war with the settlers; as the result, the settlers asked president Roberts for military assistance. President Roberts assisted the Marylanders; therefore, the joint military campaign which included the African-American colonists resulted into victory; then, in 1851, Maryland became a county of Liberia. The second president of the Republic of Liberia was Stephen Allen Benson who led Liberia from 1856 to 1864; then, he was succeeded by Daniel Bashiel Warner, who served until 1868. In 1862, the American president, Abraham Lincoln, extended official recognition to Liberia as the sovereign nation in 1862.

In the year 1865, 346 immigrants joined the African-Americans coming to Liberia after the American Civil War from Barbados. As the Americo-Liberians depended on immigrants from the nearby regions of Africa to increase the republic populations, they formed elite and perpetrated a double-tiered social structure in which local African people could not achieve full participation in the nation's social, civic, and political life. They replicated many of the exclusions and social differentiations that had limited their lives in the United States. Benjamin Anderson, a government official from their social elite, travelled into the interior of Liberia on the reconnaissance mission, signed the treaty with the King of Musardo, noticed the customs and the natural resources of these areas. Upon his return from the reconnaissance mission, he published the reports to the government of Liberia; then, government moved in to assert limited control over the inland region. In 1869, the True Whig Party was founded which became the dominant political party in Liberia and maintained its dominance until 1980. At the onset of the party formation, Edwin J. Roye succeeded James Spriggs Payne who ruled from 1868 to 1870 as President of Liberia. In 1871, Edward James Roye was removed from office and replaced by James Skivring Smith for the remaining of his term as the result of political crisis that resulted due to high-interest British bank loan suffered by the Liberian government. From 1871 to 8172, James Skivring Smith served as the interim President of Liberia followed by the former President Joseph Jenkins Roberts from 1876 to 1878. After his term, Anthony William Gardiner ruled from 1878 to 1883 and later resigned. He was succeeded by Alfred Francis Russell who completed his term and ruled from 1883 to 1884.

In 1875, a war broke out among the confederation of the Grebo People; as the result, the Liberian government asked the United States to serve as the mediator; in response, the United States emissary visited the Grebo's Kingdom; in addition, the Liberian Republic dispatched the Naval to assist the government to settle the conflict.

In 1904, the Liberian government instituted an administrative system that brought indigenous people into an indirect political relationship with the central government through their own paid officials. The Liberian officials including the republic's vice president supported forced labor of the indigenous people in 1929; in response, the international community dispatched an investigative team during this time; however, the evidence was hidden; therefore, the team did not find an evidence of force labor.

In 1944, William Vacanarat Shadrach Tubman was elected to the first of his seventh term as Liberian President and the right to vote in election was extended to the Liberian indigenous in 1946. President Tubman died in office in 1971 and William Richard Tolbert, Jr. was elected to the Liberian Presidency after finishing Tubman's unexpired term in 1972. On April 14, 1979, a rally protesting the increase of rice price ended in riot; as the result, in 1980, a military coup led by Samuel Kanyon Doe, a Liberian of non-American descent, assassinated President William Richard Tolbert and overthrew the government that had held sway over Liberia since in 1847 ending the First Republic.

In 1985, a civilian rule was restored; ironically, President Samuel Kanyon Doe remained in power as the military dictator while a new constitution was established for the Second Republic. In 1989, Charles Ghankay Taylor, an Americo-Liberian and his followers toppled the Doe-led government. This action helped precipitate the Liberian Civil War while various ethnic factions fought for control of the nation. Rebel forces executed President Samuel Kanyon Doe in 1990 and the Second Republic came to an end. In 1995, the 16-member Economic Community of West African States (ECOWAS), mediated peace treaty between the Liberian's warring factions and an interim State Council established a tentative time-table for election; then, the peace was re-negotiated. In 1997, Charles Ghankay Taylor was elected president of the Third Republic under the slogan, "He killed my fathers and mothers; however, I will vote for him." The international community was disfigured regarding such statement by the electors of Liberia's general election held under tension; however, some electors had no option but to make such statement.

The Chronometric Historiography
(1847–2018)

	Presidents Of Liberia In Chronological Order[94]
1	Joseph Jenkins Roberts: 1848–1856 Born in Virginia, U.S.A First President of Liberia Was elected six times
2	Stephen Allen Benson: 1856–1864 Born in Maryland, U.S.A Was elected four times
3	Daniel Bashiel Warner: 1864–1868 Born in Maryland, U.S.A Was elected twice
4	James Spriggs Payne: 1868–1870 Born in Virginia, U.S.A Was elected twice (2nd term: 1876–1878)

[94] Dr. Fred P.M Van der Kraaij, "The Colony of Liberia and the Suppression of the Slave Trade," accessed May 22, 2022, https://www.liberiapastandpresent.org/.

5	Edward James Roye: 1870–1871
	Born in Ohio, U.S.A
	Was elected once
	First President who deposed in a coup d'état
	Probably the first President who was assassinated
6	James S. Smith (VP)
	Completed Roye's term: 1871–1872
	Born in South Carolina, U.S.A
7	Joseph Jenkins Roberts: 1872–1876
	Born in Virginia, U.S.A
8	James Spriggs Payne: 1876–1878
	Born in Virginia, U.S.A
9	Anthony William Gardiner: 1878–1883
	Born in Virginia, U.S.A
	Was elected three times
	First President who resigned
10	Alfred Francis Russell (VP)
	Completed Gardiner's term: 1883–1884
	Born in Kentucky, U.S.A
11	Hilary Richard Wright Johnson: 1884–1892
	First Liberian President born in Africa (of American parents)
	Was elected four times
12	Joseph James Cheeseman: 1892–1896
	Born in Edina, Grand Bassa County, Liberia
	Was elected three times
	First President who died in office
13	William David Coleman (VP)
	Completed Cheeseman's tem: 1896–1900
	Born in Kentucky, U.S.A
	Was elected twice
	Second President who resigned

14	Garretson Wilmot Gibson Completed Coleman's term: 1900–1904 Born in Maryland, U.S.A Was elected once
15	Arthur Barclay: 1904–1912 Born in Bridgetown, Barbados, British West Indies Was elected three times First President who serve a four year term
16	Daniel Edward Howard: 1912–1920 Born in Buchanan, Grand Bassa County, Liberia Was elected twice
17	Charles Dunbar Burgess King: 1920–1930 Born in Liberia of Sierra Leonian parents Was elected three times Third President who resigned in office
18	Edwin James Barclay Completed King's term: 1930–1944 Born in Brewerville, Montserrado County, Liberia Was elected twice First President who served an eight year-term
19	William Vacanarat Shadrach Tubman: 1944–1971 Born in Harper, Maryland County, Liberia Was elected six times Longest serving President in the Liberian history Second President who died in office
20	William Richard Tolbert, Jr.: 1971–1980 Completed Tubman's 6th term (1971) and served his 7th term (1972–1976) Born in Bensonville, Montserrado County, Liberia Was elected once (1975) Second President who was deposed in a coup Second President who was assassinated

21	Samuel Kanyon Doe: 1980–1990
	Born in Tuzon, Grand Gedeh County, Liberia
	First President of tribal descent (Krahn), rigged the 1985 Presidential elections
	First military leader/President
	Third President who was assassinated
	Third President who deposed in a coup
	Was elected once
	6 interim Presidents during the civil war (1990's)
	Amos Sawyer (November 1990–August 1993)
	Bismarck Kuyon (August 1993–November 1993)
	Philip Banies (November 1993–February 1994)
	David Kparmakor (February 1994–September 1995)
	Ruth Perry (September 1996–August 1997)
	First female Head of State
22	Charles Ghankay Taylor: 1997–2003
	Born in Liberia (A.L Father, Gola's Mother)
	Was elected once following the end of the first civil war he had started
	Fourth President who resigned
23	Moses Blah completed Taylor's term: August–October 2003
	Born in Toweh Town, Nimba County, Liberia
	Second President of tribal descent (Gio)
	Charles Gyude Bryant: October 14, 2003–January 16, 2006
	Born in Maryland County, Liberia
	Was elected by Liberians/representatives of fighting parties and civil society during the peace talks in Ghana
	Leader National Transitional Government of Liberia (NTGL)
24	Ellen Johnson-Sirleaf: January 16, 2006–January 22, 2018
	Born in Monrovia, Liberia
	Was elected in 2005 when she defeated George Weah
	Liberia's second female Head of State
	Liberia's first elected female President

25	George Manneh Weah: January 22, 2018–Present
	Born in Monrovia, Liberia
	Was elected in 2017 when he defeated the Vice President, Joseph Boakai
	Third President of tribal descent (kru)
	Liberia's first democratically elected indigenous President

The Chronometric Historiography Analysis
(1847–1980)

From 1848 to 1980, the Liberian governance has been characterized with doubled-tiered structure of social elite, exclusions, disillusions, and differentiations that consequently marginalized the indigenous people of Liberia to participate in the social, political and civic life of the country for 133 years of aristocratic-oligarchy form of government characterized with single party system; ironically, it was called democracy. The evidence can be seen in the chronometric historiography record of the presidencies from Joseph Jenkins Roberts to William Richard Tolbert. The evidence is seen in the term column of the table and the number of frequencies that the term occurs when presidents were elected in their social elite's circle while excluding the rest of the populations from participation in government and voting rights until 1946 when President William V.S Tubman restored women suffrage. During the tenure of the Liberia's presidencies from 1848 to 1980 according to the chronometric historiography, two presidents served six terms, two served four terms, five served two terms, five served three terms, and ten served one term respectively. The tenure of services changed with the presidencies when the First Republic came to an end in 1980 after the coup d'état. From the chronometric historiography of the Liberian's presidencies from 1848 to 1980 indicates that the government of Liberia was an aristocratic-oligarchy. When President William V.S Tubman ascended to the presidency in 1944, he brought in William Richard Tolbert to serve as his Vice President for twenty years. Upon his death on July 23, 1971; then, William Richard Tolbert ascended to the presidency to complete Tubman's term before he was elected as

149

President in 1975. The completion of the dead man's term began with Joseph Jenkins Roberts and continued throughout the First Republic's tenure of administration; hence, this is doubled-tiered social elite structure called the aristocratic- oligarchy camouflaged as democracy. William Richard Tolbert was elected once; however, he served as president for nine years before he was assassinated. Joseph Jenkins Roberts and William V.S Tubman served the longest term as presidents of Liberia according to the chronometric-historiography analysis. For William V.S Tubman, he ruled Liberia for 27 years; hence, he was president for life. The greatness of any nation is tied to the philosophy of the leader. This is the reason; the Bible says that where there is no vision, the people perish. The philosophy of the founding fathers of Liberia had the slave mentality; evidentially, it was played out before their eyes which have impacted the nation negatively up to the presence. The oldest independence country in Africa that was never colonized by foreign powers remained impoverished up to the present. The present generation of Liberia cannot build on the shaking foundation the founding fathers to change the status quo. Liberia was built on the foundation of corruption from Joseph Jenkins Roberts to William V.S Tubman. When William Richard Tolbert ascended to the Presidency, after the death of his predecessor, he made a move to deal with corruption in government before he was overthrown. William Richard Tolbert was a smart guy who envisioned greatness for Liberia; unfortunately, the rally for the increase in rice price set the stage for his assassination by the People Redemption Council government. The shaking foundation built over the period of 133 years of aristocratic-oligarchy leadership, has created the vacuum for criminals to be held accountable for corrupt practices because impunity is buried. Corruption in government is the norm of any government that lacks democratic values; therefore, aristocracy, oligarchy, dictatorship, monarchy, totalitarianism, authoritarianism, communism, socialism, and the list goes on are synonymous to corrupt governments based on historical evidence. Democracy is fragile; therefore, it takes people who believe in their value systems and want to keep their true identity among the community of nations to be democratic. Where justice is denied, democracy dies automatically; for this reason, even the Great United States of America has internal rivalry due to systemic racism being played out before her eyes. Recently, President Joseph Biden had meeting with 120 nations on the issues of democracy being tested in the world. China and Russia who happen to be super powers are guilty of human rights abuses; realistically, the presidents of China and Russia are presidents for life; therefore, anything that is democratic, they will become opposition to it. It should be cognizant that dictatorship is also rooming over Africa. Military dictatorship is gradually reviving in Africa. It started with Mali; continued with the Republic of Guinea; then, the Democratic Republic of Congo. The military has overthrown the civilian democratically elected governments in these nations with the notion that they want to bring change while labeling the civilian governments as corrupt. Democracy is fragile; therefore, democratic values system is the continued fight that never ends. Liberia is transitioning to democracy; unfortunately, she has not achieved 10 percent to be democratic. Disparity is seen across the Liberian community with reference to the unequal distribution of wealth to the masses. The Liberian government must deal with the salary issue of government officials. It is the doubled-tiered structure of elite set up and an organized crime to stop the masses access to health care delivery, education, development, social services, and among others when government officials' salaries are depleting factors to these services stagnation. What should have been used for the masses, it is being allocated to so-called government officials' salaries. The Liberian government is allocating millions of United States dollars to salary payment to government officials while the rest of the populations remain in endless poverty. This is not democracy because social justice is being denied in the nation. God is against injustice in the land especially when the poor has been marginalized in the land. History is being repeated by the children of the indigenous of the land and the crime that was committed by the settlers for 133 years against their ancestors is being repeated by them against their own people.

Prographónosticism:
Examination of the First Republic
(1847–1980)

Aristocracy emerged from the Greek word *Aristokratia* that signifies the rule of the best; therefore, this ideology cognitively and historically emerged from the Greek philosophers, Aristotle and Plato who both considered aristocracy to be the best type of governance after naming timocracy, democracy, and tyranny.[95] Their ideology is based on the assumption that aristocrats are special class of people historically considered to be the elites and best on ruling accordingly as considered in the Greece's society. Aristocrats are class of eminent citizens who belonged to the upper class and deemed best qualified to rule the people. On the other hand, oligarchy is the rule of the chosen few who are rich and privileged. In oligarchy, the rich rules the poor because they are the ones entrusted with the power to rule; therefore, oligarchy is the degenerated version of aristocracy since the two types of governances are polarized on two axes based on ideology. Oligarchy is corrupt while aristocracy is the best governance according to Aristotle and Plato based on history. Whether which one is the best, it is debatable based on individual differences according to behaviorism. One can tell whether the government is the oligarchy or aristocracy based on the practices of the government.

In the nation, oligarchy and aristocracy can exist together as aristocratic oligarchy; characteristically, such group is considered rich, powerful, and people who perceive themselves to be qualified to rule the rest of the people they considered poor and unqualified to lead based on their social statuses. From 1847 to 1980, Liberia had existed as the aristocratic oligarchy. The freed people of color who arrived in Liberia in 1822, formed a doubled-tiered social structure of the elites, exclusions, disillusions, and differentiations and retroactively marginalized the indigenous people of Liberia to participate in the social, political, and civic life of the country

---

[95] Graham Maddox, "The Prospects for Democratic Convergence: Islam and Christianity," *Political Theology* 16, no. 4 (2015): 305–328.

for 133 years until this group was overthrown in 1980 via cote d'état. This was the group who left the United States of America as the result of inequality, injustice, and systemic racism perpetrated against them. Despite of their experiences as slaves in the United Sates, they perceived the indigenous as third class citizens. These people were taken in hammocks by the indigenous people from one township to another township during their national tour of Liberia. The indigenous were called *protos* or plebeians as named in ancient Rome. The government that ruled Liberia from 1847 to 1980 was an aristocratic-oligarchy camouflaged as democracy; therefore, the government that ruled Liberia from 1847 to 1980 is the opposite of democracy.

It has been said that Liberia was built on Christian principle; realistically, Liberia began with people who had historical Christian root; on the contrary, they did not practice the principle of Christianity. Joseph Jenkins Roberts who emigrated from the United States at age 20 to Liberia; his family was deeply religious and had the desire to evangelize the indigenous people of Africa; however, it does not tell history that Joseph Jenkins Roberts who served as the first Lieutenant governor of the commonwealth and the first president of Liberia was a Christian. Jehudi Ashmun, who served as the American Colonization Society's agent for the colonists between 1822 and 1847 was the Methodist missionary-religious leader and social reformer from New England who became involved in the American Colonization Society's effort to repatriate freed African-Americans to Africa. Stephen Allen Benson who became the second elected President of Liberia after Joseph Jenkins Roberts was a Methodist Preacher. Despite of their connections to Christianity historically, the word "principle" as used, did not influence their ethics how they related to those whom they met in Liberia. The word "Christianity" indicates justice, love, self-sacrifice, and equal protection for all in regardless of race, creed, geography, religion, social status, and historical orientation. The constitution drafted by the colonists is the hybrid of the Constitution of the United States of America that advocates that all human beings are created equal and have the inalienable rights to be happy and to live peacefully. These lines of the United States' Constitution influenced the Emancipation Proclamation in America when Abraham Lincoln became President. These lines are written in the American's Constitution and are paraphrased in the Liberian's Constitution; though, the constitution has undergone changes during previous years; ironically, the people of America still dehumanized black people as slaves despite of their church attending during the time of slavery. This is religion contrary to Christianity and its applied principle; therefore, principle controls behavior of the group based on the doctrine and practice that influence it. Presently, there are Christian churches in the United States that support racism. They are called the "White Evangelicalism Movement" in the American Christian's society; however, they still preach Christ and then practice division. It is written on their churches "No black allowed on the premises." It is engrained in their DNA; therefore, they do not know the Savior. Contemporaneously, Liberia has the history of Christianity; on the contrary, the past leadership of Liberia did not practice Christianity. To be connected to the church does not make one the Christian; on other hand, to be called the Christian is based on obedience to the Scripture. William Richard Tolbert was the Baptist and became the President of the Baptist Alliance of the world; ironically, he was polygamous and made human's sacrifice. Ritualistic killing in Liberia has root from the people of the First Republic; though, several had Christian's background in the Americas.

The former President, Ellen Johnson-Sirleaf, a United Methodist, says effort to declare Liberia as the Christian State would create division among the citizens based on religious beliefs. Former President Ellen Johnson-Sirleaf made this statement in 2008 when she addressed the United Methodist General Conference in Fort Worth, Texas, United States of America. She made the statement when she submitted the report of the Constitution Review Commission to the National Legislature on August 18, 2015 five months after the Commission met in Gharnga and approved a proposal to make Liberia a Christian country. She made this statement in the eight-page letter to the Liberian Senate. She said that the founding fathers of the republic did not put into the Liberian constitution a declaration of Christianity as the national religion. " The constitution has always allowed freedom of religion and worship without seeking to prescribe one religion as the official religion," she said adding that Article 14 of Liberian Constitution correctly separates State and religion and provides that the republic shall establish no specific religion" On quote.[96] The former President Ellen Johnson-Sirleaf's letter was yet to be discussed by the National Legislature to hold a referendum if Christianity should be declared a national religion; even though, the senate is dominated by Christians. Bishop John G. Innis, the Methodist, opposed the proposal and said that it would bring problems in Liberia. "Jesus did not force anyone to join Christianity; therefore, there should be no provision in the Liberian constitution declaring Christianity as the national religion" on quote. President Ellen Johnson-Sirleaf and Bishop John G. Innis are hundred percent right. You have people in government who are placed as legislators; unfortunately, they do not know the constitution of the land neither the country's history. They did not synthesize and analyze the implications of their decision to make Liberia a Christian country that was not built on the principle of Christianity; hence, this is hypocrisy. These guys should deal with social injustice in the land instead of bringing trouble to the people of Liberia. Muslims and Christians live size by size as brothers and sisters in Liberia; therefore, there is no need to bring problems among them due to religious issues. Their decision to make Liberia the Christian country has no rationale and does not align with the democratic society and the Bible based on history. States can interfere with religious belief and thus pollute the sanctity of religion. It happened in the days of Constantine, the Roman's Emperor, when he declared Christianity as the state religion between 306 and 337 AD and thus influenced how the church conducted her religious affairs.[97] He

---

[96] Richard Peck, "General Conference Acts on Wide Range of Issues," accessed August 24, 2022, https://www.umnews.org/en/news/general-conference-acts-on-wide-range-of-issues.

[97] Francis Opoku, "Constantine and Christianity: The Formation of Church/State Relations in the Roman Empire," *Ilorin Journal of Religious Studies* 5, no. 1 (2015): 17–34.

appointed his government officials as Bishops to sit on the seats of the religious clergies and thus polluted the church of the living God. States and religion are separate meaning that no government in the democratic society shall impose religious beliefs on the populations that government serves; however, it does not forbid the populations including religious people from participating in national politics across all cultures as democratic values are adhered to. True religion can isolate evils in society; therefore, religious people are entitled to exercise their political franchise in national body politics.

The Facets of Oppression

Moses writes, "Therefore, say to the children of Israel: "I am the Lord; I will bring you out from under the burdens of the Egyptians. I will rescue you from their bondage, and will redeem you with an outstretch arm and with great judgments (Exod 6:6 NKJV).The above text is the culmination of the prophecy recorded in Genesis 5:13 prior to the declaration made to Moses to fulfill the Abrahamic Covenant when God called Moses as the potential deliverer to the enslaved Israelites under the dominance of the Pharaoh of Egypt. The Bible declares that as the children of Israel moved to Egypt due to famine in Canaan Land, they started to increase in populations; consequently, the Pharaoh of Egypt feared them; as the result, he enslaved them fearing that Israel might one day oppose them as they become many. Oppression might be the alternative answer to decrease their numbers and dominance; therefore, he enslaved Israel.

Psychologically, there are three factors responsible for the leadership's fear of the inferior generation; influentially, these factors did influence the Pharaoh of Egypt decision to enslave the Israelites. These three factors are generic and do influence any leadership that wants to maintain dominance over the inferior generation. Namely, the Pharaoh had the fear of the unknown, the Pharaoh wanted to gain cultural superiority over Israel, and the Pharaoh's desire was to maintain dominance over Israel. In simplicity, the Pharaoh was xenophobic, ethnocentric, and oligarchic in his psychological mode. Based on historical evidence, these factors do influence how leadership in the dominant culture relates to the subordinate group (sub-culture). The birth of dictatorship, aristocracy, oligarchy, and similar manifestations of bad governance is the result of xenophobia, ethnocentrism, and oligarchy. When the settlers arrived in Cape Mesurado, Liberia, they put the Bassa people at gun point in order to take the land for the initial settlement. The people could not resist them because they had gun; therefore, they surrendered their people land to the settlers. As the settlers settled, they gradually asserted effort to control certain territories of Christopolis, Monrovia. Psychologically, the settlers knew that they were the minority group and the people they met in the land might one day oppose them; therefore, they established a doubled-tiered elite structure of exclusions, disillusions, and differentiations and proactively marginalized the people of Liberia to participate in the social, political, and civic life of the country for 133 years of rules. Xenophobia, ethnocentrism, and oligarchy can exist on governmental level as the sub-culture and dominant culture. In the case of the Liberia's situation from 1848 to 1980, it has existed as the sub-culture. The sub-culture is part of the dominant culture and it is usually composed of the minority group who wants to maintain dominance over the majority group. The aspiration for the sub-culture or the minority group to maintain dominant control perpetually over the majority group is the result of birth of xenophobia, ethnocentrism, and oligarchy. It happened in Egypt during the enslavement of Israel and in South Africa during the Apartheid government.

Xenophobia

Xenophobia is defined as the fear of strangers also known as the fear of the unknown in the broader sense based on behavioral psychology. Prior to 1994, immigrants from elsewhere face discrimination and violence in South Africa. Contrary to expectations, the incidence of xenophobia increased between 2000 and March 2008, at which at least 67 people died in what were identified as xenophobic attacks. In May of

2008, a series of attacks left 62 people dead; although 21 of those killed were South African citizens.[98] During these incidences, the South Africans rooted and burned down businesses that belong to foreigners with the fear that foreigners are taking their jobs. Xenophobia can exist internally and externally in government. Politicians fight each others to maintain dominance due to the fear of the unknown known as xenophobia. This is one of the reasons the ruling party in the country can use other means to get rid of those she thinks are opposed to her rules in order to maintain perpetual dominance in the country. Xenophobia is the birth of totalitarianism in the world. Xenophobia is the enemy that makes a leader to get into dirty psychological mode and thus commits atrocities against the people he or she is leading. It is an enemy to the leadership self-esteem because it leads to the downfall of the leader and even causes his or her death. Dictatorial regimes are seen across the globe due to xenophobia which can cause the government to fall. Xenophobia gives birth to ethnocentrism and oligarchic form of leadership in society. The settlers were xenophobic; therefore, they developed the oligarchic form of government in order to marginalize the land owners in Liberia from 1848 to 1980; hence, the status quo changed five percent when William Richard Tolbert was overthrown giving renaissance to representative democracy, ironically, it was a camouflaged democracy from 1980 to 1990 during the deposed President Samual Kanyon Doe's regime. The First Republic was characterized with xenophobia and similar manifestations of marginalization in the land. The Pharaoh of Egypt enslaved the Israelites due to xenophobia; therefore, xenophobia is the facet of oppression deployed by the dominant or sub-culture to maintain dominance in power.

---

[98] Michele Sparati/AFP via Getty Image, "South Africa: Widespread Xenophobic Violence," accessed August 24, 2022, https://www.hrw.org/news/2020/09/17/south-africa-widespread-xenophobic-violence.

Ethnocentrism

Ethnocentrism exists when the sub or the dominant culture feels cultural superiority over those she is ruling. Ethnocentrism can exist across all cultures in respective of governments, in-groups, families, and the list goes on. One of the countries in the world that is ethnocentric is the United States of America. America feels cultural superiority over other nations with reference to health care, technology, education, or government. With reference to education, if one obtained a degree outside of America, it does not have weight in America unless one has attended her university or college or take the equivalent examination that satisfies the degree. If one graduated outside of America and wants to matriculate into the American school, one's credential must be evaluated by an accredited and a recognized institution in America before such credential can be endorsed by the university the student wants to matriculate. The failure to evaluate the credential is the stumbling block to matriculation. This is cultural educational superiority. It works in America because it is attached to the accreditation awarded to the school; therefore, the failure to adhere to accreditation rules can lead the institution to lose it. It is the system puts into place and all universities or seminaries that are accredited must play by the rules to remained accredited or lose the accreditation.

The indigenous of Liberia were not educated to lead or did not have the idea about government as did the settlers; therefore, their culture was a sub culture as compared to the culture the settlers brought from the United States of America; in this light, the sub culture that should have been inferior became the dominant culture in Liberia. This is one of the reasons, the settlers organized themselves as the social elite and excluded the rest of the populations to participate in the social, political, and the civic life of their country because they felt superior to the people they met in the land. The fear of the unknown known as xenophobia can lead one group to feel that her culture is superior to the other group and therefore becomes oppressive; for this reason, xenophobia gives renaissance to ethnocentrism in domestic and national leadership. The practice of xenophobia and ethnocentrism in body politics can lead to insurrection in the land. Dictatorship governments have fallen in the world due to xenophobia and ethnocentrism. It is the matter of time; eventually, the sub culture that is marginalized will revolt contingently. The coup d'état in 1980 in the Liberian political history was the result of the amalgamation of the happenings that occurred between 1847 and 1980.

Oligarchy

The last facet of oppression as discussed in this monograph is called oligarchy. Oligarchy is the form of government wherein the minority group who is rich and privileged is entrusted with the power to rule the poor. The Liberian government since independence from 1847 to 1980 had been characterized with oligarchy. It was a doubled-tiered social elite structure that permeated the Liberian society and excluded the majority of the populations from the political, social, economic, and civic life of their country. Everything written in the 1847 Constitutional Convention with reference to the Liberia's Constitution and Declaration of Independence favored the doubled-tiered social elite of exclusivism, disillusion, and differentiation. It was one of the reasons that after the coup d'état of 1980, the 1847 Constitution was suspended by the People Redemption Council's government and the new draft Constitution was adopted and written in 1986 with changes made to the old led by Dr. Amos Sawyer and the 25–members delegated committee.

Oligarchy can exist in governmental sector as in-group called sectionalism to deny the masses from the immunities that belonged to them. In the context of the in-group situation, members of the group selected to benefit politically, socially, and economically, will feel superior to the dominant culture because they received the dollars monthly while the rest of the populations live in endless poverty. This is an in-group oligarchy set up within the governmental sector to marginalize the rest of the populations and therefore deny them of social justice due to the centralization of the wealth to the selected few in the country. There is an in-group modified oligarchy in the Liberian government at present. It is the modified version because the wealth is given to senators and representatives who were elected by their people during general election as compared to the one that existed from 1847 to 1980. The members of the in-group will continue to be superior in the country because the wealth is being allocated to them through astronomical salary payment. What should have been allocated for developments, education, health care, social services, and among others to serve the masses is going into individual's pocket. The economy of such nation will never recover because the wealth is in the hands of the selected few and those selected few alone cannot grow the economy of the country alone. Economic development is the unanimous consented effort by all in the country. Vice President Dr. Howard Taylor made a remark during the opening of the rehabilitation center built by Senator Abraham Darius Dillon. In her remarks, she asked other law makers to build similar things in their districts. The Vice President including government officials know that something is wrong with the Liberian's government with reference to salary's issue and it must be fixed. Leadership without vision for the nation due to the lack of patriotism is dangerous and sinister. Every corrupt government is characterized with in-group oligarchy. The leadership of such in-group does so to protect herself and to maintain dominance over the majority group. Oligarchy is oppressive; therefore, it can manifest physicality and leads to insurrection in the country. This is proof historical indicator when President William Richard Tolbert, Jr. pursued a policy of suppressing opposition. Dissatisfaction over governmental plans to raise the price of rice in 1979 led to protest demonstrations in the streets of Monrovia. The deposed President William Richard Tolbert ordered his troops to fire on the demonstrators; consequently, seventy people were killed. Rioting ensued throughout Liberia leading to a military coup d'état on April 12, 1980. The deposed President William Richard Tolbert was killed during the coup d'état with several of his ministers marking the end of the First Republic.[99]

Prographónosticism:
Examination of the Second Republic
(1980–1990)

When Aristotle and Plato named the forms of governments, they named timocracy, democracy, and tyranny and said that aristocracy was the best rule among the three. What is discussed in this section of the monograph is the difference between dictatorship and tyranny. Tyranny is the form of government that is handled by a single ruler who oppresses people with absolute power while dictatorship is the type of governments that is ruled by a group of people, whereas the final verdict is yielded by the head of the council. Sometimes, tyranny and dictatorship can exist together based on the behavior of the head of the government taking into consideration the complexity of the ruler due to unpredictability of the behavior. In some instances, the dictator can change into a tyrant based on personality characteristic changes in behavior mode; in this light, he or she runs decision without the consensus of the council's members. When General Thomas Quiwinkpa's coup d'état failed in 1985 and Journalist Charles Beyans played his journalistic role during the coup's transition, the deposed President Samuel Kanyon Doe ordered his execution without the approval of the council's members when his power was revived. When he rigged the general election in 1985, he ordered the SECOM's chairman to declare him as the winner; though, Jackson F. Doe won the election; therefore, the SECOM's chairman had no option; instead, he had to declare the deposed President Samuel Kanyon Doe as the winner of the general election. The deposed President Samuel Kanyon Doe was both a dictator and a tyrant. A tyrant can be crueler than the dictator because his decision has no second opinion. After the coup d'état in 1980, the

---

[99] "Liberia Forward," accessed December 24, 2021, https://www.liberiaforward.org/history-of-liberia.

deposed President Samuel Kanyon Doe wanted to execute 200 members of the Tolbert's government officials after he has executed 26 supporters during the gun battle at the Executive Mansion. His decision received an objection as members of the People Redemption Council disagreed to the numbers of people the deposed Samuel Kanyon Doe wanted to execute; eventually, thirteen members cabinet of the Tolbert's dethroned regime was put to the firing squad behind the military barrack in Monrovia. The deposed President Samuel Kanyon Doe was both a dictator and a tyrant who had no respect for the constitution of the republic and human rights. During his tenure of the presidency, he has no respect for religious and press freedom. He ordered the beating of religious people and the death of anyone whom he perceived as opposition to him. He kept closed to his tribesmen and certain ethnic group he perceived favored his rule and consequently carried out reprisal against the ethnic groups he perceived as opposed to his rule. The deposed President Samuel Kanyon Doe-led government was tyrannical, dictatorial, and tribalistic. He sent his troops at the onset of the rebel's invasion of Monrovia to massacre the civilian population who sought refuge at the Lutheran church. The deposed President Samuel Kanyon Doe would have done better for Liberia had he not turned into dictator and tyrant because he had a developmental mindset for the country.

The climax of the end of the Second Republic culminated in 1990 marking the assassination of the deposed President Samuel Kanyon Doe. The amalgamation of the factional wars that internally and externally displaced Liberian refugees and killing over 250,000 of the populations was a senseless war. The war was characterized with complexities of warring factions who fought to control the nation leading to deadlock in peace talks beginning with the Summit at Yamoussoukro. The proliferations of weaponries in the nation were the result of the multiplicities of warring factions that made the war more complex. This can be seen in the chronometric historiography record with reference to the onset of the war beginning with the 1990's interim presidencies ranging from one to six interim presidents. This is how the complexity of the Liberian insurrection had been prior to the general election held in 1997. After the assassination of President Samuel Kanyon Doe and the general election held, the Liberian insurrection took on different morphology at which peace was in utopia until Charles Ghankay Taylor resigned from office in 2003. After the election of President Ellen Johnson-Sirleaf, ECOMOG backed by the United Nations remained in Liberia to monitor the fragile peace. The Liberian insurrection became apparent to be senseless because the target of the war was no longer the focus; instead, it became a control of power instead of national interest. The installation of six interim presidents as seen in the chronometric historiography record speaks volume of the complexity of the Liberian Civil War. War is never good and should be discouraged by any group in the nation. War is discouraged in the nation when injustice and corruption are dealt with and perpetrators of the crimes are brought to justice.

Xenophobia, Ethnocentrism and Oligarchy in the Second Republic

The subjects of xenophobia, ethnocentrism, and oligarchic characteristics of leadership do exist in domestic and national leadership in body politics. These facets of oppression are common generically with all totalitarian form of leadership. They do exist consciously and unconsciously in the leadership with reference to sectionalism and tribalism in domestic and national leadership body politics across all cultures. While they serve as oppressive tools used against the subordinate group, they also serve as tools to the downfall of leadership. It is just the matter of time; not sooner later, the oppressive ruler will expire timely. The Liberian government during the Second Republic from 1980 to 1990 had been characterized with xenophobia, ethnocentrism, and oligarchic form of leadership. These facets of oppression are psychological tools that begin with the leader's mindset; therefore, they are pervasive and tend to permeate into the psychological code of the leader and eventually make the individual to develop prejudices against his or her subjects. This speaks volumes of their pervasiveness into the core of the leader's behaviorism. Primarily, the leader's downfall begins with xenophobia; then, it sets him or her up for the psychological crisis wherein he or she creates an in-group oligarchy (sectionalism and tribalism). The reason of the creation of the in-group is the result of the fear that certain people in the government are opposing him or her; therefore, they might seek his or her downfall. Such psychological mode is not healthy for the opposing party in the country; then, the crisis climaxes wherein the oppositions are arrested and jailed, some are missing and never seen, while some are falsely accused of treason, journalistic freedom is buried, freedom of speech is abolished, or the constitution of the country is dead. Xenophobia leads the ruler to create the in-group within the government so that this group will become a protection to him or her. The issue of tribalism and sectionalism begins to surface in his or her leadership in different dimensions. In most instances, the obvious will be tribalism.

The terminology "tribalism" exists with all ethnic groupings in regardless of leadership; therefore, everyone is tribalistic across all societies in respective of cultures and historical orientations; therefore, tribalism is not all bad and it is not all good. The goodness or badness of tribalism depends on the level of practices of the doctrine and the leader's mindsets. Tribalism is an organization, culture, or beliefs of a tribe. It is a strong feeling of identity and loyalty to one's tribe or group. To remain un-tribalistic is to not belong to an ethnic group; obviously, everyone does belong to an ethnic group. When members of the tribes begin to feel that they are superior to other ethnic groups in the nation; then, tribalism forms a degenerative version called ethnocentrism; as the result, this tribalism becomes bad because it divides, destroys, and rules. Ethnocentrism is the belief that one's culture is superior to the other groups in the nation; for this reason, what is actually called tribalism in the government is the bad governance that begins with ethnocentrism; therefore in contrast, tribalism deals with identity while ethnocentrism deals with cultural superiority. The manifestation of tribalism in the negation mode in practice is called ethnocentrism; therefore, it is ethnocentrism that gives birth to bad tribalism in the group. The dictator that is tribalistic will use his or her power to oppress those whom he defined as the unknown that pose threat to his or her leadership. Every dictator is afraid to die; for this reason, he or she will use oppression as the tool to put his or her opponents down or even kill them. The creation of the in-group oligarchy (tribalism and sectionalism) is the result of xenophobia in leadership body politics. In the case of the in-group oligarchy, the tribe or the race in power or the ruling party becomes the oligarchy in the government as define inferentially; therefore, the oppressed as identified are enemies to the ruling party as defined by the dictator. In the case of the Liberian's situation, the deposed President Samuel Kanyon Doe was at war with the people of Nimba due to xenophobia; therefore, he used oppression to keep them down through systemic execution of his opponents and the massacred of the children at the onset of the Liberia's Civil War. This helped fueled the Liberian Civil War that led to his assassination in 1990. The Second Republic leadership was characterized with xenophobia, ethnocentrism, and the in-group oligarchy. How can one describe the Third Republic leadership at present to be? Every corrupt government is characterized with one of these facets of oppression across all cultures.

Prographónosticism:
Examination of the Third Republic
(1990 to present)

Nations of the world are indecisive to welcome democratic values in their governances predominantly those nations that did not start with democratic values. The nation of Liberia for 133 years of rules had exhibited as single party system from Joseph Jenkins Roberts to William Richard Tolbert prior to the 1980 coup d'état. The Liberian government had been camouflaged for these years as democracy; on the contrary, the country was run under the aristocratic-oligarchy leadership. The misrepresentation of the various counties in the government did not reflect democratic values; though, the government was named "democracy" based on its theoretical characteristics as opposed to practical ramifications. The 133 years of rules of government were characterized with the family ruling Liberia instead of representative democracy. As Liberia transitions from single party system to multi-party democracy, Liberia is faced with dilemmas. These dilemmas are realities Liberia must recognize, analyze, evaluate, and put into place practical resolution in order to transition well. One can dress a monkey with a coat suit; naturally, the monkey remains a monkey despite of the outside transformation. Countries that did not practice democratic values from the beginning; however, they want to transition to democracy fit this analogy for the monkey's situation; so, it is Liberia. To deal with the dilemmas, Liberia must deal with injustice, recognizes that she is a novice to democracy, and realizes that she falls short of democratic values. It is impossible to treat any illness without proper diagnosis of the problem. The manifestation of these problems in the Liberian government can be seen when security forces crack down on peaceful protest, the practice of injustice in criminal and civil cases, the lack of check and balance among the three branches of government, and the failure of the government to redress the demand from peaceful protesters and the lack of equitable distribution of wealth to the masses. Based on the functions of the government as previously discussed in this monograph, the government of Liberia falls short of her functions with reference to the restraining of evil and keeping national security for all. The ongoing ritualistic killings and the killing of the auditors with no arrest made indicates human rights abuses and camouflaged democracy in the country during President George Manneh Weah's administration.

The Liberia's Dilemmas

The Injustice

It has been argued in President George Manneh Weah's administration that it would bring problems in the nation if former combatants and corrupt leaderships who are guilty of human rights abuses and economic crimes in Liberian are brought to justice through the Economic and Criminal Court system; hence, such move would break national peace and damage the reconciliation in the country. The government has ignored justice in the land under the disguised of national reconciliation. Such decision is the direct act of ignoring democratic values in the land and consequently putting citizens' lives at risks. There are consequences of ignoring justice in the land. It will make criminals who are guilty of human's rights abuses to resurface with similar past behavior in different hidden fashions due to the lack of deterrence. At this time, they themselves might not be involved directly; instead, they will send second party to carry out their criminalities posing insecurity in the land. This is one of the reasons rampant ritualistic killings have increased in Liberia because criminals feel secured and can commit crimes with impunity due to the lack of justice in the land. The refusal of the government to establish the court encourages criminals in the land to continue their criminalities due to the lack of deterrence. Justice denied in the land is equivalent to the increase in criminality. The stealing of the billions of the Liberian dollars at the Central Bank, the killing of the auditors with no arrest made, and the continued ritualistic killing in Liberia is the result of the government refusal to establish justice in the democratic society. One does not have strong democratic society in the absence of justice. When government refuses to restraint evil in the land, it can lead to security breakdown; consequently, peaceful citizens become the prey for evil doers. This way, criminals have tested the weakness of the government and showed up with no fear of impunity because government has refused her fiduciary responsibility and made citizens vulnerable. National security for all is the characteristic of the stable democratic government. Democracy means justice for all; therefore, government should play her fiduciary responsibility to her citizens in order to maintain a democratic society free from another civil war. Liberians know very well what the civil war has done to this country up the present; therefore, citizen's refusal to speak out will make corrupt government to continue to rule. The below statement is the epiphany of Rev. Jagaye Karnley of the Catholic Diocese of Cape Palmas, Liberia. He writes,

> Lest we forget: It was on Christmas Eve 1989 that the trajectory of Liberia's history changed when an avalanche of violence, murder, unbridled destruction and looting descended on the country for fourteen years up to 2003. Remote and proximate causes in Liberia's history from the 1820's to 1989 are responsible for the civil war. The active and passive actors in the theater of the war were both internal and external. It was a struggle between the beasts of evil and darkness and the angels of good and light. But the hope of peace ultimately prevailed in August 2003 over the gloom and despair of war. We have since then seen and experienced the tangible and intangible dividends of peace, democracy and good governance. It is however abundantly clear that Liberia is no longer on the progressive trajectory it embarked upon beginning in 2003. The evidence of this is in the serious issues of corruption and accountability that hang over some officials of the past and current administrations like the Sword of Damocles. Corruption negatively impacts development. Liberia is on the trajectory of retrogression and death because of greed and corruption. This and many issues from the country's past and present that have not been decisively addressed will continue to

undermine peace, democracy, and development. Liberia needs to seriously embark on the path of healing and reconciliation once again. One way forward is honoring the sacred memory of all victims of the civil war. Moreover, holding people accountable for their words and action in the civil war should be given the serious attention it deserves.[100]

The Young Democracy

Apostle Peter writes,

> Submit yourselves for the Lord's sake to every human authority: whether to the emperor, as the supreme authority, or to governors, who are sent by him to punish those who do wrong and to commend those who do right. For it is God's will that by doing good you should silence the ignorant talk of foolish people. Live as free people, but do not use your freedom as a cover-up for evil; live as God's slaves. Show proper respect to everyone, love the family of believers, fear God, honor the emperor "(1 Pet 2:13–17 NIV).

From the above text, it can be deduced that God supports democracy, that Christians and non-Christians alike represent God in the context of democratic values that are not in opposition to biblical values, that Christians use their freedom responsibly, and that Christians fear God, love the family of believers, and honor the human leadership. Since Liberia has a young democracy and still in the process of transitioning, things are not going to change overnight; therefore, citizens are admonished to exhibit tolerance; however, they should remain steadfast towards

---

[100] Ibid.

dramatic change to the betterment of Liberia. Christians and non-Christians alike should speak out for justice; however, they are admonished to remain in the context of God's governing authority as described in the above text. The Christians' approach to such situation regarding change should be passive resistance as allowed by the constitution of the land.

After 133 years of single party system, Liberia has transitioned to democracy after the civil war; however, Liberia has a young democracy. This is one of the reasons; one sees law enforcement posed in the street to stop peaceful protest when the constitution of the land has said that citizens have the right to peaceful gatherings. Young democracy might not be used to such because leadership feels threatens that protest will turn into unrest that threatens their security. This is obvious because protest might turn violent when law enforcement wants to make arrest of the protesters. Both protesters and law enforcements are novices to democracy in the young democratic setting like Liberia; therefore, there is uncertainty in the mind of the current leadership of the land; paradoxically, the leadership has failed to play by the rules according to democratic values. Liberia has the slogan of democracy; on the contrary, the government is far from protecting democratic values because justice is being denied. The players in the area of free speech have also abused freed speech. People who are involved in freed speech have insulted the President's mother due to hate. Why insult the President's mother? Ethically, it is wrong to do so. Freed speech comes with responsibility; therefore, insulting the President's mother is the manifestation of hate and such individual who aspires for leadership in the land is not qualified to lead; in this light, electors need to be careful how they elect politicians into public office. Change comes gradually; therefore, it is going to take time for Liberia to transition to true democracy. Liberia is trying democracy; however, there are elements in the government who have some levels of control over the people; on the contrary, they do not support democratic values. Citizens of the land including government officials are novices to democratic values in Liberia. Every democracy is fragile; however, it requires people who put the country and its people primarily above personal interests to keep the fragile democracy from collapsing. This is one of the reasons the American democracy though became fragile in 2020 election but was able to regain prominent because the people put their country and its people primarily above personal interest. Democracy is fragile; nevertheless, it stands provided the people put personal interest aside. Democracy is the government of the people and cannot be personalized and be camouflaged as totalitarianism. The invisible slogan of totalitarianism will test democratic values; however, it takes the people of the land to stand up and to protect the values in the midst of conflicting and competing personal interests for the common good of all.

The Camouflaged Democracy

Camouflaged democracy is the democracy disguised as democracy; on the contrary, such democratic leadership finds it difficult to practice democratic values. Most nations that transition from other forms of governments other than democracy can find it difficult to adhere to the norm of democratic values. There are indicators on the globe of camouflaged democracy. For example, the Republic of Guinea was once ruled as one party system; then, the leadership transitioned into camouflaged democracy; on the contrary, it found it difficult to remain practicing democratic values. Camouflaged democratic systems can be characterized with systemic arrest of politicians, corrupt practices in government with impunity, the lack of justice for the victimized, and various manifestations of inequalities in the country. In the structural democratic make-up, the balance of power with reference to the branches of government as the constitutionality of the Liberian Constitution is against equilibrium when it comes to checks and balances in powers; therefore, the executive branch tends to influence the legislature and the judiciary, when each should be autonomous. In the camouflaged democracy, the executive branch of government tends to overrule and to overstep the other two branches of government; as the result, members of the other branches of government are vulnerable to persecution should any members resist or serve as opposition to the executive branch. In most camouflaged demo-cratic systems, the executive controls all; therefore, the two branches are usually scapegoats in the administration. In reality, the people who voted their representatives into power to represent them are actually misrepre-sented in the government because the people who are representing them are being bought by the executive branch or are afraid to speak out for fear of being persecuted or even killed. In the camouflaged democracy, the citizens of the country are vulnerable to systemic inequalities because the government is the opposite of democracy. The word "democracy" signifies government of the people and for the people characterized with represen-tations in the context of constituencies within the sub-political divisions of the nation; on the contrary, camouflaged democracy is the government of the select few. Such government can be the in-group oligarchy char-acterized with sectionalism or tribalism. In the camouflaged democracy, the wealth of the nation is stolen by the select few; therefore, the wealth is not distributed and the in-group oligarchy will always fight against democratic values in order to protect her interest. Over the 132 years of rule as one party system prior to the assassination of President Williams Richard Tolbert, Liberia had been operating as camouflaged democracy dressed in the aristocratic-oligarchy rule where family members of the executive branch of government controlled key governmental sectors in the land. From J. J Roberts to William R. Tolbert, the common people were represented in the military and served as body guards to the elites. It was one of the motivations that led to the overthrow of the Tolbert's government; then, Liberia transitioned into another dictatorship form of government during the deposed President Samuel Kanyon Doe's regime. At this time, the government became tribalistic and tended to marginalize other ethnic groups in the country by carrying out reprisal against the ethnic groups through systemic execution of their leaders in government and atrocities against the people of Nimba. This led to the sixteen years of civil war in Liberia that destroyed lives and property. After the civil war, the camouflaged democracy continues in Liberia up to the present. One contemplates why there has been no change to fully embody democracy in Liberia despite of the sixteen years civil war? Some of the perceived answers to this question could be, the leadership who led the war probably did not have a goal and present leaderships of Liberia are not being patriotic due to greed.

In the Liberia camouflaged democratic system, the executive branch of government tends to overrule and to overstep the legislature and the Judiciary branches. The president is treated as *demi god*; therefore, he or she is perceived by the common people to have owned everything in the land. This is one of the reasons presidents don't live up to the value system of democracy and can steal with impunity because psychologically, the people of the land think he or she owns all. It has been said by many in Liberia that Liberia is an elephant meat; therefore, when someone ascends to the presidency, he or she has to cut his or hers. This has to change. Liberia is the only country that allocates special budget to the president for development; therefore, all developments taking place in Liberia are being attributed to the president as if the resources belong to him or her. Such budget should have been allocated and given to the Ministry of Public Works for development. Liberia has a camouflaged democracy; hence, it is deceiving and lacks the characteristic of being democratic. Who decides the budget of Liberia? Camouflaged democracy is dangerous because it never lives out to democratic values and can turn bad when it is not eradicated. In the camouflaged democratic system, the issue of ethical standard in government for government officials with respect to corrupt practices and sexual misconducts are in Utopia and are never the subject on the agenda. Ethics should be taken seriously when it comes to electing people to public office. Senators and law makers in Liberia need to develop bills of laws in additional to the Constitution of the land to become laws in the Constitution with reference to budgets, ethical issues regarding holding public office in Liberia, and among others if Liberia will become a democratic society. Christians are encouraged to enter the government to bring these changes; hence, allowing the heathens to rule always is the problem to the land of Liberia.

The Corrupt Practices

After twelve years of leadership of the former President Ellen Johnson-Sirleaf, she handled over power for the smooth transition of democratic leadership; however, she has been criticized for the failure to reduce poverty and to crack down on corruption in Liberia. She has defended her son who has been accused of corrupt practices and has gone ahead to influence the disestablishment of the Economic and Criminal Court in Liberia using her influence in President George Manneh Weah led government understanding that when the court is established in Liberia, she, the son, and other governments' officials will be implicated. It should be made known that it was unlawful for the former President, Ellen Johnson-Sirleaf to employ her son in the Liberia's government; therefore, she broke the Liberian's Constitution ignoring the practice of nepotism in the government. According to the Liberia's Constitution of 1986, Chapter II: General Principles of National Policy, Article 5 (c), states that steps shall be taken, by appropriate legislation and executive orders, to eliminate sectionalism and tribalism, and such abuses of power as the misuse of government resources, nepotism and all other corrupt practices. The former president's action to employ her son in the government to steal government's resources is the gross abuse of her power and the misuse of government's resources. It is the crime that is punishable by law when the president leaves office. It takes the incumbent president to prosecute his or her predecessor regarding such crime when he or she takes office; unfortunately, the incumbent President is far from doing so in Liberia because he or she is coming to embezzle.

Justice denied in the land is the increase in criminality; for this reason, President George Manneh Weah's administration has followed the foot step of her predecessor, Ellen Johnson-Sirleaf, due to corrupt practices. The epiphany of his corrupt practices can be seen in the stolen of the 25 billion Liberian dollars at the Central Bank, the complexes he has built for himself, and among others. The political history of Liberia from 1847 to the present is being replayed repeatedly by past and present leaderships of Liberia; therefore, corruption has become the network of chain in the progressive mode; hence, it takes justice to break this chain in order to change the status quo.

Former President Ellen Johnson-Sirleaf leaves a mixed legacy especially when it comes to maintaining the fragile peace in the Third Republic and helping women to be listed in the military coupled with the protection of women in the Liberian society. Despite of the above legacy, the allegation of corruption against her and her son has overshadowed her legacy. Based on the 2016 assessment with reference to the Corruption Perception and the Human Development Indexes from Transparency International, Liberia ranks 90th out of the 176 countries and remains the country that is really underdeveloped. Poverty level and unemployment especially among the youth remain high making Liberia one of the world's poorest nations. Despite of the international community's support of Liberia backed by the United States' government, the former President, Ellen Johnson-Sirleaf could not deal with poverty in Liberia as the result of corrupt practices. Corruption undermines democracy, national peace, and retards infrastructures and human developments in the land. The proliferation of arm insurrections in the world is the result of corruption in governments.

The Corruption Perceptions Index ranks countries and territories based on how corrupt their public sector is perceived to be. A country or territory's score indicates the perceived level of public sector corruption on a score; therefore, 0 indicates highly corrupt while on the score of 100 indicates very clean. The Corruption Index for Liberia remained unchanged at 28 points in 2020 from the 28 points in 2019. According to the 2022 forecast, the Corruption Index for Liberia is expected to reach 31.0 points by the end of 2021.[101] In the Corruption Index, the lowest the number, the corrupt the sector is and the higher the number, the clean the sector is. According to the report, the government of Liberia fight against corruption has declined recently. Corruption remains the

---

[101] Transparency International, "Liberia Corruption Rank, "accessed August 24, 2022, https://tradingeconomics.com/liberia/corruption-rank.

major problem in Liberia. To deal with corruption, past leaderships must be brought to justice to account for the resources they have stolen from Liberia so that the incumbent leaders will not do the same due to deterrence. Justice denied in the land is the refusal to bring past leaderships to justice to account for the resources stolen beginning with the former President, Ellen Johnson-Sirleaf and onward. To make the Third Republic distinct from the First and Second republic, the incumbent leader after 2023 general election must bring past leaderships to justice regarding corruption. The refusal of the incumbent leader to bring past leaderships to justice with reference to corruption is the indication that Liberians are not prepared to change the status quo.

The Theological and Political Foundation of Liberia Political History

Apostle Paul writes, For everything that was written in the past was written to teach us, so that through the endurance taught in the Scriptures and the encouragement they provide we might have hope" (Rom 15:4 NIV).

The above text puts history into context as the blueprint used in this life to make adjustment how an individual makes informed decision in domestic and national leadership. Apostle Paul moved by the Holy Spirit said that what an individual has read in history with reference to events is the blueprint an individual uses to make judgment on the current situation in decision-making; unfortunately, humans are polarized on two axes to repeat bad history. The past known as *prographō* in Greek as used in the biblical text is the blueprint that teaches humanity past history underscoring the potentiality of similar manifestation as history is concerned. From the First and Second Republic in the context of the Liberia's situation, what have Liberians learned from the political history? What applied teaching can the present leadership of Liberia applies to her political ambition? Why should aspirant politicians apply the applied teaching? Aspirant politicians should apply the teaching because the applied teaching is the blueprint they can use in now situation to remain on course so that the mistakes the past leaders had made and fallen, they should not be trapped in the same snare. Apostle Paul said that through the encouragement the Scripture provides, we might have hope. The word "hope" in Greek is called *elpida*. *Elpida* is confidence; therefore, in simplicity, history teaches humanity what direction to take and provides her hope when similar epiphany is resurfacing in her midst to guide her make appropriate decision remedial; therefore, leadership becomes conscious judgmentally to make the appropriate decision for the salvation of the masses. In the context of the development of the doctrine of *prographónosticism,* the past, the applied teaching, and the hope the teaching provides define and reference the specificities what happened in the First and Second Republic to guide leadership modifies behavior in the Third Republic when making decisions. The past, the applied teaching, and the hope are analogies of history leadership can use as blueprint to make decision in body politics in the now situation in the Liberia body politics. Based on the historical perspectives with reference to the Liberia's political history, *prographó* or the past becomes the blueprint leadership can use as reference to make decision on the current situation that references the past. Analogically, if an individual were to build a decent house with reference to the dimensions, the kind of materials, the cost of the materials, the labor involved, and the estimate to build the house, an individual would need the house blueprint to carry out the project. The reason of the blueprint is tied to the decision-making whether he or she would start construction. The blueprint represents the practical experience to direct him or her, how, where, when, and to what extent he or she should go about building the house. Analogically in the context of the Liberia's situation, the present leadership of Liberia should use the past to serve as stepping stones to direct her decisions on domestic and national leadership. This is the reason it is impossible to use someone else's blueprint to make decision on personal life situation or else an individual could take a decision that goes wrong. It reminds Liberians of the young democracy incomparable to the American mature democracy; therefore, Liberia cannot use the American's blueprint nor other nations in the world to make decision.

America is the democratic society and tends to preach democracy in the world; however; it does not mean that all nations that aspire to be democratic should use the American's blueprint. In the democratic society, there are good and bad values that democratic nations can adopt or discard. When it comes to social justice system, every nation needs to define social justice in her context based on the values systems. Social justice has to do with allowing people access to wealth, privileges, and rights according to individualism. Every citizen in Liberia has the right to freedom of speech, education, healthcare, equal protection, and the right to live happily according to the constitution of the land. These rights are inalienable rights that should not be denied by anyone in the land. On the other hand, citizens do not have the rights to abortion and homosexuality; though, some do it in secret; however, it is not legalized in Liberia as some States in the United States have legalized them. These things are immoral; therefore, they should not be practiced among mankind according to the Divine; nevertheless, in some democratic societies like the United States of America, these things are allowed because they are rights of citizens according to the social justice system as defined by the United States of America's contextualization. It has become rights for some citizens who want to practice them instead of becoming unnatural and abomination before God. Despite of their moral falloffs, America still influences some nations who aspire to practice democracy in their nations to legalize them. The decision to leave conservative values and to follow liberal values systems has made some nations to reject democracy. In the American political arenas, there are two divides called conservatism and liberalism. Conservatives are against abortion, homosexuality, and other manifestations that depict similar epiphany; while, liberals are for abortion, homosexuality, and other manifestations that depict similar epiphany; therefore, the American politics is polarized on two axes; consequently, the politicians use these divides to preach to their audience whom should vote them during general election. President George

Manneh Weah understands this psychology; therefore, he goes around in the various counties to mingle with the common people in order to over-shadow his bad practices regarding corruption in order to get their votes. Politicians need to understand audience's political motivation before winning voters to their sides during general elections. Politicians need to understand the doctrine of *prographónosticism* in order to draw a line of demarcation between the past and the present. The present government of Liberia cannot use the blueprint of the former President Ellen Johnson-Sirleaf administration and become successful in leadership because one of her bad legacies she left behind that is being documented is corruption; so, are the other governments that had existed in Liberia from 1847 to the present; similarly, no government of Liberia who comes into power after the 2023 election and beyond can follow the blueprint of the past governments and become successful to better Liberia.

From our previous study in this monograph taking *progonosticism* into consideration, one learned that xenophobia is an enemy to domestic and national leadership; consequently, it influences the leader to have fear of the unknown. Xenophobiais the mind game that plays on the leader to have wrong views about people; therefore, it leads to similar manifestations of oppressions in domestic and national leadership. The proliferation of dictatorship in the world is the fear of the unknown in leadership. Leaders must deal with xenophobia in order to make good leadership. The Pharaoh of Egypt oppressed the Israelites through enslavement as the result of xenophobia. The South Africans rooted and burned down foreigners' businesses in South Africa due to xenophobia. Dictatorial regimes are seen in the world today as the result of the fear of the unknown. The failure of leadership to deal with the fear of the unknown can lead the leader to have misjudgment about people's cultural values; as the result, the individual will have considered other people's cultures insignificant leading to cultural superiority. This ideology can lead the sub-culture to develop a doubled-tiered elite structure and therefore proactively marginalizes the rest of the populations in the country using oppression.

Ethnocentrism leads to the development of the class system in the community of nations; therefore, when the settlers arrived in Liberia in 1822 during the tenure of their administration, they developed the class system and marginalized the indigenous of Liberia for 133 years. The marginalization was the result of the sub-culture that became ethnocentric and xenophobic to the rest of the populations of Liberia. This is one of the reasons, there were force labor in Liberia as which the indigenous were called *protos* or plebeians; therefore, leadership of any country must avoid the psychological snare of ethnocentrism to avoid class system. The failure to deal with ethnocentrism can lead one group of people to consider herself to be the superior group and might marginalize the dominant culture to participate in the social, economic, and political life of the country. Ethnocentrism can exist in the in-group, the sub-culture, and dominant culture in the nation. This form of political-social structure that is created when people become ethnocentric leads to oligarchy. Members of this group consider themselves rich and superior to others in the land. They believe that the poor should not be given leadership. The power is in the hand of those that have the money or are privileged and not based on those values that qualify them to lead. Oligarchy is corrupt; therefore, it is degenerative version of aristocracy according to Aristotle and Plato.[102]

Apostle Paul said that, what we learn from the past, we can use them to make decision on the current affairs based on experience and history. From the political history of Liberia, the audience, including politicians, learned that the decision the founding fathers of Liberia took to marginalize the rest of the population was the result of xenophobia, ethnocentrism, and the institutionalized oligarchy. Any movement that operates in this manner can fall. It is the matter of time because the people will have known and risen against the movement. Xenophobia, ethnocentrism, and oligarchy are *prographó* Liberians can learn from in history because they serve as teaching, the platform of endurance, and the instruction they provide so that leadership may make the right decision on domestic

---

[102] "Tyranny, Democracy, and the Polity: Aristotle's Politics "accessed August 24, 2022, https://fs.blog/aristotles-politics/.

and national issues (Rom 15:4). Their political expediency, reality, future promising for the masses, and its stability as one people, one nation, and one government for all depends on how they treat the past to relate to the present; unfortunately, the present and the past leaderships continue to replay the history of the past that does not help Liberia and its people.

Responsive Actions Required

The author of Proverbs writes, "Where there is no vision, the people perish: but he that keepeth the law, happy is he" (Prov 29:18 KJV). The responsive actions required for Liberia, calls for the visionary leadership; therefore, electors need to assess politicians before voting them into public offices in order to keep the visionary leadership in check; unfortunately, Liberian people don't know whom to vote into public office. Prior to the 2017 general election, I witnessed the young people being interviewed why they were voting for the president. The common answer to the question was I love him; therefore, I will vote for him. You don't vote for politicians because you love them; instead, you vote for politicians who fuel your political motivations that positively affect the masses; for this reason, Liberian people need education to vote politicians into public office who care about the nation and its people. When the Republic of Ghana was engulfed with corrupt practices, it took Jerry Rawlings to eradicate corruption in the Republic of Ghana because he was a visionary leader. The visionary leader cares for the peoples' well-being; therefore, he or she denies himself or herself of any resources that belong to the country; for this reason, the word "corruption" is far away from the person who stands against what he or she thinks is abominable in the society. Corruption is an abominable practice that denies the masses from receiving services accorded them. Corruption is an enemy of social justice in the country; therefore, it denies people from receiving services accorded them. Citizens died from diseases, are unable to gain educational services, and are unable to live balanced lifestyles as the result of someone's embezzlement of resources that belong to the masses.

Visionary leader cannot do such because he or she is not interested in the death of citizens. The Scripture said that where there is no vision, the people perish. The visionary leader has the capacity to think and to plan the future with imagination and wisdom. Everything he or she does is consumed by his or her vision. His or her words, imaginations, actions are dictated by the vision he or she carries within. He or she sees prosperous future for the nation and its people and implements programs to revive it; therefore, it is unlikely for such individual to do something contrary to what will destroy his or her dream about the nation and its people. The author of Proverbs said, "He that keepth the law, happy is he "(Prov 29:18b). Godly vision is controlled by ethics because law has to with guidance and happiness; therefore, country that aspires for transformation for the betterment of its citizens needs to put politicians into public offices who have adopted some guidelines regarding ethical behavior. Does the president of the nation including government officials have the right ethically to have multiple sexual partners? Such leadership is an irresponsible leadership; therefore, what will the Liberian people expect from such leadership? He or she is living without being guided by ethics; therefore, he or she is opened to wrong doing and will embezzle the country's resources to support those multiple sexual partners. Vision is guided by ethics; therefore, its goal is to deliver happiness to the people; on the contrary, where there is no vision, the people die. This is the reason people die every day emotionally, psychologically, and physically in the corrupt nation due to the lack of visionary leadership. In the Liberia's context, the responsive actions required by the incumbent leadership to fulfill the visionary leadership include envisioning, patriotism, and the eradication of astronomical salary.

Envisioning

Domestic and national leadership should be characterized with seeing the future prosperous of the country and sincerely acting in the interest of her posterity; therefore, envisioning becomes the core accelerator to energize the vision leadership to see the broken system and therefore proactively decides to fix it. Understanding the political historical orientation of Liberia with reference to the foundational basis, Liberia has been built on corrupt practices; therefore, in order to fix the broken systemic systems requires the visionary leadership characterized with selflessness. Liberia was founded by the generation who had experienced dehumanization due to slavery that culminated into inequality, injustice, disparity, and among other manifestations of social injustices. Having this marginalized group of such dehumanized experience, the psychological tendency probable in most instances will be to extend her anger to others as the result of post traumatic stress disorder (PTSD) experienced during slavery in the America. Eventually, upon their arrival in Liberia in 1822, the settlers had confrontations with the aborigines coupled with some resistance; however, based on their sophistication with respect to weaponries for war, they overcame the resistance and eventually asserted their effort to take some territories from the inland leading to the development of the commonwealth of Liberia. Their experience in America as slaves coupled with the struggle to find a place in Africa became synergistic episode creating the psychological modes of xenophobia, ethnocentrism, and oligarchy leadership; consequently, this led to the creation of doubled-tiered elite structure of exclusions, disillusions and differentiations in order to marginalize the people of Liberia to participate in the social, political, economical, and civic life of the country. The past dehumanized experience clouded their vision and disabled them to see the people of Liberia with equal justice; therefore, patriotism was never envisioned because they saw Liberia as the land conquerable based on privilege of rule and consequently built the nation on corrupt practices; therefore, these people did not adopt the correct practice disconnect from the past experience in America as slaves. This is the human nature explicably exemplified in this situation. Leaders who had come to power came with the same mindset and therefore had committed crimes with impunity even when they left office. Justice is lacking because Liberia was built on injustice, inequality, corruption, and similar manifestations. What should the present leadership of the Third Republic do to be different from the First and Second republic? To build Liberia as a democratic society that will prosper in Africa, the systemic practices of corruption that have occurred in the First and Second Republic should be eradicated. The present leadership of the Third Republic cannot build on the shaking foundation the founding fathers had laid. The indicators are seen in the present leadership with reference to disparity in wealth distribution with reference to education, healthcare delivery, developments and among others. The constitution of the land affirms that citizens are entitled to receive the above immunities; unfortunately, these disparities will continue to be seen as the result of corrupt practices in the land. To change the status quo, the present leadership of the Third Republic should be a visionary leader disconnect from the former leaderships.

Patriotism

The words "patriotism" and "nationalism" are used sometimes together to give weight to an argument being presented; however, the two words differ in definition and practice; nevertheless, writer uses them sometimes together and close the argument that the two words should be adopted to give the meaningful relationship between a patriot and a nationalist based on practices. Complementation is the ideology presented in using the two words side by side; therefore, using one can complement the other. Based on historical evidence as behavioral psychology is concerned, adopting the two words practically to complete an argument is misleading because one is polarized on evil and selfishness while the other is polarized on good will for its people, nation, and for others' well-being. Nationalism is selfish and evil according to historical evidence as stated in the following paragraphs. "So it is the human condition that to wish evil to one's neighbors" said Voltaire. The rise of nationalism across the world, especially in the US, the UK, Russia, China, Germany, France, Hungary, and Italy is alarming. Nationalism is poisonous idea; for it is a feeling of superiority over others and hostility towards other nations. It naturally leads to interventionism, conflicts, and wars.[103]

Based on the above quotation, nationalism is linked to national birth of the individual that is inherently tied to the individual's commitment for his or her fatherland. The German's nationalism empowered Hitler to execute war on the entire globe and later brought shame to the Germen's people when Hitler massacred six million Jews in the Holocaust. Nationalism was also the factor in the 1990's that the Serbs massacred Muslims in Bosnia and Kosovo that was globally televised. Nationalism is destructive based on these historical evidences. George Santayana said, "Those who cannot remember the past are condemned to repeat it." The nationalist only cares for the nation he or she belongs to by birth; unless, all others are secondary to his or her agenda. In other word, it is impossible to be patriotic and to be nationalistic at the same due to conflict of interest. Being patriotic to the core is equivalent to breaking the norm for nationalism to the core. On the other hand, patriotism is the care for one's nation including others who are not related to you by national inheritance; on the contrary, nationalism only cares for one's nation while leaving out others. The colonists that arrived in Liberia in 1822, were not citizens of Liberia by birth; therefore, by national inheritance, their interests were not tied to the development of Liberia; nor could they practice patriotism because they did not carry the DNA for Liberia national birth; consequently, they isolated the people of the land for 133 years of rules due to the lack of patriotism. Patriotism is the care of one's country, people, and the care for its neighbors. To move Liberia to the better place on the globe, the present generation cannot build on the foundation of the founding fathers of Liberia because they did not leave a good legacy that the present generation can build on. Someone said that Liberia is like an elephant's meat; therefore,

---

[103] Lisa Schlein, "UN Rights Chief: Rise of Extreme Nationalism Threat to Global Peace," accessed August 24, 2022, https://www.voanews.com/a/un-rights-chief-rise-of-extreme-nationalism-threatens-global-peace-/4443998.html.

when you get there, you should cut your portion. The past leaders, who ruled Liberia, had cut theirs; therefore, refusing to cut yours, you will live in perpetual poverty when you leave office. This statement influences every politician who wishes national leadership of Liberia. Only true patriot will refuse to practice corruption because he or she cares for the people of Liberia. The true patriot gets his or her goal achieved when the future leaders of Liberia get educated, citizens get treated when they get sick, better housing, security and justice for all, development projects executed for the masses, and road networks are connected to make farmers and business people get their goods to the market; hence, only vision-patriot leader can have these on his or her mind.

Astronomical Salary Eradication

According to Transparency International, corruption is the intentional misuse of public resources for personal gain. It hurts everyone whose happiness depends on the integrity of people in a position of authority. When coupled with weak government systems and elites looking to take advantage of their power, corruption prevents the average citizen from accessing quality public goods and services like education, health care, or protection.[104]

The goal of general elections in the democratic system is to elect people who will fulfill their fiduciary responsibility to the electors. Representation means carrying out the demands, proposals, and aspirations of the citizens while delivering their aspirations to the Legislative Assembly during governmental sessions. That's being said, electors have the power to tell the central government what to do provided the representative is delivering to the central government the aspirations of the citizens during sessions. Liberia has organized corrupt practices when it comes to salary payment to government officials. This is an intentional misuse of public resources

---

[104] ASJ, "Association for a More Just Society, "accessed August 23, 2022, https://www. asj-us.org/?gclid=EAIaIQobChMIkJqe3dTf-QIVLtSzCh0vVwEPEAAYASAAEg-JQHPD_BwE.

that deny the ordinary citizens access to health care, education, protection, and the necessity for life. How can the Liberian people eradicate such organized crime in the Liberian society? The issue of astronomical salary can be addressed through citizens' involvement since the representatives and senators have become opposition to salary's reduction. The constituencies who have elected them into public offices during general elections can prevail on their representatives and senators using the medium of constitutionality. In this monograph, I have suggested few guidelines how to go about resolving this problem constitutionally. According to the Liberia's Constitution, Chapter II: General Principles of National Policy, Article 5 (c), states that citizens shall take steps, by appropriate legislation and executive orders, to eliminate sectionalism and tribalism, and such abuses of powers as the misuse of government resources, nepotism and all other corrupt practices.[105] Astronomical salary paid to representatives and senators monthly is the misappropriation of government resources that consequently denies ordinary citizens to benefit from health care, education, security, and among other necessities for life. According to Chapter I: Structure and State of Liberia's Constitution, Article 1, on quote: "All power is inherent in the people. All free governments are instituted by their authority and for their benefit and they have the right to alter and reform the same when their safety and happiness so require. In order to ensure democratic government which responds to the wishes of the government, the people shall have the right at such period and in such manner as provided for under this Constitution to cause their public servants to leave office and to fill vacancies by regular elections and appointments.[106] In this article, astronomical salary paid to government officials monthly jeopardizes the happiness of ordinary citizens due to social injustice being played out against citizens; therefore, the Liberia's Constitution has empowered citizens to change this astronomical salary payment through the law. This is an organized crime created against the

---

[105] Amos Sawyer, "Constitute: 1986 Liberia's Constitution," accessed December 19, 2021, Online: https://www.constituteproject.org/constitutions?lang=en.

[106] Ibid.

Liberian people; hence, they were elected to serve the Liberian people instead of exploiting them. According to Chapter XII: Amendments, Article 91, states that this Constitution may be amended whenever a proposal by either (1) two-thirds of the membership of both Houses of the legislature or (2) a petition submitted to the legislature by not fewer than 10,000 citizens which receive the concurrence of the two-thirds of the membership of both Houses of the Legislature, is ratified by two-thirds of the registered voters, voting in a referendum conducted by the Commission not sooner than one year after the action of the Legislature.[107]

If the salary payment to representatives and senators is the law, it can be changed by the citizens of the country without the involvement of the representatives and senators according to option (2) of the constitution-ality. It requires leadership put into place amongst the citizens of Liberia to make awareness to the voters according to their electoral districts. The leadership put into place by citizen volunteers is required to write a peti-tion outlining the issues of astronomical salary as the flaw. Once the doc-ument is written, have 10,000 citizens' signatories on the document who are qualified voters and have the document submitted to the Legislature. The registered voters whose signatories are on this document and who will vote to repeal this law should form two-thirds of the voters in the repre-sentative and senatorial controlled districts each. This document should be reviewed by the Legislature and acted upon according to law so that the referendum will be organized by the Election Commission of the country for voters to decide salary payment to representatives and senators. If there is the law in the Constitution that determines their own paid salary, it will be changed automatically once the citizens have casted their bal-lots to vote against it; then, the change will be made by the Constitution Review Committee of the country. If it is not a law, they will be liable for criminal offense against the Liberian people and restitution payment made to compensate the damage created by the administration. This is

---

[107] Ibid.

representative democracy; therefore, no one in the land including the president is immune to the law.

Solutions Recommendations:
The CED Formula

While the conclusion of the issue of the Liberia's political history is established, this monograph has adopted the CED formula for solutions recommendations. The CED formula is highly recommended for the readers to adopt since they are recommended solutions to the present problems of Liberia; therefore, they are solutions aspiring candidate can adopt in national leadership of Liberia in order to address the current situation that undermines democracy and peaceful co-existence in the land. These solutions recommendations constitute the constitutionalization, the educationalization, and the denationalization of the Liberia's constitution in order to eradicate corruption. Constitutionalization is the process of making the constitution of Liberia accessible to individuals and institutions on hard copy or online platform while educationalization is the teaching of the constitution to individuals and institutions via traditional classroom environment or online platform in order to inform the general public; additionally, denationalization is the process of getting rig of corrupt practices in government via anti-corruption committee in order to bring perpetrators to justice on corruption charges. The CED formula is highly recommended; therefore, citizens are encouraged to adopt these solutions recommendations to the Liberia's situations.

The Law's Constitutionalization

The constitutionalization of the law is the act of making the law accessible and available to everyone in the country through various media feasible and accessible. The constitution of Liberia is the blueprint by which the country is run; however, the law made to run the country is hidden from ordinary citizens when it has not been made accessible to them. Sometimes, it appears that people who have been elected as representatives and senators may know little about the constitution of the land. The instrument made to run the country is never put into effect in obscurity unless it is made known to the people for awareness; hence, it becomes the document of no virtues because leaders in the government will break the laws and they are never held accountable even when they leave office. The constitution becomes the written blueprint; however, it never guides how leaders conduct themselves during public service due to the ignorance of the constitution. For instance, the Liberia's Constitution, Chapter II: General Principles of National Policy, Article 5 (c), forbids tribalism, sectionalism, and corrupt practices in government; on the contrary, the government of Liberia is engulfed with corruption on the daily basis; ironically, no one has faced charges in the government with reference to corrupt practices. The law has been written to govern the nation for guidance, security, and happiness of the citizens; unfortunately, it has not been applied to fulfill what it has been written for. When laws written to fulfill these goals are ignored, it brings problems in the nation; therefore, criminals in government feel comfortable to commit crimes with impunity. We cannot maintain stable environment and democratic society for all when the law is not enforced. The United States of America understands how laws are useful to peaceful co-existence of her populations; therefore, she applies the law in order to hold perpetrators of the crimes accountable in order to maintain stability. The example is seen in the January 6, 2020 Capital's riot at which the federal government has arrested over four hundred people; hence, some are serving prison sentence between five and ten years.

The misapplication and non-enforcement of the Liberia's Constitution is the clear manifestation seen in the former administration led by Ellen Johnson-Sirleaf regarding corrupt practices at which she has not been brought to justice; though, the constitution provides that once the president leaves office, he or she should be held accountable for the criminalities committed provided the incumbent leadership starts the process. President George Manneh Weah could not indict her because he is guilty of the same criminality. The former President Ellen Johnson-Sirleaf and the lists that follow will be held accountable for crimes committed as Liberia is changing gradually to become democratic society. The incumbent president for 2023 general election and onward should be the candidate responsible to bring perpetrators to justice regarding corrupt practices in the Liberian government.

The issue of constitutionalization is required to provide the constitution to everyone in the country via hard copy or via website so that everyone can read the Constitution. It is the document of guidance; therefore, it should be made accessible to everyone in country who can read. Exposing the constitution to the people informs the public and creates the state of anxiety in government officials who are involved in wrong doing because the public will have known and proactively responded to their wrongs via whistle blowing. Constitutionalization is warranted to expose the Liberian public to the constitution of the country.

The Law's Educationalization

According to the Liberia's constitution, Chapter1: Structure and State, Article One, states that all power is inherent in the people and all free governments are instituted by their authority and for their benefits and they have the right to alter and to reform the same when their safety and happiness so require. Article Two states that the constitution is the supreme and fundamental law of Liberia and its provisions shall have binding force and effect on all authorities and persons through the Republic of Liberia. In these articles, Article One empowers citizens to exercise the law in the situation where changes are needed to affect their happiness and living condition positively while Article Two presents and guarantees the constitution as the working manual of the country. That's being said, the country cannot be run well when government officials are breaking the law with impunity. It is like operating the machine without observing the rules in the operational manual how the machine is operated. Two probable things are liable to happen; hence, the operator might get injured or the machine might get damaged. Metaphorically, this is contemporaneous to the country when people violate the law with impunity; consequently, citizens are going to get injured economically, emotionally, and socially. It is obvious that senators and representatives have been elected for representation; ignorantly, some might not know the constitution. No one knows their goal of running for public offices when they are unsighted to keeping the constitution and are unable to deliver the services to the people who have elected them. Recently, the Spoon TV visited the Pledeyee Township of 2021 in Nimba County in order to interview the residents. During the interview, the residents told Spoon TV that the district has only one mud palm covered school building in the province when there are several schools going children in the township. Mr. Kpan who has been elected as senator in 2020 Special Senatorial election has been the representative in the district for the past nine years; unfortunately, he did not deliver any services to the people who elected him while serving in this position; catastrophically, he has been elected by the same people to become senator when he did not perform the job as the representative during the nine years tenures; caution, there are several of Mr. Kpans in the Liberian government; similarly, nothing they have delivered to their people. Mr. Kpan's actions have two probable causes; primarily, he does not know his job descriptions as the representative. The second probable cause is, he knows his job descriptions; irresponsibly, he has failed to perform his fiduciary responsibility to the district. Based on the above analysis, the constitution should be taught to people who desire public office or learning it should be the requirement to holding public office. It is necessary for aspiring politicians to know what expectations are required of them before holding government jobs.

The Corruption's Denationalization

The systemic corruption established in Liberia's institution since 1847 to the present is the result of the degradation of the Liberian society; hence, corruption undermines national peace and leaves the country undeveloped perpetually resulting into endless poverty. Considering Liberia with reference to national resources, Liberia should have been the developed country in Africa. With reference to civilization post marking imperialism in Africa, Liberia became a land in Africa that had the first arrival of people who happened to have come from the civilized society and had never been colonized by foreign country. Liberia being founded by the freed people of colors did not experience imperialism as compared to other countries in Africa who had to fight for independence. The date of independence as the sovereign nation in Africa via the American Colonization Society is the *prographó* (past history) that Liberia was never colonized by a foreign nation. Despite of these, Liberia was not built on the foundation of justice due to systemic corruption seen since its foundation. To change this systemic corruption, corrupt practices in government must be denationalized. The term "denationalization" is the process of transferring an asset from public ownership, specifically ownership by a national government to private sectors. Corruption is a non-material asset that can be transformed to material assets when the crime is committed by the perpetrator in both government and private sectors. When politicians who aspire to hold public office, own corruption before holding government jobs, psychologically, corruption become systemic in the institution and consequently undermines national peace and development. Understanding the root causes of instability in the world, corruption must be denationalized to avoid imminent conflict in the Liberian society; hence, the denationalization of corruption is everyone's responsibility. To denationalize corruption in the country is to eradicate corruption permanently via systemic arrest of people in institutions who are involved in corrupt practices. Someone once said that Liberia is an elephant's meat; therefore, politicians must cut theirs when they get into public office. This statement is diabolical; therefore, corruption must not be practiced in the land. Corruption is the criminal act; unfortunately, there are past and present presidents in Liberia who are criminals; paradoxically, they are still called presidents. The Liberia's Constitution has labeled institutionalized sectionalism, tribalism, and corruption as the national crimes punishable by law when the president leaves office; ironically, the law is written as the instrument of the State as stated in the preamble; on the contrary, the law is theorized and not enforced. Criminals are running for government jobs to embezzle because the law of the land has not been applied; however, it is well written. Democratic values have not been kept nor solidified to avoid fragility of the society as the result of injustice in the land. This is the reason government officials take oath before they are inaugurated into the office; hence, the oath taken is the affirmation that he or she will uphold, protect, and keep the constitution of the land. The failure to uphold, to protect, and to keep it is breaking the constitution which is punishable through prison sentence, fines, or death. To denationalize corruption in Liberia, two solutions recommendations have been proposed; hence, they include the establishments of the Anti-corruption Committee and the Informed Committee.

The Anti-Corruption Committee

The organized Anti-corruption Committee shall be set up to constitute representatives from the thirteen sub-political divisions of the country to fight against corruption. This group is the humanitarian and advocacy group set up for advocacy on behalf of the Liberian people. This committee shall be organized, registered, and incorporated with the Liberian government to be functional and legitimate. This committee shall have access to declassified government financial records, records of government autonomous agencies, financial records of companies who do business with the government, and the revenues the country accumulates monthly. The committee needs these records to fight against corruption. The accessibility to these documentations positions the committee strategically to do research, to strategize plans, and to put into action plan how she identifies perpetrators of corruption and refers them to the Justice Department of the state's government for prosecutorial measures.

The Informed Committee

The second duty of the Anti-corruption Committee is to set up the Informed Committee within the Anti-corruption Committee. This committee shall be the in-group set up to educate voters the characteristics of politicians who should represent them and shall teach the constitution of Liberia to create educational awareness. The committee shall do so via information dissemination through organized seminars within the thirteen sub-political divisions of the country. During these conferences, the seminarians will be taught how they develop standards and expectations for their districts and have them submitted to politicians who want their votes during general elections; reasonably, electors should not vote for politicians in the vacuum. The politicians must promise the electors expectations achievable when they are elected into office and such expectations must be fulfilled during their tenures of administration. People who run for public office must have platform presented to the electors during campaign and must promise the electors those expectations achievable when they are elected into office. The people of Liberia shall be educated by the Informed Committee prior to provincial and general elections how and whom they vote for into public office; hence, in representative democracy, citizens should be educated why they vote for politicians in elections.

The Liberia's Elephant Meat

According to Lev Vygotsky, the Russian teacher and psychologist, that culture is the primary determinant of knowledge acquisition; therefore, he argued that children learn from the beliefs and attitudes modeled by their cultures.[108] From his philosophy of education, he developed the Socio-cultural Theory of Cognitive Development of children in the field of education. Complementarily, Erik Erikson, the ego psychologist, states that children learn through social interaction; therefore, he developed the

---

[108] Colin Lewis, "Ritual Education and Moral Development: A Comparison of Xunzi and Vygotsky, " *Dao* 17, no. 1 (2018): 81–98.

Psychosocial Theory of Cognitive Development of children in the field of education.[109] The two theories are closely intertwined; contemporaneously, the former advocates for cultural influences on learning while the later advocates for relational influences on learning; therefore, the common denominator between the two is cultural learning. Based on the above philosophical views of Lev Vygotsky and Erik Erikson, we can deduce that children are absorbed learners in the sense that what they see the elders do is what they practice immediately during their play times; cautiously, educators or parents need to know what they do before their children. Lev Vygotsky and Erik Erikson's statements are also true of adults whose brains are wired differently than children. Their theories explain the porosity, the fragility, and the complexity of the human beings when it comes to behavioral modes; in this light, boundaries should be set via good legislations to guide human's behavior in society. The emulation of bad behaviors others have adopted from bad actors against democratically elected governments recently regarding the over throw of the civilian governments, originated with Mali, followed by the Republic of Guinea; then, the Republic of Sudan, fulfills Lev Vygotsky and Erik Erikson's prophecy regarding human's behaviors. Military dictatorship is roaming over Africa; for this reason, America has huge tasks before her since she preaches democratic values in the world. The military in Mali has overthrown the democratically elected government; similarly, the military in Guinea and Sudan have done the same. What Lev Vygotsky and Erik Erikson have said about what children are when it comes to learning also affects adults proportionally; therefore, adults will do what others have done due to polarization of evil or good based on the choices that influence their decisions; therefore, human's behavior is affected by the psychosocial and socio-cultural effects in regardless of history, creed, religion, race, or geography. This is one of the reasons, good legislations (laws) should be put into effect to guide human's behavior in society; hence, those who break the laws should be punished in order to set deterrence.

---

[109] Eugene L. Thomas, "Values Psychosocial Development" (Westport, Conn: Aubum House, 1994), 3–12.

The elephant's meat situation with reference to corrupt practices in Liberia should be treated in this manner to say farewell to corruption. The statement "Liberia is an elephant's meat" teaches two negativities that aspiring politicians eventually will adopt when they are elected into public office. The pathological statement[110] "Liberia is an elephant meant" is seen in the Liberia's political history since 1847 to the present regarding the embezzlement of government's resources by government officials. The practical ramification about this pathological statement is demonstrated by the past and present governments of Liberia since 1980 to the now even when the coup d'etat had taken placed followed by the sixteen years civil insurrections. Past and present presidents of Liberia have committed crimes with no fear that they will be punished because Liberia is an elephant meat and those elected into public office should cut theirs before leaving office. This must stop; hence, it takes all Liberians united with one voice and one action to hold past and present leaderships accountable for these crimes committed against the Liberian people. Can you imagine how many Liberians have died due to lack of access to health care and other necessities for life because an individual has stolen the resources and therefore undermined financial accessibility to those health institutions in the country? Corruption has a criminal liability that equates to misdemeanor and felony; therefore, the deaths of those people should be attributed to the doings of politicians who have stolen government resources and denied citizens' access to social justice.

During the former President Ellen Johnson-Sirleaf's presidency, corruption overshadowed her legacy despite of maintaining the fragile peace in Liberia. When President George Manneh Weah ascended to the presidency, corruption has gone for the worst because he is not afraid to do what his predecessor had done. The elephant meat's statement controls the incumbent leader's psychological mode and drives his or her behavior when he or she gets into the presidency. The negative influence created by the elephant meat's statement include: (1) the psychological disorder for the incumbent

---

[110] Malcolm Galloway and JajTaiyeb, "The Interpretation of Phases Used to Describe Uncertainty in Pathology Reports," accessed August 23, 2022, https://www.hindawi.com/journals/pri/2011/656079/.

leaderships, and (2) the continued wrong doing in the Liberia's society regarding corrupt practices.

The Psychological Disorder

On the average, politicians who are running for public office in Liberia during general elections suffer from psychological disorder due to the statement that "Liberia is an elephant's meat especially the presidency. The psychological disorder tends to influence their ethics with reference to how they handle public property when they are elected into the presidency. It has become the norm for incumbent presidents of Liberia that once they are elected, they own the nation and everything in it. Psychologically, this is coded in their psychologies no matter what their religious affiliations are. There is no fear of God despite their church attendance; hence, they find it as the opportunity to cut the portion of their elephant's meat. Their psychosocial and socio-cultural responses when they ascend to the presidency are influenced by the past behaviors of their predecessors. This is the reason; corruption has become the generational trend since 1847 to the present. During the presidential debates in 2017, the former Vice President, Joseph Nyumah Boakai, said that corruption is the cancer that is hunting Liberia; therefore, something must be done about corruption. The development of the astronomical salary during the tenure of the former President, Ellen Johnson-Sirleaf's administration is influenced by the pathological statement that "Liberia is an elephant's meat." The former President did well to create the platform for representative democracy in Liberia; on the contrary, the administration has done the worst to allow her government to create such salary for government officials. The creation of such salary was premeditated and planned based on the statement that "Liberia is an elephant's meat." The astronomical salaries given to representatives and senators are briberies given indirectly; hence, this is called sectionalism in the Liberian government, the restriction of interest to a narrow sphere; undue concern with local interests for pretty distinctions at the expense of the general well-being of the people of Liberia. The wealth that should have been given to the various districts for development is being diverted to representatives and senators in Liberia. This undermines their ethics and the masses that live in these districts become the victims of social injustice in the land. Senator Abraham Darius Dillon recognized such social injustice in the country and proposed that salary being reduced and the remaining spread out for development. His recommendation was opposed by some elements in the government; nevertheless, the people who live in these districts can change the status quo about salary's reduction; hence, the resolution is being proposed in this monograph. Someone should take the responsibility to change corrupt practices in Liberia via legislation. Astronomical salary is the organized crime created by the past leadership of Liberia called corruption; therefore, something must be done about this crime that is killing Liberia.

The Misdeeds

According to the Executive Director, Mr. Matthias Yeanay, the Institute for Research for Democratic Development (IREDD), as interviewed on Spoon TV held January 17, 2022, said that ninety percent of the laws passed by the legislature come from the president of Liberia, George Manneh Weah. He said that the Liberia's Legislative Assembly is weak; therefore, the legislature is not working accordingly; instead, the legislature branch is working for the President instead for the people who have elected her. This is contradictory to the Liberian democracy; contrary, the executive branch is making laws and giving them to the legislature to have them passed; hence, this action is against the Liberia's constitution with reference to check and balance, functions, and separation of powers among the three branches of government as revealed in Chapter I: Structure of the State, Article 3.[111]

The Institute for Research for Democratic Development, IREDD, does evaluate the activities of members of representatives and senators in the Liberian government with reference to how members contribute

---

[111] Constitute, "Liberia's Constitution of 1986," accessed August 23, 2022, https://www.constituteproject.org/constitution/Liberia_1986.pdf?lang=en.

to discussions during sessions of the Liberian Legislative Assembly.[112] According to IREDD's Executive Director, Mr. Matthias Yeanay, said that most of the law makers that attend meetings during sessions do not contribute to the discussions; instead, they only pay attention in meeting and continued agreeing to proposals from the President's desk without opposition; therefore, the ten percent of laws that is legislated by the legislature has not been passed; instead, they sit on the President's desk and yet to be passed by the senate to become laws. In this chapter, I have proposed the establishment of the Anti-Corruption Committee and the Informed Committee to fight against corruption and to educate voters what caliber of politicians they should vote for during general elections. Most of these guys who are running for representative and senatorial positions are opportunists; therefore, electing them into office will only be adding to the present problems of Liberia. Opportunists are not useful; therefore, they do not have meaningful platforms in the interests of the people they claim to represent; instead, they are looking to grasp something to fill their pockets. The practical example is President George Manneh Weah; hence, the indicators are seen right before the eyes of the Liberian people with reference to the complexes he has built for himself using government's resources less than two months when he took office; hence, he refused to reveal his assets to the Liberian people when he was asked to do so. The Law makers who do not contribute to discussions are bought already due to the astronomical salary these guys received monthly. Liberia has thieves instead of credible government because the people who elected these guys into office lack representation in the central government. These guys are decorations and opportunists and are making fun of the Liberian people. How can they justify the pay they are taking monthly when they cannot pass one law to affect their constituents? This is flaw in the Liberian government that is hurting the Liberia's population.

---

[112] "The Institute for Research for Democratic Development, IREDD, "accessed August 23, 2022, https://www.devex.com/organizations/institute-for-research-and-democratic-development-iredd-98812.

The elephant's meat statement is the psychological disorder that influences aspiring politicians to adopt when they come to power thereby leading them to continue the misdeeds in the Liberian society. To deal with the elephant's meat statement which has created the psychological disorder to influence incumbent leader to practice misdeeds, corruption must be punished according to the law. Past presidents who are still alive and have been alleged to have carried out corruptions should be brought to justice according to the law as revealed in the constitution, Chapter II: General Principles of National Policy, Article 5 (c).[113]

Ethical Reflection

Liberia is a young democracy; therefore, some aspiring politicians are novices to democracy and democratic values; as the result, there are fights seen amongst members of the political parties in Liberia who should become the standard bearers for their parties during Presidential General Election especially those parties that lost in the presidential election recently. This gives ground to the ruling party to hold the political ground in the various political subdivisions of Liberia. Voters who want to take turn or change direction to vote differently at this time are confused what decision to take. If voters cannot see credibility amongst the opposition parties, they will decide to keep the corrupt ruling party into power in Liberia. This is the dilemmas in the Liberia political body politics because politicians are opportunists who want to get into power to continue the bad legacy of corruption from the predecessor; inferentially, this is one of reasons there are power struggle amongst them. The subject of corruption and ritualistic killings in Liberia are issues that are engulfing the nation. Ethically, corruption and murder are crimes punishable by God; however, corruption and ritualistic killings in Liberia have become normal. This reminds the audience with reference to who is responsible to keeping national security in Liberia? The government of Liberia has

---

[113] Ibid.

the fiduciary responsibility to have criminals deterred through systemic arrests in order to keep national security for all; hence, the failure to do so is the relinquishment of fiduciary responsibility.

CHAPTER VII
AMERICANIZATION

Chapter Overview

Americanization defines the state of characterization of what makes up the character or the nationality of Americans; therefore, in the context of americanization, this section of the monograph delineates the interconnectivities between America and Liberia while discussing the American political history and body politics in the spotlights. Liberia being a unitary state as opposed to a federal state, there are interconnectivities between Liberia and America with reference to branches of government, foreign relations, colonization, commerce, democracy, membership to international organizations, bilateral representation, and body politics; therefore, based on these interconnectivities that resonate with the commonalities of Liberia to that of America, it is expedient to study the American body politics inclusive taking into consideration liberalism and conservatism as seen across the American body politics since Liberia endeavors to practice representative democracy; meanwhile, this section of the monograph covers the American political history with reference to conservatism versus liberalism, racial discrimination, white evangelicalism in the American body politics, role conflicts between white evangelicalism and the Republican party, the liberal stance of the Democratic Party on abortion and homosexuality, the roles of the church in body politics, and the rationale of the separation between state and religion. At the conclusion, the author has developed a reflection on the chapter to redress the subject in order to pin a mental picture in the mind of the reader for personal subjective reflection.

Interconnectivities between the United States and Liberia

The emergence of the nation Liberia is rooted in the United States of America as the result of the Emancipation Proclamation declared by President Abraham Lincoln in 1863 when tension intensified between the Northern and Southern States of the United States during American Civil War. The result of the Emancipation Proclamation led to the formation of the American Colonization Society to repatriate people of color to the continent of Africa; therefore, Liberia was chosen to repatriate freed slaves who thought could not be integrated into the American society due to disparity that resonated with racial issues and social injustice. Over the past 133 years of Liberia's existence, Liberia has faced episodes of challenges of compliance and resistance with respect to Pan-Africanism, new policy direction toward socialism, the end of the First Republic due to coup d'état, the intensification of armed conflicts, and the genesis of the Third Republic; connectively, the United States of America has been the major player and the interventionist direct and indirect in these past and present incidences militarily, economically, and reconciliatory.[114]The issues of United States Liberia relations, the United States assistance to Liberia, the bilateral economic relations, membership to international organizations, and bilateral representation interconnect the United States of America to Liberia; therefore, the issue of interconnectivity between Liberia's body politics to that of the America's warrants their study alongside. The United States of America diplomatically established relations with Liberia in 1864 after Liberia had declared its independence from the American Colonization Society. After 133 years of rules, the party that controlled its independence from 1847 ended in 1980 via coup d'état led by the late

---

[114] Niels Hahn, "Two Centuries of US Military Operation in Liberia: Challenges of Resistance and Compliance" (Alabama: Air University Press, 2003) 3–192.

Samuel Kanyon Doe. From 1980 to 2003, Liberia has experienced misrule and insurrection until a fragile peace began in 2005 after the presidential election that resulted to the former President Ellen Johnson-Sirleaf being elected as President for the post-war Liberia. The latest national election held October 10, 2017 led to the election of President George Manneh Weah. Based on democratic values Liberia tries to endorse, the United States has continued to partner with government donors, international organizations especially the World Health Organization and civil society in order to galvanize the Liberia health care system; therefore, the United States assistance and engagement are critical to Liberia's long-term development that resonate with the interconnectivity.

Other areas of the United States assistance are focused on fostering democratic progress, improving capacity, transparency, accountability of institutionalized governance, promoting broad based market-driven economic growth, improving access to education and health services, professionalizing the Liberia's military and civilian security forces, assisting Liberia build capacity to plan and to implement, and sustaining its development efforts to each governmental sector.

With reference to bilateral economic relations, Liberia is eligible for preferential trade benefits under the African Growth and Opportunity Act. Its revenues primarily come from rubber, iron ore, and its maritime registry program (fishery, seafaring, and military). Liberia's United States owned and operated shipping and corporate registry is the world's Second-largest United States exports to Liberia including agricultural products, vehicles, machinery, optic and medical instruments, and textiles. The main imports from Liberia to the United States include rubber, allied products, wood, art and antiques, palm oil, and diamonds. The United States government and Liberia have signed a trade and investment framework agreement and both are members of the United Nations, International Monetary Fund, and the World Bank.[115]

---

[115] CIA World Factbook Liberia Page, "U.S Relations with Liberia," accessed August 23, 2022, https://www.state.gov/u-s-relations-with-liberia/.

History of the American Political Parties

The oldest party founded in 1828 in the United States is the Democratic Party; then, the Republican Party followed in 1854; however, the histories of the two parties are intrinsically connected with reference to background and the Founding Fathers.[116] Based on diverse political views of the Founding Fathers, two factions of the parties emerged eventually. George Washington, Alexander Hamilton, and John Adam thus established the Federalists; ideologically, the Founding Fathers of the Federalists sought to ensure a strong government coupled with central banking system with the national bank while Thomas Jefferson and James Madison, the Founding Fathers for the Democratic Party; ideologically, they advocated for a smaller and decentralized government. During the emergence of the 19th century, the Democratic-Republican Party gained prominent due to her victories in general elections; as the result, the Federalists gradually faded leading to dissolution. Due to the popularity of the Democratic-Republican Party, the Party had no less than four political candidates rivaled against one another in the presidential election of 1824. During this election, John Quincy Adam won the presidency, in spite of Andrew Jackson winning the popular vote. This sparked political division within the Democratic-Republican Party and eventually caused the party to split into two. After the split, Andrew Jackson, who was against the existence of the Bank of the United States and largely supported States' right and minimal government regulation, became the leader of the Democratic Party. With reference to political opposition, the Whig Party stood in the opposition to Jackson and the Democrats and supported the National Bank formation.

The donkey in the Democratic Party's logo is said to derive from Andrew Jackson's opponents who called him a "jackass." Jackass is the word that refers to the male donkey and the nickname that describes

---

[116] Abraham and Mary Lincoln, "Political Party Timeline: 1836–1864, "accessed August 23, 2022, https://www.pbs.org/wgbh/americanexperience/features/lincolns-timeline/.

an unintelligent or foolish person. Andrew Jackson embraced it unconsciously; as the result, it has become a symbol of the Democratic Party.

In the mid-nineteenth century, the issue of slavery became political
in the American body politics. The Democratic Party internal views on
the issue of slavery differed. Southern Democrats wished for slavery to
be expanded while Northern Democrats argued that this issue should be
settled on the local level and through popular referendum. This brought
the Democratic Party the infighting and made Abraham Lincoln who
belonged to the Republic Party to win the presidential election of 1860.
This was different version of the Republican Party that was founded by a
group of Whigs, Democrats, and other politicians who had broken from
the respective parties in order to form a party based on anti-slavery model.

After the inauguration of Abraham Lincoln, tensions between the
Southern and Northern States became high causing the American Civil
War to break out in 1861. During the civil war, seven Southern States
formed the Confederate States of America and fought for detachment from
the United States; however, the Union won the war and the Confederacy
was formally dissolved. The issue of slavery was at the center of political
disagreement during the civil war leading the Republicans to fight for
abolition of slavery; therefore, Abraham Lincoln signed the Emancipation
Proclamation in 1863. At this time in history, the United States South
was predominantly Democratic and held a conservative, agrarian-overfed,
and anti-big business values. The majority of the Northern voters were
Republicans, many of whom fought for civil and voting rights for African-
Americans. After the war, the Republican Party became oriented towards
economic growth, industry, and big business in the Northern States at
the onset of the 20th century. Many Republicans gained financial success
in the 1920s until the stock market crashed in 1924 leading to the Great
Depression in human history.

During the Great Depression, many Americans blamed Republican
President, Herbert Hoover for the crisis; therefore, he lost the election to
the Democrat, Franklin D. Roosevelt. To get the country back on track,
Roosevelt introduced and launched the progressive government-funded

social programs, ensuring social security, improved infrastructure, and minimum wage. Southern Democrats, whose political views were more traditional and conservative, did not support Roosevelt's liberal initiatives; instead, they joined the Republican Party. Roosevelt's progressive, liberal policies play an important role in shifting the Party's political agenda to look like the modern Democratic Party today. Roosevelt died in 1945 and the Democrats stayed in power with Harry S. Truman in the White House. He continued to take the Democratic Party in a progressive direction with a pro-civil rights platform and desegregation of the military forces, thereby gaining support from a large number of African-American voters, who had supported the Republican Party previously because of its anti-slavery platform.

The Democratic Party stayed in power until 1980, when Republican Ronald Reagan was elected as President. His social conservative politics and emphasis on cutting taxes, preserving family values, and increasing military funding were important steps in defining the Modern Republican Party platform. Following Reagan's two terms in office, his Vice President, George H.W. Bush was elected as his successor in the White House. Since then Republicans and Democrats have taken turns in the White House. In 2008, Democrat Barack Obama was elected as the first African American President. One of the Obama's most political achievements was the reforming American health care with the Affordable Care Act called Obamacare. After the two terms in office, he was succeeded by the Republican, a well-known business man Donald Trump who was elected in the White House in 2016. Two of the main accomplishments on Trump's agenda was providing tax reliefs and to establishing strong borders in order to reduce undocumented immigrants entering the United States. In 2020 Presidential General Election, Democratic Party's previous Vice President for former President, Barack Obama, Joseph Biden was elected as the 46th President of the United States.

Brief History of the American Political Parties and Ideologies

In the political arenas with reference to the American political platform, ideologies of the political beings influence the decision they will
make that directs them to particular party that appeals to their political
emotions; therefore, it is with those who belong to the Republican or the
Democratic Party on the political spectrum that defines their decisions
and behaviors toward the parties.[117] Ideologically, the two major political parties of America correspond closely with conservative and liberal
ideologies. These ideologies influence the United States policy debates
with reference to foreign and national issues that often resonate with the
appropriate amount of government intervention in the economy and
social behavior of the people. Despite of the strong correlation between
individual's ideology and the party he or she belongs to, Americans hold
array of opinions on the economic and social issues that don't always agree
neatly on to the simple "left-right wing" ideology that dictates individual
beliefs on multiple dimensions on the political spectrum of the left and
right wings' ideologies corresponding to liberal and conservative views.

With reference to conservatism, conservatives tend to believe that government should operate on the States or local level. They favor minimum
government intervention and private sector-based solutions to problems
solving. They believe that government imposes restrictions on contraception, abortion, and homosexuality. Based on their beliefs, conservatives
are said to fall on the "right wing" of the axis of the political ideologies.
The Republican Party supports conservative ideologies and falls on the
"right wing" of the axis of the political spectrum.

With reference to liberalism, liberals tend to believe that government
should intervene into the economy and provide a broad range of social
services to ensure the well-being and equality across society. Liberals
believe that government should not regulate the private sexual or social
behavior of the populations. They are said to fall on the "left wing" of

---

[117] Ibid.

the axis of the political ideologies. The Democratic Party supports liberal ideologies and falls on the "left wing" of the axis of the political spectrum.

With reference to progressive ideology, liberal and progressive are interchangeably by many; however, some have argued that the two words are different. Those who believe the terminologies as separate believe that liberals tend to protect the disadvantaged populations from discriminations while progressives believe that it is the government's responsibility to address past wrong doings and bring reform to systemic problems as the result of those disadvantages that caused them.

With reference to communitarianism, this ideology supports legislation that supports the need of the community over the rights of the individual. This group in the American body politics is economically liberal; however on the other hand, it is socially conservative. This group carries the ideologies of the Republican and the Democratic Parties.

The third largest party in the United States founded in 1971 by people who felt that the Republican and Democratic Parties no longer represented the libertarian intentions of the founders is called Libertarian Party; hence, libertarianism tends to favor limited government intervention in the personal, social and economic issues of the populations.

The fourth largest political party in the United States founded in 2001 is called the Green Party. With reference to the Green Party's ideology, it tends to favor strong federal government's intervention. The politician who supports this ideology often runs on the platform of grassroots democracy, non violence, social justice, and environmentalism; therefore, the Green Party's ideology is the hybrid of the Democratic Party's ideology.

The last political party's ideology in the United States is called nationalism. Nationalists' ideology tends to promote the interests of their nation and often believe in the superiority of their nations over others. This group is the hybrid of all the political party's ideologies in the United States; therefore, such group believes in interventionalism and can be the threat to patriotism based on historical evidence across the globe.

Brief History of Liberalism and Conservatism

The ideologies liberalism and conservatism emerged and developed during the French Revolution and the Napoleonic era.[118] The terminologies have recurred throughout the political history of the 19th century in the world influenced by European philosophy. During the era of change, the two ideologies drew a contrast between those who agitated for reform and those who inclined to protect existing values of society against what they saw as a destructive and corrosive influence. Prior to the renaissance of these ideologies, the group called "liberals" initially existed as a political party in Spain in 1810 when the French occupation prompted the gathering of an independent Cortes in Cadiz. At this gathering, the delegates split into two groups and became known as the *Liberales* and *Serviles*.[119] The *Liberales* were in favor of reform while the *Serviles* were against reform. The *Serviles* wished to continue the Spanish tradition of absolute monarchy while at this gathering, the *Liberales* won and wrote the constitution of 1812 paving the way for parliamentary election for the monarch, freedom of the press, and other radical measures. The delegates at this gathering included members from the Latin America, where the independent movements were already under way. The ideology on the other axis birthed the term "liberation" followed by the other ideology called " conservative" used after the restoration of the monarch in French for those in favor of the reactionary backlash aims to mend the damage perceived to have been done by French revolution principles. Both ideologies are within the traditions much older than the immediate circumstances which bring into existence. The liberal emphasizes on reason, education, secular values and personal liberty while the conservative loves of tradition, established order and ritual has its roots far back in the Christian culture of the Middle Ages. Underlying the intellectual

---

[118]Robert E. Brown, "Liberalism, Conservatism, and History" (Michigan: Michigan State University Press, 1963), 317–326, accessed August 22, 2922, https://www.jstor.org/stable/23737551.

[119] Ibid.

differences of opinion, there is immediate and divisive political agenda played out. The liberals advocated for a redistribution of wealth whiles the conservatives' ancient ideals, frequently have something of their own to conserve. These words have won most lasting connection with two British political parties, where the distinction between them is somewhat blurred. They are used in a much clearer sense in Catholic countries in the 19ᵗʰ century, particularly in Latin America where anti-clerical liberals struggle, usually without much success, against conservatives allied with the powerful church of Rome.

Political Campaign and White Evangelicalism

Bend writes, "What do Barack Obama and Saral Palin have to do with your mental health? In the past, I have literally seen people whose bodies are in knots and whose friendships and family relationships are completely strained due to an election. People become imbalanced, stressed-out, irritable, and potentially aggressive to those who do not share their views."[120]

The above statement narrates the roles played by politicians with reference to conservatism and liberalism on body politics and their effects they have on political adherences. Politicians use ideologies during campaign to win the supports of those who belong to their ideologies of political spectra in order to win the majority votes. In the American body politics, Democrats are considered liberal on the political spectrum while Republicans are considered conservative; therefore, despite of their religious affiliations, these ideologies tend to influence their political beliefs. Democrats, who attend church belonging to the Catholics or the Protestants, tend to support the social and sexual behaviors of the American populations with reference to abortion and homosexuality, and individual rights that are opposed to conservative's stance. On the other hand, the Republicans, who are conservative generally tend to go against

---

[120] Gulf Bend Center, "Liberal Morality VersusConservative Understanding the Difference Can Help You Avoid Arguments," accessed August 23, 2022, https://www.gulfbend.org/.

the liberal's stance concerning these ethical issues that are considered destructive and corrosive in the American society; therefore, there are political and religious wars that are psychologically being fought in the American body politics during political campaign. Both parties use their ideologies as leverages to win general elections; contemporaneously, politicians use their ideologies and their political convictions during political campaign to win the support of their audiences. The former President, Donald Trump; even though, he does not represent true conservative values, has used conservative ideologies and messages during the campaign to win the white Evangelicals and the Catholics votes during 2016 general election. The issue of conservatism among the Republicans and the White Evangelicals has brought role conflicts between the White evangelical churches of America and the Republican Party with respect to the legislation of morality that has instigated roles conflict between the Republican Party and the White Evangelical churches of America. Do the White Evangelical churches that seem to support conservatism based on religious beliefs actually represent conservative conviction? Why made some Protestant churches of America to support liberal ideologies with respect to abortion and homosexuality? These questions are answered in this monograph.

Bend writes, "Some of what makes political disagreements tense is the sense that many people believe that those people who disagree with their own position "don't understand. They think that if they could just figure out a better way to communicate what makes their policies and their politicians a superior choice over opponent policies and politicians that the "misguided" people they are speaking with would somehow come around to their way of thinking. The sense that the other side does not understand what is really important leads to immense frustration and sometimes to anger and anxiety."[121]

The above quotation explains the complexity of human's misconception with reference to behavior and how political campaigners endeavor

---

[121] Ibid.

to establish relationships with their potential supporters; for this reason, everyone should know that liberals and conservatives think differently. Understanding this as politicians will alleviate lot of immense frustrations and the traumas politicians and their adherences encountered when they lost general elections. Understanding such and acting in context is the indication of maturity and can lead to peaceful transfer of power when the sitting president or ordinary politician is defeated in general election.

The American historians have been concerned with reference to the roles of the White Evangelicalism in the American politics especially when they supported overwhelmingly Donald Trump in 2016 presidential election when the moral life of Donald Trump does not represent the culture of Christianity based on past history on his assault on women and the numerous divorces he had had.[122] Based on public concern coupled with the American historians' concern, six questions were asked by the public to the American historians to find the motivation behind why White Evangelical Churches in America are always supporting the modern Republican Party. The questions presented were survey questions; therefore, each of the historians responded to the questions. From the answers given by the historians independently, the community found among the answers that favored racism that has to do with segregation and desegregation of the American public schools; although, there are other factors that are tied to ethical issues such as abortions, homosexuality, and feminism. Historian Martin writes,

> In recent history, several critical turns and factors have led the overwhelming majority of the White Evangelicals to move toward the modern Republican Party. One factor in this shift was the modern civil rights era and the black freedom struggle. The Brown V. Board Supreme Court decision outlawed the segregation of public schools. In turn, a number of White Evangelical communities opened

---

[122] The American Historian, "Evangelicalism and Politics," accessed August 23, 2022, https://www.oah.org/tah/issues/2018/november/evangelicalism-and-politics/.

private schools as a way to oppose school desegregation, framing their hostility to Brown V. Board as an expression of religious freedom other than a defense of racial segregation. Elementary and secondary schools such as Revered Jerry Falwell's Lynchbury Christian School and collages such as Bob Jones University became known as segregation academies.

The question why, the White Evangelical churches in America supported former President, Donald Trump during the 2016 general election when he does not represent Christian value is the fact that the White Evangelical churches support racism based on the evidence as stated in the above quotation. The quotation from one of the historians as quoted above in response to the survey question the public posed to determine the motivation behind why White Evangelical Churches of America do support the modern Republican Party is rooted in racism and other factors that have to do with abortion and homosexuality. When some States in the United States decided to desegregate public schools to make them inclusive for both black and white people, the White Evangelical Christian churches in the United States decided to form private elementary, secondary, and colleges to keep their students white. It is unthinkable that people who call on the name of Jesus can still be engrained with racism. This is the actual truth that still exists in the United States of America in regardless of some church going people. The Protestant Churches of America on the other hand stand on different polarities of the axes; therefore, there are divides between the Protestant churches and the White Evangelical churches of America when it comes to civil rights, social justice, and the issues of race.

The quotation above speaks volume on their stance on racism in America. Donald Trump is believed to be racist; though, his supporters disagreed with the label; nevertheless, his action speaks very clearly and no one can deny it. It should not be surprise that some White Evangelical churches of America supported Donald Trump because he agrees with their stance on abortion and homosexuality; however, some supported him because he is the racist. The Republican Party and the White Evangelical's stances on conservative values are excellent; on the other hand, their stances on racism and the Republican Party refusal to agree with the Democratic Party to enact gun safety control laws in the United States to minimize gun violence do not support conservative values according to the norm of conservative Christianity. One does not become true conservative if one hypocritically believes in one conservative Christian's value; on the contrary, one refuses to believe and to uphold the others. One cannot be the follower of Jesus; however, one refuses to live up to Christian's value. This is the flaw in the Republican Party; even though, the party has identified herself to be conservative in the American body politics. This makes some members of the Republican Party including the White Evangelical churches to be what they are not based on conservative values. When it comes to helping the marginalized communities of America in order to minimize both economic and social disparities, some members who are Republicans in Congress usually oppose these positions; on the other hand, the Democratic Party usually supports these positions to help the marginalized communities of America.

The modern Republican Party that has labeled the Democratic Party in America as liberal and corrosive to conservative values, has taken the back seat on the issue of social and criminal injustices toward the marginalized community of America and refused to enact safety gun's law to minimize gun violence; however, she has presented herself to be good; on the contrary, she opposed those positions considered as humanitarianism. The Democratic Party labeled as liberal; evidentially, the party represents such moral fall off; however, she preaches against social injustice with reference to the distribution of wealth in favor of the marginalized community. If the Republican Party is the party of Abraham Lincoln; then, she should stand for those values Abraham Lincoln stood for. The behavior of the modern Republican Party towards the marginalized community has caused the black protestant churches of America to join the Democratic Party and consequently support liberal position on the issues of abortion and homosexuality. The conservative flaw seen among the modern Republican Party on the issues of injustice with reference to social and criminal justices has made the black people who initially supported the Republican Party to take different position during general election. If the Republican Party believes to stand for conservative values; similarly, she should also stand against gun violence, racism and inequality in the American society. Members of Congress who constitute the Republican Party do so when they agree with the Democratic Party in passing gun's law that alleviate gun violence in the United States. Members of the Republican Party cannot allow their political expediencies to overshadow their conservative values they claimed to be when children had been massacred at Sandy Hook Elementary School, Rob Elementary School and numerous public assemblies in the United States.

Flaws in the American Republican Conservatism

The ideology regarding conservatism is tied to religious Christianity. Conservative practices values in the context of the Christian religion based on historical evidence; therefore, conservative values are tied to the practice of doctrine that has to do with righteousness, good will toward humanity, and negating those values considered as corrosive and destructive. In the American political arena, there are two divides on the spectrum based on these values systems that influence the party's decision on both domestic and foreign policies. The Republican Party is known as the party that practices conservative values; therefore, she is against abortion and homosexuality and other manifestations that show such abominable behavior in society; however, there are flaws seen in the Republican Party based on her response with reference to social and criminal justice system in the American society. One of the flaws seen in the party is the opposition to services offered to the middle class that promote her well-being. In congressional decision making, members of congress of the Republican Party often oppose those services that help the marginalized community such as government health insurance, food stamp, and stimulus package that the federal government should be held responsible to provide. This party is always in supportive of the rich people in America and careless about the middle class. If she is truly conservative and stands for Christian values, which defines her to be, it is necessary that she supports those services that help the marginalized community based on religious values as the doctrine of conservatism teaches based on the Scripture (Jas 5:15–17). This is one of the conservative's flaws in the Republican Party. The Democratic Party who is labeled as liberal in the American body politics does advocate on behalf of the vulnerable populations; therefore, she usually passes legislations in the interest of the middle class; in opposition, most of these bills are opposed by the Republican Party. When it comes to gun legislation to control guns in America due to gun violence, the Republican Party often opposes it despite of people being killed in mass shooting. Understanding that America is the gun culture, even those who attend church who consider themselves to be conservative do not actually represent conservative values when it comes to passing gun's law to alleviate gun violence in the American society. The present modern Republican Party is camouflaged with past attire of conservatism; on the contrary, the majorities of members do not practice conservative values based on political expediencies.

The Sandy Hook Elementary School shooting at which 29 school children were massacred; proactively, the Democrats advocated that gun legislation be passed regarding universal background check for gun carriers in the nation; in opposition, the Republicans opposed the proposal; ironically, the Republican Party is claimed to be conservative. Conservatives should not oppose law that helps reduce gun violence in the United States; on the contrary, they often oppose gun safety laws in the United States. What then is conservative value? Standing against corrosive behavior in order to maintain moral value for the salvation of the human society should define conservatism; ironically, if the Republican Party, who claimed to be conservative can oppose gun legislations to reduce gun violence; then, there is a conservative flaw that goes against conservative values that is proportionally opposed to Christian values; then, religion with reference to Christian conservatism is undefined; consequently, it is also misapplied to practical living in both the religious and the secular worlds. This is one of the flaws seen in the Republican Party with reference to opposing laws that reduce gun violence in the United States.

The Republican's stance against the manifestations of ugliness considered as corrosive or destructive in the American society is good with reference to abortion and homosexuality; hypocritically, they refused to stand against the other ugliness with reference to supporting gun legislation to minimize gun violence and disparities seen in the American society. This is not true conservatism; instead, it is hypocrisy played out that undermines the prosperity and peace of others. Conservatism is synonymous to true religion and should stand against violence nature in any society. Apostle James defined true religion as taking care of orphans and widows (Jas 5:15–17); hence, conservatism should represent true religion; therefore, the Republican Party needs to redefine her practice regarding conservative values if she chooses to carry this image as partisans. When Donald Trump lied regarding the 2020 presidential election, some members of the Republican Party supported his lie up to the present; therefore, they have passed laws in their controlled States to marginalize the voters of color during election because they believe in Donald Trump's lie that the election was stolen. Conservatives should stand for the truth; on the contrary, some members of the Republican Party have supported this lie; even though, they know that it is a lie. True conservatives should support legislation that minimizes gun violence in the American society and should oppose or disagree with lies perpetrated by members of the party. There are few members in the modern Republican Party that believe and practice conservative values on the average.

Can States Legislate Morality?

The question whether state can legislate morality should be defined in two contexts. Primarily, morality should be defined in the context of society on two polarities. These polarities of ethical decision include relativism and absolutism because what could be considered morally wrong in one society relatively could be considered morality right for another society; therefore, the issue of morality becomes complex looking at the two divides based on the human's behaviors; as the result, morality should be defined in two contexts. The two poles presented in morality become complex to define morality in the context of societies; however, considering biblical morality makes it simple to define morality disregarding humanistic approach. Primarily, to get the situation settled with reference to whether government has the power to legislate morality, one must first consider the absolute. The doctrine of absolutism teaches that there are intrinsically objective moral truth and value system according to the moral law; therefore, true morality should be defined in the context of this universal value system which originates with God according to the Ten Commandments (Exod 20:1–20). The laws in the Ten Commandments should be the template used as the metrics by government to legislate morality knowing that not all laws enacted by men can support morality that relates to absolute truth; therefore, laws legislated by government can become immoral in society based on social justice or individual rights. This makes it difficult for government to legislate morality that has to do with absolute truth in society. If government agrees that every law passes should be absolute across all cultures as defined by the moral laws; then, the government might be infringing on the individual's conscience and then tends to undercut its own legitimacy with reference to the other side of the law that talks about individual's liberty in the democratic society. Even in the Muslim's nations that enforce the *Sharia's* law regarding morality in the context of the Islamic religion, the people who live in these nations still find it difficult to keep these laws. According to biblical history, God gave the moral law to Israel via Moses; unfortunately, the children of Israel found it difficult to live by the law due to the sinful nature. The law was the school master to direct them to God; on the contrary, it did not empower them to live it; therefore, it took the atonement substitution sacrifice of Jesus Christ on the cross to make mankind to live for God through grace. No one is justified by keeping the law except through grace that comes through Christ. The Old Testament legislated morality through the Mosaic Covenant; however, Israel was unable to live the law. The legislation was given by God through Moses; however, men did not legislate morality; instead, men tended to enforce the law. Can government legislate morality? Government can use the moral law as the standard for living to enforce morality; on the other hand, government cannot legislate morality because she will be infringing on the individual's conscience and thus misses the way God planned it from the beginning. God, who created the heaven and the earth does not infringe on the individual's conscience to violate him or her because He created mankind as the free moral agent to choose between the right and the wrong. God is holy, omniscience, omnipresence, and omnipotence; however, He does not force anyone to keep His law. Had He done so, He would have prevented sin in the Garden of Eden.

The God of the Bible does not force anyone to obey His law; on the other hand, He gives mankind freedom of choice despite of his omnipotence, omniscience, and omnipresence nature that defines His transcendence nature among the gods of the world; therefore, religious movements that legislate morality and force it on their subjects should be questioned if they are serving God, the Creator. Equally so, government might tend to legislate morality based on the moral law; however, government does not have the right to legislate morality and force it on the citizens. God is the only person who is qualified to legislate morality; however, based on abortion carried out in the United States and similar manifestation of wrong doings, legislation of morality amongst the Republican Party has become politicized since the Republican Party is known to be conservative in the American body politics. Politicians in the Republican Party who aspire to run for public offices usually use the platform of conservatism to appeal to voters. Donald Trump used it; therefore, he was able to win the White Evangelical's votes during the 2016 presidential election despite of his conservative flaws. In their fights against abortion and similarly manifestations of destructive nature contrary to conservatism, the Republican Party has passed laws in their controlled States in America to legislate morality with reference to abortion. This is the fight seen in America between the Republican Party and pro-abortion movement; however, the Republican Party has been successful in passing the laws in their controlled States to hinder those who are in the constant habit of killing children through abortion. Abortion is the business in America; therefore, some medical practices are specialized to abort children. This has become income business because the present generation cannot live without having sex; however, the consequential of illicit sexual activities can lead to unwanted pregnancy. This is the roles conflict between the church and the Republican Party in the American body politics when it comes to the legislation of morality based on the party's conservatism.

In her fights against abortion, homosexuality, and similar manifestations, the Republican Party tends to legislate morality in her controlled States with reference to passing laws that prohibit pro-abortion's right activists to exercising their individual's liberty as defined by the American destructive social justice system regarding individual's right. These laws passed to legislate morality are tried in the court systems to be challenged based on the individual's liberty as constitutionality is defined in the American's context. Despite of the party's effort to legislate morality, the pro-abortion rights activists still fight back through the court system to claim and to protect their individual liberty; therefore, it has become the normal lifestyles to abort babies. It does not appear to be wrong doing; therefore, abortion has become the lifestyle of those who endorse and support it. The Democratic Party, who is liberal, supports the pro-abortion rights activists in order to get their votes during general elections; therefore, morality has become politicized by both the right and left wings based on the party's ideologies that affect both national and foreign issues how each makes decision at home and abroad respectively.

Roles Conflicts

Understanding that conservatism sprang from orthodox Christianity, it is extrapolated that both Christians and those who are identified to carry such value system do work together to support the endeavor; therefore, the issues of role conflicts between the White Evangelical Christian Community of America and the conservative Republican Party are validated; therefore, the White Evangelical Christian Community of America tends to influence the American politics by using the conservative Republican Party to legislate morality when it comes to abortion and homosexuality. The Republican Party is used as the tool for the White Evangelical Christian Community to act on her behalf since she endorses morality based on the Christian's stance. The reader of this monograph could be concerned why the Christian community described in this monograph, is described using racial language. The reason is that, there is the great divide between the White Evangelical Christian Community of America and inclusive Protestant Churches that comprise both white and black people. The White Evangelical Christian Community of America is the racial group who is saying that black people could take her place in America if they are endorsed. This group goes to church; however, she is still influenced by racism; therefore, she views people of colors as criminals, drug addicts, homosexuals, and the lists goes on. It is very clear that the former President Donald Trump is found in this group based on his corrosive languages against people of color. On his slogan "Make America Great Again" is influenced by his racial ideology that black man became President of America; therefore, America became degraded when black man entered the White House. This was inconceivable for him; therefore, he was fighting back to make sure that it never happens again. His inconceivability was tested again when the black woman was designated as the Vice President of the United States of America. His fight to overturn the 2020 presidential election via multiple courts cases and followed by the January 6, 2021 riot was influenced by his inconceivability and corrosive ideology of racism. It is not surprise that the White Evangelical Christian Community of America supported his endeavor to win election in 2016 because the group and Donald Trump carried racial ideology in the United States.

The issue of role conflict exists; therefore, instead of the church preaching salvation to the lost people that are considered pro-abortion activists and homosexuals, the White Evangelical Christian Community of America is using the conservative Republican Party to preach the message through legislation of morality. The church has politicized the Gospel and entered the political arena. It does not help the pro-abortion activists and homosexuals to change based on the methodologies the church has adopted. On the other hand, some Protestant churches of America especially those comprising of the black people have allied themselves with the liberals, the Democratic Party, to vote them into office since the Democratic Party usually advocates for the vulnerable populations. They vote the liberals into office not because they endorse abortions and homosexuality; instead, the party described as liberal, tends to practice true religion according the Bible while those who have declared themselves to be conservatives, are far from practicing the values. The message of conservatism is preached without love; instead, it is preached with hypocrisy, hate, and lack of examples among those who preach it.

The reason the Republican Party usually wins the White Evangelical Christian Community's votes during election is tied to her stance on morality coupled with racism. The White Evangelical Christian community had voted for Nelson Dixon, Ronald Regan, George Bush, and Donald Trump consistently because these past presidents defined themselves to be conservative in the American body politics.

The Amalgamation of States and Religion

The definition of the separation of the church and States as revealed in the Amendment Clause of the United States' Constitution defines the Roman's situation as evidence when Emperor Constantine became Emperor of Rome from 306–337 AD. Many of the Roman's Emperors that came before Emperor Constantine were hostile to Christianity; therefore, they persecuted Christians in blood bath. Emperors Nero, Domitian, Marcus Aurelius, Diocletian and others succeeded one another with bloody bath persecutions of Christians. At the emergence of Emperor Constantine prior to the era of the previous blood thirsty emperors, Constantine had encountered huge military rivalries in his struggles; nevertheless, he had been successful to defeating his rivals in battles; therefore, Emperor Constantine attributed his victory to God's intervention; as the result, he became converted from paganism to Christianity. After his conversion, Emperor Constantine introduced religious tolerance in the Roman Empire and consequently adopted Christianity as the States' religion. His adoption of the Christian's religion made Christianity to expand and many of the Roman's officials became part of the Christian church as the result of Constantine's conversion; however, some said that his conversion was not sincere; instead, it was a pretence and politically motivated. It was under Emperor Constantine that the Nicaea's Creed was adopted after he had convened a meeting of the Council of Nicaea in 325 AD for the empire wide meeting of church leaders to discuss various doctrinal controversies. Among the doctrinal controversies was the issue on the Trinity that emerged. The controversy emerged as the debate between the heretical Arius and the Christian Theologian Athanasius of Alexandria regarding the Doctrine of the Trinity. In the doctrinal controversy, heretical Arius believed and propagated that Jesus, the son and God, the Father are of different substance while Theologian Athanasius believed and propagated that Jesus, the son and God, the Father, are of the same substance (*homoousion*). This was the theological contest between Arius and Athanasius with reference to the Doctrine of the Trinity; hence, at the close of the debate, Athanasius won the contest based on his exegetical approach using the Greek text as the evidence from the Bible that God, the Son and God, the Father are of the same substance. It was under

Constantine that the Doctrine of the Trinity was debated, clarified, and established as the Christian doctrine biblically leading to the adoption of the Nicene Creed to form part of the Christian belief in 325 AD after the Synod conference of 250 bishops of the Council of Nicaea.

The downside of the inclusion of the church and the States as the mutual body operative brought the world into the church and defied the church.[123] The influence of the people whom Emperor Constantine appointed as bishops and placed them in the church to lead polluted the church because the people did not have the Spirit of God to lead a spiritual organization. It can be learned from history that States and church should exist independently as the political and spiritual body instead of mutually existing in rituals, practices, and lifestyles because they are conspicuously different when it comes to rituals, practices, and lifestyles. Apostle Matthew writes to authenticate this statement, "No one sews a patch of unshrunk cloth on an old garment, for the patch will pull away from the garment, making the tear worse. Neither do people pour new wine into old wineskins. If they do, the skins will burst; the wine will run out and the wineskins will be ruined. No, they pour new wine into new wineskins, and both are preserved" (Matt 9: 16–17 NIV). The above passage describes while States and religion are incompatible to exist mutually based on rituals, practices, and lifestyles. States and the church are incompatible in rituals, practices and lifestyles; however, people who attend the church, are part of the government and therefore have the right to exercise their political franchise in government; hence, it does not forbid Christians from participating in body politics of their nation by virtue of their citizenship rights. The phrase, "separation between States and religion" defines that no government of the country is allowed to declare a specific religion and to impose it on the people. It speaks of freedom of religion in the democratic society.

---

[123] Ibid.

Ethical Reflection

The subjects on abortion, homosexuality, and gun violence have been politicized on the ground of political expediencies by members of the Republican and the Democratic Parties than considering the bad effects that are engulfing the American society morally, spiritually and catastrophically. Politicians on either side the political wings of the Republican or the Democratic Party are preaching their ideologies that appeal to these issues in order to win their potential adherences who agree with them and might support them in general election. The Democratic Party that is considered liberal knows that abortion and homosexuality are affront with objectively universal moral acts and punishable by God; however, she endorses them for political expediencies; similarly, the Republican Party that is considered conservative knows that gun violence has become epidemic in the American society; nevertheless, she has the obligation to work with the Democratic Party to pass safety gun laws in order to alleviate gun violence; on the contrary, she has opposed the Democratic Party to passing safety gun laws for political expediencies to win voters who are pro-gun rights activists. They have considered their positions in the government important than the lives of the Americans who have been killed daily in mass shooting. Allowing an eighteen year old child to be an adult to own gun whose brain is still undergoing development is a disaster in the American body politics regarding the right to bear arm. These flawed laws in the American's Constitution should be revisited and amended for the betterment of the American society.

CONCLUSION

Apostle Paul's literary universal address to the Christians of Rome has been considered as an interpolation by some biblical scholars; however, taking a review of previous chapters of the book of Romans before chapter thirteen, the passage under discussion cannot be defined as an interpolation. Apostle Paul's address to the Roman Christians to submit to civil authority is universally addressed to the great audience beyond; though, it had been directed to specific audience and seen situational. According to textual study of Romans chapter thirteen verses one to seven, the Greek text refers to both secular and spiritual authorities indicating inclusivity and universality of the commandments in the context of the recipients and the addressees. Looking at the historical cultural context, the time period Apostle Paul wrote this letter things had not yet deteriorated in Rome; however, Emperor Claudius had already expelled the Jews from Rome. When Apostle Paul addressed this letter, the Jews were returning to Rome; however, there were Gentiles Christians who remained in Rome after the expulsion that practiced Christianity. These Gentiles believers worshipped in house churches when Apostle Paul had written the letter while the returned Jews gathered in the Synagogues; therefore, there were two designated places of worships in Rome when Apostle Paul had written the letter; for this reason, the letter was addressed to both Jews and Gentiles Christians in the Roman Empire. No sooner will Emperor Nero begin to persecute the Christians in blood bath that he had accused them of being the new cult after Emperor Claudius had died and Nero had ascended to the throne. He will start the persecution of the Christians after the great fire on July 18, 64 CE.[124]

Apostle Paul's address to the Christians to submit to civil authority was crucial when King Nero will have begun Christians' persecution. It was advisable for the Christians not to be rebellious for their lives to be saved since the government that was ruling was autocratic. His address to the Roman Christians to submit to the governing authority did not define what kind of governments to submit to; therefore, Christian's submission to the governing authority is universal; hence, submission should not infringe on God's ordinance to make believers sin against God; therefore, caution should be taken when submitting to the governing authority. During this time, there was emperor worship in Rome; for this reason, preaching Jesus would cause one's death; hence, the emperor was the god of Rome and he demanded worship. Apostle Paul's address for the Roman Christians to submit to the governing authority was necessary taking these events into consideration. His address was specific to the impeding situation; however, his address is also inclusive and universal of all people since government is ordained by God to maintain law and order in society; hence, there are cross references and proof texts that provide the existence of civil authority in the world to prove the inclusivity and the universality of the address to the universal audience of all times.

Hermeneutics is the science of biblical interpretation; therefore, in the context of the foundational text, the tool of hermeneutics called exegesis is being adopted to define Romans chapter thirteen verses one to seven using the methodologies in the context of history, textual analysis of key words, and proof texting. The methodologies have been employed in this monograph to lay the foundation of the argument introduced formerly in the introductory section of the discourse. The use of the Greek tools has helped defined, explained, and interpreted the text.

The primary holisticity defines the roles of government and citizens in the community of nations; meanwhile despite of the biblical functions of

---

[124] M. De Lipman, "July 18, 64 CE: Great Fire of Rome," accessed August 23, 2022, www.nationalgeographic.org.

government, there are other functions such as the provision of health care delivery, development projects, and education that government is required to provide other than restraining evil and the provision of national security for all. While it is obligatory that government provides these services; reciprocally, citizens are also required to honor civil authority and to pay taxes as defined by the biblical text.

Understanding the biblical view of wealth does ease traumas in the materialistic world as illustrated in the biblical text concerning the love for money, the case of the rich ruler analogy, and Zaccheus, the tax collector, who promised to pay back two times what he had defrauded his victims; on the contrary, the rich ruler was captivated by his riches and refused to share with the poor; though, he desired to enter heaven based on his interrogation. He was not willing to let go his riches. Many in this dispensation are found in this category of the rich ruler; on the other hand, few are found in the Zaccheus's case.

The issue of wealth redistribution is rooted in the Old Testament practices with reference to the Year of Jubilee to close the wealth gap between the buyer and the seller of the land after 49 and half years. The issue of Jubilee in the Old Testament is contemporary to social justice system in today's government when government decentralizes wealth through education, health care delivery, development projects and among others. These are fiduciary responsibilities government has towards her citizens; however, government will be unable to distribute the wealth when corruption becomes the norm of the government; hence, corruption will deplete resources and make them inaccessible to citizens. The subject of biblical and social view of justices varied with reference to practice, theory, and application in the democratic and religious setting; similarly, they varied with adherences and the proponents while democratization defines social, biblical, criminal, and environmental justices; even though, democratization seems to conflict with biblical justice based on the human's element since democracy and theology are incompatible based on doctrine, core values, beliefs, and practices; however, some democratic values are in alignment with biblical values. For example, democracy is against oppression based on its core values and eventually advocates for individual's rights; similarly, biblical justice advocates for the individual's freedom. The dichotomy between social and biblical justice is defined by absolutism and relativism positions in decision making when it comes to ethics. Biblical justice is absolute and has to do with ethics and integrity; on the other hand, social justice is relative; therefore, laws enacted to reflect values and guide behavior in social justice systems can be flawed. For example, in some democratic societies, individual has the right to practice abortion and homosexuality. This right is contrasted with biblical justice since biblical justice is tied to righteousness; therefore, abortion and homosexuality are not allowed in biblical justice since they do not reflect righteousness; instead, they are abominations and punishable by God. This is the flaw side of social justice system that is incompatible with biblical justice; therefore, democracy and theocracy conflict with values system as social and biblical justice conflict based on doctrines and practices. That's being said, not all democratic values and practices are wrong. Social justice that constitutes privilege, opportunity, and individual's right is contrary to the facets of biblical justice that constitutes restorative and retributive justices. What seems to be a privilege, opportunity, and individual's right might not agree with the practices of orthodox Christianity. Individual's right might undermine the Scripture and eventually become abominable to societal society in the court of the divine. These social justice facets such as privilege, opportunity, and individual's right can become countercultural biblically depending on how they are exercised in the democracy. Individual constitutional right to kill unborn babies through abortion in the United States according to Roe V. Wade is the social justice system that goes against biblical justice; therefore, this sin is punishable via retributive justice punishment. In the case of social and criminal justices, individual's right exercised can have criminal liabilities depending on the law changing dynamics. For example, Roe V. Wade that has given women constitutional right to kill unborn babies has been nullified by the federal government recently; for this reason, states have been empowered to enact their own law regarding abortion. Some States in the United States have gone ahead to bind abortion; for this reason, abortion that was allowed under the umbrella of individual constitutional rights according to Roe V. Wade has now become a criminal act equal to murder punishable in the court of the law. The effect of criminal justice has limited the effect of social justice in the States that abortion has now become a criminal act. With reference to the criminal and biblical justices, they both agree when it comes to criminal punishment. The facets that constitute biblical justice system are found in the criminal justice system; however, different terminologies and approaches to the justice system are different from the approaches in the biblical justice. Environmental justice that resonates with the environment does influence social, biblical, and criminal justice systems universally since geographically, humanity is intrinsically and geographically connected in regardless of race, history, creed, and religion.

Jurisprudence is the study of the philosophy of ethics and laws; therefore, jurisprudence examines the contrasts between ethics and laws since laws can become flawed and question integrity that relates to ethical standard based on the practices of the human cultures. The flawed nature of laws that question integrity tends to go against the moral goodness of society calls for civil disobedience; therefore, not all governments should be obeyed due to the flawed nature of laws that does not dictate the ethics of God. Apostle Paul's address on the subject of submitting to the civil authority does not undercut compromising with the government to do wrong contrary to the Scripture. Apostle Paul has been general in his address; nevertheless, there are scriptures and incidences in the Bible that have allowed civil disobedience.

The principles of ethics as defined in the monograph constitute beneficence, nonmaleficence, autonomy, and justice. The former two emerged during the era of Hippocrates while the later two evolved during medical practice. The four fundamental principles of ethics reflect values and guide human's decision. Beneficence signifies doing good to all while nonmaleficence signifies doing harm to no one. While it is true that these fundamental principles of ethics reflect values and guide human's decision, human being should be autonomous and capacitated to make decision without the third party intervention. That signifies that to be autonomous, the individual should be mentally sound to make decision in order not to harm others in the exercise of the individual's liberty. In the event of being autonomous, truth-telling, informed consent, and confidentiality are required to make the individual capable of self-determination.

The subject of Christian's military enlistment is substantiated in the Scripture; therefore, Christians can be assured that serving in the military to protect life and property under the umbrella of keeping national sovereignty is endorsed and ordained by God. While the Christian and non-Christian military enlistment is endorsed and substantiated in the Scripture, the applied ethics of absolutism and relativism does influence how the military conducts herself during arm conflict.

Liberianization in the Liberia's body politics defines the characterization of what makes up Liberian or the nationality; therefore, the existence of the First, Second, and the Third republics in the Liberia's body politics defines liberianization from 1847 to the present. As Liberia had existed as the aristocratic-oligarchy from 1847 to 1979 prior to the coup d'état in 1980, the nature of such government for 133 years of rules was influenced by xenophobic and ethnocentric ideology that permeated the Liberian body politics leading to the marginalization of the dominant culture. Upon the settlers' arrival, they created a double-tiered of exclusivism, differentiation, and disillusion leading to the marginalization of the members of the dominant culture to participate in the political and the civic life of Liberia for 133 years of rules. The synergism of the events from 1847 to 1979 culminated into coup d'état ending the First Republic followed by ten years of dictatorial regime; then, the Second Republic ended in 1990 after the overthrow of Samuel Kanyon Doe. Despite of the sixteen years of civil conflict, the past history of corruption and ritualistic killing has been replayed in Liberia; hence, Liberia faces the dilemmas of injustice, young democracy, camouflaged democracy, and corruption in government. To alleviate these dilemmas, Liberia needs the leadership that has vision, patriotic, and is willing to eradicate corruption by bringing perpetrators of this act to justice. Similar recommendations are being proposed in this monograph with reference to the constitutionalization and educationalization of the Liberia's constitution and the eradication of corruption.

Americanization defines the characterization of Americans in the context of the American body politics as delineated in this monograph. In the context of the American political ideologies, both Democratic and Republican Parties make decisions that affect both national and foreign policies based on the ideologies each party carries. The ideologies also drive what kind of messages each party preaches during campaign; therefore, these divides control the polarity of the American political agenda how the country is administered by the ruling party ; however, based on congressional voting system, the policy agenda that come from these ideologies can be hindered by the opposition party depending on the number of candidates on the U.S. Senate and the House of Representative; meanwhile, the subject on abortion, homosexuality, and gun violence has been politicized by both parties in the American body politics; therefore, both parties use the message of conservatism and liberalism to appeal to voters on either side of the isles in order to win election. The Democratic Party that is considered liberal, represents the moral fall offs based on the practice of the doctrine of liberalism; on the other hand, the Republican Party that is considered to be conservative, misrepresents the message she preaches based on the practice of doctrine with reference to the refusal of passing safety gun laws to alleviate gun violence and supporting programs that help the middle class; therefore, there is flaw in the American Republican Party when it comes to practicing the doctrine of conservatism; for this reason, the Republican Party lacks conservative values when it comes to gun control in America; meanwhile, the subject of legislation of morality in the nave of the Republican Party tends to appeal to the Christian community especially the White Evangelical Christian Community to vote for the Republican Party as role conflict emerges in their fight against abortion.

APPENDIX

Early Settlement of Liberia 1830

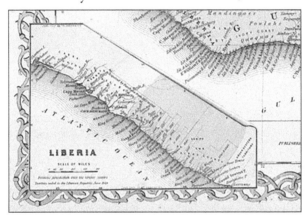

Early Settlement of America 1830

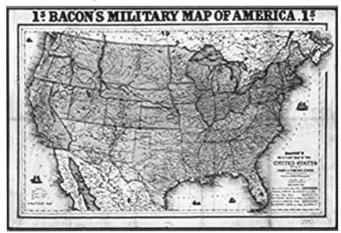

SELECTED BIBLIOGRAPHY

Abraham and Lincoln, Mary. "Political Party Timeline: 1836–1864." Accessed August 23, 2022, https://www.pbs.org/wgbh/americanexperience/features/lincolns-timeline/

Allen, Douglas. *The Philosophy of Mahatma Gandhi for the Twenty-first Century*. Lanthan: Boulder: New York: Toronto: Plymouth, UK: Lexington Books, 2008

Armstead, Kayla. "Branches of Ethical Philosophy." Accessed August 24, 2022, https://study.com/learn/lesson/ethics-philosophy-overview-branches.html

ASJ, "Association for a More Just Society." Accessed August 23, 2022, Https://Www.Asj-Us.Org/?Gclid=Eaiaiqobchmikjqe3dtf-Qivltszch0vvwepeaayasaaegjqhpd_Bwe

Borggren, Erik. "Romans 13:1–7 and Philippians 3:17–21: Paul's Call to True Citizenship and to Gaman," *The Covenant Quarterly* (Online), no. 1 (2015): 1–16.

Brown, Robert E. *Liberalism, Conservatism, and History*.Michigan: Michigan State University Press, 1963,https://www.jstor.org/stable/23737551

Calvin, John. "Commentary on Romans 13:1". "Calvin's Commentary on the Bible."Accessed August 30, 2021, https://www.studylight.org/commentaries/cal/romans-13.html. 1840-57

Chalmers, Matthew. "Rethinking Luke 10: The Parable of the Good Samaritan Israelite," *Journal of Biblical Literature* 139, no. 3 (2020): 543–566.

Chames, Ruth. "US History Textbooks: Help or Hindrance to Social Justice," *Church and Society* 78, no. 4 (1988): 48–58.

Chisholm, Robert B. "Rizpah's Torment: When God Punishes the Children for the Sin of the Father," *Bibliotheca* 175, no. 697 (2018): 50–66.

CIA World Factbook Liberia Page, "U.S Relations with Liberia." Accessed August 23, 2022, https://www.state.gov/u-s-relations-with-liberia/

Clark, Adam. "Commentary on Romans 13:1"."The Adam Clarke Commentary." Accessed August 29, https://www.studylight.org/commentaries/acc/romans-13.html. 1832

Coffman Burton, James. "Commentary on Romans 13:1". "Coffman Commentaries on the Bible".Abilene, TX: Abilene Christian University Press, 1983–1999. Accessed August 30, 2021, https://www.studylight.org/commentaries/bcc/romans-13.html

Collin Son & CO. LTD, William."Dictionary.com." Accessed June 19, 2022, https://www.dictionary.com/browse/government

Constitute, "Liberia's Constitution of 1986." Accessed August 23, 2022, https://www.constituteproject.org/constitution/Liberia_1986.pdf?lang=en

Dodoo, Lennart. "VP Howard Taylor Tours and Inspects The Mother of Light, Liberia Inc. Rehabilitation Center." Accessed June 28, 2022, https://frontpageafricaonline.com/news/vp-howard-taylor-tours-and-inspects-the-mother-of-light-liberia-inc-rehabilitation-center%EF%BF%BC/

Fair Fight Initiative, "Jim Crow Laws." Accessed July 7, 2022, htts://www.fairfightinitiative.org/jim-crow-laws

Fleming, Donald C. "Commentary on Romans 13:1". "Brideway Bible Commentary." Accessed August 29, https://www.studylight.org/commentaries/bbc/romans-13.html. 2005

Galloway, Malcolm and Taiyeb, Jaj. "The Interpretation of Phases Used to Describe Uncertainty in Pathology Reports." Accessed August 23, 2022, https://www.hindawi.com/journals/pri/2011/656079/

Gaffney, Adam and McCormick, Danny. "The Affordable Care Act: Implication for the Health Care Equity." Accessed June 20, 2022, https://pubmed.ncbi.nlm.nih.gov/28402826/

Gouli, Katerini&Karellos, Nicholas. "Children Behind Bars: A Voice for Greece's Juvenile Offenders," *Road to Emmaus* 7, no. 1 (2006): 39–49.

Gardner, Andrew. "Students and the Study of Religion: The Extra-curricular Origins of the World Religions Paradigm," *Implicit Religion* 23, no. 1 (2020): 54–62.

GK Today, "Four Branches of Ethics." Accessed August 28, 2022, https://www.gktoday.in/topic/four-branches-of-ethics/

Gueullette, Jean-Marie. "Hippocrate, Jesus, Freud, Still: Fondateursd'UneActiviteTherapeutique,?" *Theophilyon* 20, no. 2 (2015): 353–368.

Gulf Bend Center, "Liberal Morality versus Conservative Understanding the Difference Can Help You Avoid Arguments." Accessed August 23, 2022, https://www.gulfbend.org/

Hahn, Niels. *Two Centuries of US Military Operation in Liberia: Challenges of Resistance and Compliance.*Alabama: Air University Press, 2003

Hafer, Charleton. "Exegesis of Romans 13:1–7 and Its Appropriation of the Second Republic of Zambawe," *Eleutheria* 5, no. 2 (2021): 234–257.

Hanc, Ovidiu. "Paul and Empire: A Reframing of Romans 13:1–7 in the Context of the New Exodus," *Tyndale Bulletin* 65, no. 2 (2014): 313–316.

Hayes, Pamela & Grant, Mary. "Spiritual Direction and Counseling Therapy," *The Way Supplement* 69, no. 1 (1990): 61–71.

Hendrickx, Herman. "The "House Church" in Paul's Letters," *The Theology Annual* 12, no 1 (1990–1991); 154–186.

Hirsch, Afua. "Liberia Has Sold Quarter of Its Land to Logging Companies, Says Report, "The Guardian." Accessed June

28, 2022, https://www.theguardian.com/world/2012/sep/04/liberia-sold-quarter-land-logging-companies

Huston, James L. "The American Revolutionaries, the Political Economy of Aristocracy, and the American Concept of the Distribution of Wealth, 1965–1900," *The American Historical Review* 98, no. 4 (1993): 1079–1105.

John, Russell St. "Exploring Prosperity Preaching: Biblical Health, Wealth, and Wisdom," *Journal of the Evangelical Homiletics Society* 14, no. 2 (2014): 90–91.

Johnson, James Tumer. "The Lesser Evil: Political Ethics in the Age of Terror," *First Things* 151, no. 1 (2005): 44–47.

Kendrix-Komoto, Amanda. "The Other Crime: Abortion and Contraception in Nineteenth and Twentieth-Century Utah," *Dialogue* 53, no. 1 (2020): 33–45.

Kiadii, Alfred P.B. "The Rice and Rights Riot: Social Struggle and the Quest for An Alternative Society in Liberia, Part II, The Perspective." Accessed June 28, 2022, https://www.theperspective.org/2019/0507201901.php

Kovalishyn, Mariam Kamell. "A Biblical Theology of Social Justice," *Crux* 55, no. 3 (2019): 30–39.

Koyzis, David. "[Consider] Civil Disobedience: Christians Should Submit to the Governing Authority Except When They Shouldn't," *Christianity Today* 60, no. 3 (2016): 38–45.

Kroeker, Dave. "What Belongs to Caesar: A Discussion on the Christian Response to Payment of Wars Taxes," *The Mennonite Quarterly Review* 46, no. 1 (1972): 91–92.

Law, Easten. "Complex Currents, Contemporary Perspectives, and Converging Methods: A Review of Graduate Student Research Panel at Princeton Theological Seminary's 2018 World ChristianityConference," *World Christianity* 9, no. 1 (2019): 114–121

Layhee, Patrick. "A Biblical View of Wealth and Riches," *Center for Christianity in Business.*" Accessed September 27, 2021, https://bbu. edu/center-for-christianity-in-business

Lewis, Colin. "Ritual Education and Moral Development: A Comparison of Xunzi and Vygotsky,"*Dao* 17, no. 1 (2018): 81–98.

"Liberia Forward."Accessed December 21, 2021, https://www.liberiafor-ward.org/history-of-liberia

Library of Congress, "History of Liberia: A Time Line." Accessed August 24, 2022, https://www.loc.gov/collections/maps-of-liberia-1830-to-1870/ articles-and-essays/history-of-liberia

Lipman, M. De. "July 18, 64 CE: Great Fire of Rome." Accessed August 23, 2022, www.nationalgeographic.org

Lucius, Casey. "Religion and the National Security Strategy," *Journal of Church and State 55*, no. 1 (2013): 50–70.

Maddox, Graham. "The Prospects for Democratic Convergence: Islam and Christianity," *Political Theology* 16, no. 4 (2015): 305–328.

Mackay Alexander, John. "Religion and Government, Their Separate Spheres and Reciprocal Responsibilities," *Theology Today* 9, no. 2 (1952): 204–222.

Manz, William H. "Encyclopedia of DNA and the United States Criminal Justice System," *The Catholic Library World*74, no. 4 (2004): 279–280.

May, David. "Context Is Key to Interpreting Romans 13:1–7." Accessed June 18, 2022, https://goodfaithmedia.org/ context-is-key-to-interpreting-romans-13-1-7-cms-19577/

Mettes, Susan. "Ministry after Maslow: Maslow's Hierarchy of Needs Has Leavened the Teaching in American Churches, That's a Problem, "*Christianity Today* 62, no. 5 (2018): 38–43.

Moszkowicz, David. "Michael Walzer's Justification of Humanitarian Intervention: Communitarian? Cosmopolitan?Adequate?"*Political Theology* 8, no. 3 (2007): 281–297.

Murchie, David. "New Testament View of Wealth Accumulation," *Journal of the Evangelical Theological Society* 21, no. 4 (1978): 335–344.

NC Department of Health and Human Services, "Social Services." Accessed June 20, 2022, https://www.ncdhhs.gov/divisions/social-services

Opoku, Francis. "Constantine and Christianity: The Formation of Church/State Relations in the Roman Empire," *Ilorin Journal of Religious Studies* 5, no. 1 (2015): 17–34.

Payne, Michael. "What Can Church History Tell Us about the Debate between Just War Theory and Pacifism and What Does This Mean for the Church Today," *Eleutheria* 5, no. 2 (2021): 2017–233.

Peck, Richard. "General Conference Acts on Wide Range of Issues." Accessed August 24, 2022, https://www.umnews.org/en/news/general-conference-acts-on-wide-range-of-issues

Perry L. Samuel and Whitehead L. Andrew. "Christian America in Black and White: Racial Identity, Religious-National Group Boundaries, and Explanations of Racial Inequality," *Sociology of Religion* 80, no. 3 (2019): 277–298.

Pennoyer, Robert M. "No Surrender: To Defend Reproductive Rights, First Protect Church State Separation," *Church & State* 74, no. 2 (2021). Accessed June 29, 2022, https://www.au.org/church-state

Peter, "Tax in the Early Days of the Roman Republic." Accessed June 1, 2021, https://academy4sc.org/video/the-roman-republic-separation-of-powers/?hsa_ver=3

Point Park University Online, "The Types of Criminal Punishment." Accessed June 29, 2022, https://online.pointpark.edu/criminal-justice/types-of-criminal-punishment/

Praise Ministries Interdenominational Prayer Bible Study Forum, "Praise Ministries Prayer Forum," accessed November 13, 2021, https://praiseministriesprayerbiblestudyforum.wordpress.com/

Reuss, Henry S. "Taxes, Income and the Distribution of Wealth," *Christianity and Crisis* 35, no. 10 (1975): 139–145.

Sayer, Amos. "Constitute: 1986 Liberia's Constitution." Accessed December 19, 2021, https://www.constituteproject.org/constitutions?lang=en

Scharffs, Brett G. "the (Not So) Exceptional Establishment Clause of the United States," *Journal of Law and Religion* 33, no. 2 (20218): 137–154.

Schlein, Lisa. "UN Rights Chief: Rise of Extreme Nationalism Threat to Global Peace." Accessed August 24, 2022, https://www.voanews.com/a/un-rights-chief-rise-of-extreme-nationalism-threatens-global-peace-/4443998.html

Schhmanlhofer, Travis. "Romans 13:1–7: An Historical and Exegetical Analysis," *Presbyterion* 45, no. 2 (2019): 187–188.

Sim, May. "Rethinking Virtue Ethics and Social Justice with Aristotle and Confucius," *Asian Philosophy*, no. 2 (2010): 195–213.

Singh, Avinash. "State and Criminality: The Colonial Campaign against Thugee and the Suppression of Sikh Militancy in Postcolonial India," *Sikh Formations* 8, no. 1 (2012): 37–58.

Smalley, Martha Lund. "Mountain Archival Finding Aids on the Web," *ATLA Summary of Proceedings* 53, no. 1 (1999): 301–307.

Smith H., Shelton. "Am I Not a Man and a Brother: British Missions and Abolition of the Slave Trade and Slavery in West Africa and the West Indies, 1786–1838," *Church History* 42, no. 2 (1973): 290–291.

Sparati/AFP via Getty Image, Michele. "South Africa: Widespread Xenophobic Violence." Accessed August 24, 2022, https://www.hrw.org/news/2020/09/17/south-africa-widespread-xenophobic-violence

Sshaban Alfa, Abdur Rahman. "Liberia Senator Takes Pay Cut, Donates $10,000.00 Monthly Constituency." Accessed June 28, 2022, https://www.africanews.com/2019/08/16/liberia-senator-takes-pay-cut-donates-10000-monthly-to-constituency//

Starkman, Dean , Shiel, Fergus , Diaz-Struck, Emilia and Boland-Rudder, Hamish , "Frequently Asked Questions about the Pandora Papers and ICIJ." Accessed June 29, 2022, https://www.icij.org/investigations/pandora-papers/

frequently-asked-questions-about-the-pandora-papers-and-icij/?g-clid=EAIaIQobChMI4PC5_ezR

Streater, David. "The Emergence of Liberty in the Modern World: The Influence of Calvin on Five Governments from the 16th through the 18th Centuries," *Churchman* 110, no. 1 (1996): 90–92.

Thayer, Joseph Henry . "Thayer's Greek Lexicon." Accessed August 27, 2022, https://biblehub.com/greek/1849.htm

The Analyst, "Liberia: Reform Lease Policy," *Editorial.* Accessed June 28, 2022, https://allafrica.com/stories/200408260378.html

The American Historian, "Evangelicalism and Politics." Accessed August 23, 2022, https://www.oah.org/tah/issues/2018/november/evangelicalism-and-politics/

Timm, Jane. "Pope Francis Calls for Wealth Redistribution." Accessed June 26, 2022, https://www.msnbc.com/pope-call

Thomas, Eugene L. Values Psychosocial Development. Westport, Conn: Aubum House, 1994

Thomas, Robert L. "NAS Exhaustive Concordance of the Bible with Hebrew-Aramaic and Greek Dictionaries." Accessed May 22, 2022, https://biblehub.com/greek/4270.htm

Thompson, Evan. "Cheat Sheet: 10 Common Forms of Government." Accessed June 19, 2022, https://thebestschools.org/magazine/common-forms-of-government-study-starters/

Transparency International, "Liberia Corruption Rank." Accessed August 24, 2022, https://tradingeconomics.com/liberia/corruption-rank

Tuggy, Dale. "Theories of Religious Diversity," *A Peer-Reviewed Academic Resource.* Accessed June 19, 2022, https://iep.utm.edu/reli-div/

Universal History Archive/UIG via Getty Images, "American Bomber Drops Atomic Bomb on Hiroshima." Accessed July 13, 2022, https://www.google.com/amp/s/www.history.com/.amp/this-day-in-hist

Van der Kraaij, Dr. Fred P.M. "The Colony of Liberia and the Suppression of the Slave Trade." Accessed May 22, 2022, https://www.liberiapa-standpresent.org/

Williamson GM., Hugh. "A Christian View of Wealth and Possession: An Old Testament Perspective," *Ex auditu* 27, no. 1 (2011): 1–19.

_____"Tyranny, Democracy, and the Polity: Aristotle's Politics." Accessed August 24, 2022, https://fs.blog/aristotles-politics/

_____" The Institute for Research for Democratic Development, IREDD." Accessed August 23, 2022, https://www.devex.com/organizations/institute-for-research-and-democratic-development-iredd-98812